Immigration, Stress, and Readjustment

Immigration, Stress, and Readjustment

Zeev Ben-Sira

Foreword by Elihu Katz

PRAEGER

Westport, Connecticut
London

Library of Congress Cataloging-in-Publication Data

Ben-Sira, Zeev.
    Immigration, stress, and readjustment / Zeev Ben-Sira ; foreword
by Elihu Katz.
        p.   cm.
    Includes bibliographical references and index.
    ISBN 0–275–95632–6 (alk. paper)
        1. Emigration and immigration—Psychological aspects.
    2. Immigrants—Psychology.   3. Stress (Psychology)   4. Adjustment
    (Psychology)   5. Social integration.   I. Title.
    JV6109.B46   1997
    155.9′42′0869—dc20   96–20687

British Library Cataloguing in Publication Data is available.

Library of Congress Catalog Card Number: 96–20687
ISBN: 0–275–95632–6

First published in 1997

Praeger Publishers, 88 Post Road West, Westport, CT 06881
An imprint of Greenwood Publishing Group, Inc.

Printed in the United States of America

The paper used in this book complies with the
Permanent Paper Standard issued by the National
Information Standards Organization (Z39.48–1984).

10 9 8 7 6 5 4 3 2 1

Contents

Foreword

The Academic Work of
Zeev Ben-Sira

Zeev Ben-Sira was a man who did not waste time. He began academic work about twenty-five years ago, after completing a distinguished career in the army. The day after becoming a civilian, he started on the dissertation that would make him a medical sociologist, and he never stopped. Even though we know better, we like to romanticize the inspiration that characterizes the work of artists and scholars; but we all know that the best of them fix time for their work. For the twenty-five years of his affiliation with the Guttman Institute of Applied Social Research and membership in its Executive Committee, Zeev was the very model of how not to waste time, how to harness time for creativity.

Ben-Sira led a life of work that adds up, that fits together. This is no small achievement, I should add, since one of the rules of work at an institute for applied social research—as distinct from a university—is to address the problems that are brought to you by others, not just those you choose for yourself. How one weaves these strands together—whether one leads one or two lives, as a pure or applied scientist—is the mark of the man. Without ever saying no to a project that came to his desk from outside, Zeev managed to subsume most of these under the umbrella of his overarching concern with problems of coping with stress. His location at the Institute gave him empirical access to the real lives against which to examine and develop the theories he shared with his colleagues in the sociology of medicine—especially Aaron Antonovsky—and to conceptualize them in the forms developed by Louis Guttman and his disciples. These were the golden years of the Guttman Institute; Zeev made the most of them and gave the best of himself in return.

Reading and rereading his work, I prefer to think of Zeev as a sociologist of social problems to which he applied the functional models of disease taken from medical sociology. From this point of view, all problems, no matter how organic, have social and psychological etiologies, threats to equilibrium, inadequate and misleading information, copings and denials, victims and would-be therapists, internal and external resources, processes of exchange, and a cost-benefit calculus. He applied this thinking to his work on such diverse problems and crises as aging, chronic disease, the threat of hereditary disease, bereavement, disability, Russian immigrants to Israel, social reaction to Russian immigrants, public sanitation and hygiene, even to the crisis of the Jewish people from which Zionism arose as a coping mechanism, and now to the crises of the Jewish people arising from Zionism.

Zeev proceeded by first diagnosing the nature of the problem for himself. Take, for example, his analysis of aging in his book *Regression, Stress, and Readjustment in Aging* (Praeger 1991). In addition to the organic components—themselves influenced by society and psyche—he analyzed attitudes towards aging in modern, achieving, competitive societies, and the likelihood that aging persons and their associates, formal and informal, would internalize these attitudes. He analyzed the waning resources available to the aging person: the weariness or absence of the spouse, the declining patience of primary groups, the reticence of the help-givers. His ideas were informed, I should add, by extensive reading in each of the problems he addressed. He conceptualized the problem with the aid of mapping sentences, which served him very well, because he was precisely interested in making the simple complex. By means of the causal models embedded in the facets of his mapping sentences, he emerged with typologies of the variety of processes and conditions of aging. He could discuss a particular pattern of aging without losing sight of the entire variety. Similarly, by means of the facets he used to typologize illnesses or forms of health-maintaining behaviors, he could keep both their similarities and differences in mind. Thus, he could show in what ways heart disease, obesity, and respiratory and intestinal disease are similar and different and how they might, therefore, be expected to evoke different coping mechanisms.

Having conceptualized the problem for himself, the next step was to collect data to validate the conceptualization empirically. It is nice to note that one of his earliest papers set out to test a Guttmanian reformulation of Maslow's sequence of societal needs, to see whether Israelis ordered their problems in Maslow's terms, and to test the hypothesis that different levels of need preoccupied people located differently on the scale of socio-economic status. But let us return to aging, or, for that matter, any of the other problems he addressed. With respect to each, Zeev asked: How do people view their susceptibility to a threatening problem? How salient is their concern with it? Does salience lead to despair or denial or stress, or to coping through an attempt to understand the nature of the threat? And, finally, does the threat appear preventable? In other words, says Zeev, if you smell smoke, do you deny it or assume that "It can't happen to me," or do you allow its salience to occupy you enough to understand that it might be a fire, that you are not to panic, that there are professionals in charge of treating such things, and the like? These latter are the kinds of people in whom Zeev saw the potential for mobilizing internal and external resources, people who believe in themselves and their social environments, and who have a good chance of regaining their balance. In addition to the sociology of medicine and of social problems, maybe there is some spirit of the Israeli army in this theory, and not a little of Zeev.

Zeev's most recent book—the one before us—is about the stressful absorption of Russian immigrants, which he conceptualizes as a disequilibrating experience for both the immigrants and the absorbing society. He tells us about the relatively poorer health of the immigrants compared with veteran Israelis. He shows that their health improves, still falling short of the veterans, but that their morale declines, especially for those who discover that *aliya* may no longer be the highest priority of Israeli Zionism. Comparing immigrants by year of arrival (1990–1994) he infers that the high point in their positive feelings is in the second year, and that it declines thereafter. This may be related, one suspects, to another important finding—that assistance from formal agencies of absorption and rehabilitation are positively correlated with more successful integration. He expresses surprise that this source of external support is far more effective than the kinds of internal resources that best help to overcome other kinds of crises. Indeed, says Zeev, education works *against* the new immigrants, in that those of higher education are more disappointed in the new society, and thus that education acts as a stressor rather than as a facilitator of integration.

The concern with resources for coping occupied Zeev continually. He was interested in the resources people have stored within themselves and the usual advantage of socioeconomic status. He took particular interest in the supportive role of primary groups, especially the spouse, who makes a great deal of difference in most processes of readjustment after trauma, and also in certain forms of preventive action, such as smoking cessation. He explored the coping regimens that people adopt for themselves under different circumstances and how people may do the right things for the wrong reasons, and the wrong things for the right reasons.

Zeev had a particular interest in external agencies of coping. Doctors, nurses, social workers, support groups, mass media, even political parties are evaluated in turn. The medical establishment interested him most. In this, he joined sociologists of *aliya*, who from the very beginning, noticed that the doctor and the health clinic is the address to which people bring their problems and learn to present them as somatic. Doctors often fail to respond, Zeev reminds us, because they search only for organic problems and do not recognize, or fear to recognize, the affective problems underneath; they do not respond for fear of creating dependence, or because they share society's view of the wastefulness of investing in the aged, the disabled, and so forth. Social work may be the right answer, Zeev suggested, but its professional autonomy is compromised in the shadow of doctors and nurses; nor do social-work professionals have a clear-cut repertoire of what Zeev calls "resource enhancement" to replace the debilitating and dependency-creating repertoire of resource compensation that characterizes so much of what is called professional help.

If it were not for the fact that his book on Zionism preceded this one, it would be easy to show how the Russian *aliya* led Zeev to consider the crisis of Zionism. Whatever the sequence of research and writing, it is a good guess that the expectations of Russian immigrants of the Zionism they do not share led Zeev to rethink Zionist ideology. It is obvious, he claimed, that Zionism was a form of coping with the acute distress of European Jews in the nineteenth and early twentieth century, but it is equally obvious, he thought, that this successful coping has itself created a schism, between particularist and universalist conceptions of what Zionism should do next, that threatens anew the cohesion of the Jewish people. My object here, however, is not to explore this problem further, but rather to show how one thing led to the next in Zeev's work, rather than what might seem, at first glance, radical shifts of focus.

From this brief overview of a life of research, I think you will find, with me, that it is easy to agree: that Zeev Ben-Sira's work adds up—it has internal continuity and clear next steps; that he drew on, and contributed to, the two academic cultures with which he felt most kinship—the sociology of medicine in Israel, which has an important place in the world, and the tradition of facet theory of the Guttman Institute; that he was concerned with causal process but was repeatedly frustrated that his research tools were inadequate to this task; that he called attention not only to research findings but also to their policy implications and to the resources that were needed to enhance the coping abilities of individuals and subgroups; and, finally, that his work was a successful embodiment of his personality, his life experiences, and his multiple commitments to the discipline of sociology, to the profession of social work, to the practice of applied social research, and to the day-to-day obligations of all of these.

Elihu Katz
Jerusalem, May 1996

NOTE

Adapted from a talk delivered at a colloquium in memory of Zeev Ben-Sira at the Paul Baerwald School of Social Work, the Hebrew University, Jerusalem, Israel, in April 1995.

Introduction

Immigration—
A Stress-Precipitating Change

THE GROWING SIGNIFICANCE OF MIGRATION

Over the past century, migration has become an increasingly widespread phenomenon, motivated by political, economic, psychological, and ideological factors. Speaking of immigration to the United States, Doris Meissner, then Migration and Naturalization Commissioner in Washington, stated in 1993: "[M]igration is not an issue that can be solved, unless some very dramatic things change in the world. In our lifetimes we're talking about a new global reality that we have to find ways of living with and managing, and not somehow delude ourselves into thinking that we [can] make it go away" (Brownstein 1993: A20).[1]

Westermeyer (1991:127–128) contends that some hundred million people have fled their countries due to war, civil unrest, and political or religious persecution during the last fifty years. Aaronson (1984) estimates that sixteen million people were either in transit or had recently been granted asylum in a foreign country during the early 1980s. A substantial proportion of the American population is composed of refugees from World War II, the unsuccessful Hungarian and Czechoslovak revolutions, Cuba, Southeast Asia, the Middle East, East Africa, and Iran. It is likely that more than four million illegal immigrants currently live in the United States ("Great Divide" 1993). Similar statistics could undoubtedly be cited for many other countries, and certainly for Israel, which, like the United States, is a country of immigrants.

THE EFFECTS OF IMMIGRATION

Stress among Immigrants

In this book, the concept "stress" refers to a prolonged disturbance of an individual's emotional homeostasis[2] (see Antonovsky 1979). It is clear that whatever the motivation, and whether voluntary or forced, immigration produces a major change in the entire life situation of the immigrants. In Rumbaut's words, "Migration can produce profound psychological distress even among the most motivated and well prepared individuals, and even among the most receptive circumstances" (Rumbaut 1991:56). Palinkas (1982) refers to the potential for psychological stress and disorder.

However, there is a growing understanding that the stress in an individual's life situation cannot be attributed to change alone. Approaches emphasizing the stress-producing force inherent in any change (for instance, Holmes and Rahe 1967) are increasingly being challenged. Mirowsky and Ross (1989), for instance, specifically reject the importance of the psychological and social meaning of "life events" per se, that is, apart from their meaning and valence for the individual. Menaghan asserts that "accumulating research using both physiological and psychological outcome measures suggests that change per se may be neither necessary nor sufficient for the experience of stress. Rather stress occurs to the extent that . . . environmental demands tax or exceed the adaptive capacities or resources of the person, and/or environmental opportunities constrain the satisfaction of individual needs" (Menaghan 1983:158).

More specifically, Chalmers contends that the experience of stress "is the balance or imbalance resulting from the interaction of four components: internal needs and values, external environmental demands and constraints, personal resources or capabilities, and external environmental supplies and supports" (Chalmers 1981:333). In other words, the crucial questions arising from the analysis of immigration as a form of social change relate to the demands confronting individuals who undergo that change, to the stress-potential and the salience of these demands, to the personal and environmental resources these individuals have at their disposal for meeting the demands, and, finally, to the risk of disruption of their emotional homeostasis due to inadequate ability to cope—all of which may lead to maladjustment.

And, if so, understanding the stress-potential inherent in immigration-instigated change requires elucidating not merely stress-inducing factors but also stress-buffering factors accompanying that change.

Adaptation and Readjustment of Immigrants

Extensive theoretical and empirical work has been devoted to the study of the adaptation of immigrants, mostly focusing on specific aspects of this adaptation. There have been studies of occupational adaptation (Shin and Chang 1988); of inter-generational conflicts (Gold 1989); and of the process of identity assumption (Lobodzinska 1986). Of the many studies that have been devoted to the problems of emotional disturbance among the immigrants, most are limited to a few explanatory variables (see, for instance, Kuo and Tsai 1986; Palinkas 1982).

In studying adaptation, I prefer to use the more global concept of "readjustment," which refers to the restoration of emotional homeostasis as a result of successful coping with stress, as defined above (see Dohrenwend and Dohrenwend 1970). In the case of immigration, readjustment will be viewed as the outcome of meeting the demands imposed by the change inherent in immigration—that is, the successful completion of the process of immigration.

The Absorbing Society: Immigration, Change, and Stress

Immigration can also bring change to the absorbing society.[3] Shuval (1992: 123) maintains that processes of change and adaptation take place among the immigrants, but no less among individuals and groups in the absorbing society. The larger the number of immigrants relative to veterans, the larger their likely impact. Processes of adaptation, change, and readjustment are not confined to one part of the population but may be diffused throughout the social system.

Immigration may alter the social and ethnic composition of neighborhoods, towns, and occasionally even the entire society. It may affect behavior patterns in public places, at the workplace, and in residential areas. It may also have consequences in other areas of society, such as economics and politics. All these are liable to provoke intergroup polarization and tensions both between the absorbing society and the immigrants and among groups in the absorbing society. The first is alluded to by Brym, who speaks of "simmering xenophobia [in Western Europe] being fuelled by the threat and the reality of mass-emigration from the former Soviet bloc countries" (Brym 1992:387). The second can be seen in the United States, where "the anti-immigrant sentiment being generated has fueled [an] atmosphere of ethnic, racial and religious intolerance, as evidenced by . . . recent fire-bombings in California's capital, including Congregation B'nai Israel synagogue and the local offices of the National Association for the Advancement of Colored People" (Editorial, *The Daily Bruin*, November 15, 1993). In a series of newspapers articles on immigration to the United States during the same period, the author of one article states, "The intense polarization between [the] viewpoints [regarding immigration to the US] guarantees fireworks in both the state and national capital. It also diminishes the prospects that they will reach consensus on initiatives . . . and even if they do, that those measures will . . . ameliorate public anxieties over immigration visible in the polls" (Brownstein 1993:A20).

Immigration-Induced Stress and Concomitant Readjustment

Thus, understanding the stress-precipitating forces inherent in immigration-instigated change requires us to study both the immigrants and the absorbing society. The behaviors, feelings, and attitudes—including stereotypes—exhibited by members of each group are likely to affect members of other groups as well. Concomitant readjustment, then, entails incorporating the immigrants into the absorbing society and also the acceptance that all can contribute to the society. A failure to attain concomitant readjustment is apt to trigger an escalating cycle of discord.

The Need for a Theory-Based and Empirically Supported Paradigm

Despite the extensive research devoted to numerous aspects of immigration, there is still no comprehensive, theory-based, and empirically supported paradigm that identifies the factors promoting and hampering readjustment in the wake of immigration-instigated social change (Creed 1987). Such a paradigm could further our understanding of the complex effects of the changes inherent in immigration. It might also contribute to an understanding of the relationship between social change in general and stress.

The goal of this work, then, is to develop and empirically test a theory-based, comprehensive, multivariate paradigm of readjustment in the wake of immigration-instigated social change. The proposed paradigm will draw on existing approaches to the coping-stress-disease relationship (e.g., Antonovsky 1979; Pearlin and Schooler 1978) but will be developed further to enable an analysis of readjustment in the wake of immigration-instigated life change (see also Ben-Sira 1981, 1983a, 1984, 1985, 1986a, 1986b, 1988b, 1991). The paradigm is intended to provide a structured approach to the understanding of the individual and societal factors that promote or impede successful coping with the demands inherent in the process of immigration, demands that face both the immigrants and the absorbing society and consequently promote or impede readjustment. I shall then test the paradigm, using the case of Soviet immigrants to Israel.

IMMIGRATION TO ISRAEL

Israel: A Live Laboratory for the Study of Immigration

Israel is, in some senses, a live laboratory for the study of immigration. The integration of various immigrant groups into Israeli society has received extensive sociological treatment. The now-classic works of Eisenstadt (1954), Shumsky (1955), Shuval (1963) and others dealing with the mass immigration of the 1950s emphasized the "cultural gap" between "Western" (Hebrew: *Ashkenazi*) immigrants (those from Europe and America) on the one hand, and "Eastern" (also "Oriental," Hebrew: *Sephardi*) immigrants (those from Asia and

Africa) on the other, and they made predictions as to the implications of this gap for the integrity of Israeli society.

Others have investigated the absorption of immigrants from later periods. To mention just a few studies, Antonovsky and Katz (1979) conducted a multivariate research project on the problems of the immigrants from North America; Mirsky and Kaushinsky (1989) examined the difficulties of immigrant students; Hanegbi and Menuchin-Itzigson (1988) did an anthropological study of the adaptation of Ethiopian adolescents; and Weil (1988) analyzed the impact of caste ideology on the integration of immigrants from India. The immigration from the Soviet Union of the 1970s generated numerous studies: Shuval and her colleagues (see Shuval 1963, 1983; Shuval et al. 1975) carried out a comprehensive multivariate longitudinal study illuminating the problems of social and economic integration of these immigrants and of the problems of immigrant physicians. Considerable research has focused on specific aspects of the integration of the immigrants of the 1970s (see, for instance, Ben-Barak 1989; Levy and Guttman 1974; Farago 1979; Weingrod 1985).

The Peculiarity of Jewish Immigration to Israel

Between 1990 and 1992, following *perestroika*, approximately 400,000 Jews from the former Soviet Union immigrated to Israel, increasing the Jewish population of Israel by about 10 percent in a period of two years. Not surprisingly, immigration of this volume precipitated social change that affected not merely the immigrants but also the social system of Israeli society at large.

To understand the implications of this mass immigration, it is necessary to start by pointing out some peculiarities of Jewish immigration to Israel. The founding of the State of Israel is regarded as the realization of the dream of return to Zion—a dream Jews have had since the Second Temple was destroyed by the Romans in 70 C.E. Immigration is a major component of Zionist ideology and an integral part of the State's *raison d'etre* (Gitelman and Naveh 1976). As Ben-Gurion declared in 1949, "We must speed and make more powerful the stream of immigration to the utmost of our powers, for the ingathering of the exiles is the purpose of our existence" (Ben-Gurion 1969:386). Successful absorption of new immigrants is regarded, therefore, as perhaps the most important means toward achieving the national goal that Israel be the home of all Jews. Moreover, and in contrast to most other migratory movements, Jewish immigrants are seen as belonging, by definition, to the same national entity as the members of the absorbing society—namely, the Jewish people.

Immigrants to Israel: Homecoming Kinsmen or Indigenous Foreigners?

Israel's national goal of being homeland for every Jew in the world and the presumably shared identity of immigrants and veterans arouses expectations among immigrants that they will be welcomed as "homecoming kinsmen" and that they will feel more at home in Israel than they did in their countries of origin. However, several factors complicate matters and make the experiences of immigrants more frustrating than one might at first anticipate.

First is the issue of cultural differences. Though Israel is hardly a culturally homogenous society, the immigrants' cultural background, internalized during generations of distinct socialization, is apt to be perceived by the absorbing society as deviant and perhaps dysfunctional for life in Israel. Moreover, it is difficult for immigrants to develop meaningful primary social ties with members of the absorbing society if they do not have some shared cultural background (Goffman 1959:214–219; Linton 1936:80–112; Parsons 1951:3–7; Rossi 1980: 18–27). A study by Mirsky and Kaushinsky of American student immigrants to Israel illustrates this point:

When [the immigrant students] try to find a peer group within Israeli society, they are doomed to failure because of the vast differences between them and their Israeli peers. . . . Israeli students view the immigrants as outsiders and often ridicule their behavior, language and even their very decision to immigrate to Israel. But the rejection is not one-sided. This is the stage at which immigrant students tend to criticize and reject Israel and Israeli society. . . . Since very few Israelis are able to accept such an attitude, immigrant students inevitably withdraw from Israeli society into one consisting of fellow immigrants. (Mirsky and Kaushinsky 1989:737)

This passage alludes to "an escalating cycle of discord," which can lead to intergroup estrangement and even conflicts—both counterproductive to successful concomitant readjustment.

Second, in light of lingering interethnic (Ashkenazi-Sephardi) tension, the influx of a large number of Ashkenazi immigrants, who receive the modest package that government authorities have allowed for their absorption, is apt to provoke feelings of discrimination and resentment on the part of Easterners that they, who "built the country," received much less when they arrived in Israel (Ben-Sira 1988a; Smooha 1978). Such tensions have a precedent in Israel, where the wave of immigration in the 1970s was at least one of the causes of the "Black Panthers," a movement of mainly Eastern Jews protesting against what they saw as preferential treatment given to immigrants from the Soviet Union and the West at the expense of disadvantaged sectors in Israeli society (Bernstein 1979; Cohen 1980).

A third and related point is that Israel, as a welfare state, is committed to respond to problems of health, unemployment, and poverty of all its residents. The enormous burden inherent in meeting its commitment to new immigrants, however, is likely to drain resources from these other social goals.

Finally, there is some evidence that immigration is no longer viewed by Israeli society as a primary goal of Zionism (Ben-Sira 1993). Indeed, immigrants are sometimes perceived, and perceive themselves, more as "resident foreigners" than as "homecoming kinsmen." The inconsistency between the declared national goal of an "ingathering of the exiles" and the actual social and political reality may have frustrating consequences for both immigrants and veterans, consequences that hinder successful concomitant readjustment.

Applicability of the Paradigm

Given these peculiarities, can one use the case of Jewish immigrants to Israel to test a paradigm meant to apply to immigrants in general? Although this case is distinctive in many ways, the similarities to other countries are more significant than the differences. The United States, for instance, is a heterogeneous society, essentially a society of immigrants, with a policy of welcoming immigration and even viewing cultural heterogeneity as a positive element (see, for instance, DeVos 1980). And yet, the debate on the question of immigration in the United States at the close of 1993 reveals an apparently deep-seated ambivalence toward immigrants. The following passage is instructive: "In a Gallup poll taken last summer [in 1993], two-thirds of Americans said overall immigration should be reduced. . . . Consistently through American history, the public has favorably viewed earlier generations of immigrants and looked unfavorably on contemporary immigrants—often translating their sentiments into discriminatory barriers" (Brownstein and Simon 1993:A7).

This passage suggests certain commonalties between Israel, the United States, and other societies that at some stages in their history have welcomed immigrants and yet do not necessarily view all immigration positively, a fact that may lead to problems in concomitant readjustment. A systematically developed, theory-based and empirically supported paradigm may help us better understand what factors promote and impede readjustment of immigrants and, to some extent, members of absorbing societies, particularly in heterogeneous countries.

THE STUDY

The case of the immigration of Jews from the former Soviet Union to Israel served as the means of testing the hypothesized paradigm. An interview study was carried out among two cross-sectional representative samples of Israeli Jewish adults, aged twenty years or older. One sample (N = 892) consisted of veteran Israelis; for some analyses, it was subdivided into "East," if the respondent or his/her father was born in Asia or North Africa; "West," if the respondent or his/her father was born in Europe or America; and "Israel," if the respondent was at least second-generation Israeli-born. The other sample (N = 486) consisted of immigrants from the former Soviet Union who arrived in Israel between 1990 and 1993; for some analyses, it was subdivided by year of immigration. The interviews were carried out at the respondents' homes, during September and October 1993, by trained interviewers who used structured interview schedules containing the same closed-ended questions for both population groups. The questionnaires for the immigrants were translated into Russian (for further details, see Appendix A).

OUTLINE OF THE WORK

In Chapter 2, I explore the paradox of a reciprocally desirable but disillusioning change instigated by immigration and address questions regarding the stress-precipitating impact of social change instigated by immigration. I also delineate the hopes and expectations of both immigrants and members of absorbing societies and analyze the complexity of the immigration process as an extreme change in the life of both the immigrants and the absorbing society. In Chapter 3, I review current approaches to the stress-readjustment process and propose a multivariate comprehensive paradigm, demonstrating the usefulness of this paradigm for an understanding of the concomitant readjustment to the life-change instigated by immigration. In Chapters 4 through 7, I separately analyze each component of the stress-readjustment process, test it empirically, and apply it both to a conceptualization of the relevant characteristics of immigration and an elucidation of their role in concomitant readjustment. In Chapter 8, I apply Smallest Space Analysis (SSA), a multivariate data analysis method developed by the late Louis Guttman, to create an "empirical structure of readjustment," which summarizes the factors promoting and impeding the mutual readjustment of immigrants and veterans and also the interplay among these factors. Finally, I conclude with the effects of the interrelationships among intra- and intergroup components on the concomitant readjustment of both immigrants and veterans and discuss the applicability of the "structure of readjustment" to a better understanding of the factors that impede and promote readjustment in migratory movements in general.

NOTES

1. The quotation is based on an interview published in the *Los Angeles Times* as part of a series on immigration in the 1990s.

2. A short-term disturbance will be called "tension." See Chapter 3 for further elaboration of this subject.

3. Although the term "host society" is often used to refer to the country of destination of immigrants, I prefer "absorbing society" as more appropriate for describing the nature of a society that is bound not merely to house the immigrants but eventually to absorb them.

1

Immigration—A Desirable Yet Disillusioning Social Change

Immigration is a life-change generally made in order to improve the immigrants' overall well-being. And yet, there is a paradox: In the short term, at least, immigration may have profound stress-precipitating consequences (Palinkas 1982). Similarly, though absorbing societies often welcome immigration and the cultural heterogeneity it entails (DeVos 1980; Eisenstadt 1980), they may subsequently discourage immigration. There are many examples of countries or communities that initially welcomed, or even encouraged, immigration but later faced intergroup tension and hostilities and blamed the changing composition of the population for the deteriorating quality of their lives (see Brownstein and Simon 1993).

To begin to understand this apparent paradox, we must realize that immigration transforms the cultural, social, and economic systems of both immigrants and the absorbing society in ways that often differ from their expectations (Tienda and Booth 1991:51). In this chapter, I summarize the literature on the implications of immigration for immigrants and for the absorbing society.

IMMIGRATION AND ACCULTURATION

Immigration necessitates "acculturation," that is, cultural exchange resulting from continuous, first-hand contact between two distinct groups (see Redfield et al. 1936). Berry (1991) contends that acculturation is not only a group-level but also an individual-level phenomenon, which he calls "psychological acculturation." At this level, acculturation refers to changes of overt behavior and covert traits in an individual whose group is collectively experiencing cultural change.

One can study acculturation among both immigrants (whom Berry calls the "non-dominant" group) and the absorbing society (the "dominant" group).

Overall, Berry maintains that the acculturation required of non-dominant group members is likely to be greater than that required of dominant group members (Berry 1991:21). The acculturation required of the latter depends on the volume and abruptness of the influx of the non-dominant group, as well as the permanence of the immigration. In any case, however, successful completion of the process of immigration demands "concomitant readjustment" by both the immigrants and the absorbing society. If the absorbing society resists all change, the immigration is unlikely to be a success.

IMMIGRATION AND CHANGE

Immigrants must undergo changes in a wide range of areas: physical changes, such as a new place to live, different (and frequently problematic) housing; biological changes, such as different sources of nutrition, unfamiliar diseases; political changes, such as a different type of government and political procedures; economic changes, such as different types of employment, which require different know-how and skills; cultural changes, such as a different language, types of education, approach to religion; and social changes, including those involving intergroup and interpersonal relations, as well as different types of dominance. Finally, Berry (1991:22) maintains, numerous psychological changes may appear at the individual level. These include changes in behavior, in values, abilities, and motives, but perhaps also identities and attitudes toward self, one's own group, and other groups.

In a study of immigrants from Ethiopia to Israel, Hanegbi and Menuchin-Itzigsohn consider the effects of the enormous amount of cultural change that immigrants may have to undergo:

[Breakdown in the familiar social space of immigrants] can explain symptoms of deep suspicion and lack of belief in the intentions of others as a mechanism of self-defense. . . . [It] may also lead to identity confusion, which can only be resolved by a long continuous stretch of time, a clear definition of space, and understanding of process. The outer circumstances of immigration with the accompanying loss of perspective and expectation leave the [immigrant] . . . open to confusion. . . . [There are] internal and external pressures to adjust quickly, to show the outer signs of "accepting" and "being accepted." This requires two simultaneous and different sets of social codes, two different frames [of reference] in which to situate social relations and establish one's identity, a situation which too often leads to confusion and anxiety; the result—a quick external adjustment and a deep inner maladjustment. (Hanegbi and Menuchin-Itzigsohn 1988: 147–148)

Because of all the change required, immigration constitutes a change for which individuals are not likely to be adequately prepared by "anticipatory socialization" (Merton 1968).

The problems encountered by the immigrants in the absorbing societies have been a major subject of investigation for many decades. Indeed, Nann (1982) cautions on the dangers of migratory research that focuses predominantly on the harmful consequences of immigration-instigated change. One danger of such an approach is that social change will automatically be assumed to be "bad" for one's health and well-being. Another danger may be that of ignoring significant variables and factors that can explain successful adaptation and resettlement. Thus, for instance, Handlin (1951), in his classic exposition of the hardships facing immigrants, tends to emphasize the negative. In a review of Handlin's book, Tiryakian (1980) shows that Handlin's data contain significant evidence of the positive effects of immigration. Thus, I first consider to what extent change as such should be seen as the causal factor in immigration-related stress.

IMMIGRATION AND STRESS

The tremendous, usually abrupt, change in their entire life style that immigrants face is apt to exceed the capacity of their anticipatory socialization in the countries of their origin or even make it useless. Rumbaut contends that the significant amount of life-change that immigrants and refugees have to cope with, as well as their often-marginal position in the new society, can lead to "relative powerlessness and alienation," which in turn can affect their ability "to achieve life goals in a foreign world" (Rumbaut 1991:57). Srole and his colleagues, in their classic midtown Manhattan study, suggest that "psychological distance" may explain the higher rate of psychopathology among foreign-born groups, arguing that, "To compress the profound historical changes of a revolutionizing century into a few adult years of an individual life cycle may exact a high price in psychological well-being" (Srole et al. 1962:354).

There are other studies suggesting a relationship between immigration and stress. Murphy, who conducted a longitudinal follow-up study among Vietnamese (J. M. Murphy 1977), found a substantially higher level of stress among those who had been evacuated from their home villages than among those who had not been uprooted. However, he did not discuss the impact of war on emotional homeostasis. Papajohn and Spiegel (1971) studied second-generation American Greeks and concluded that the level of psychological stress of these immigrants was associated with the extent to which American values were adopted. A possible explanation is that the worth of the immigrant's native cultural orientation, which has long served as a behavioral guide, is now challenged, and perhaps even devalued, by competing American values. Kuo (1976) did research on Chinese immigrants to the United States and showed that the "cultural shock" and social isolation associated with immigration correlated positively with psychological disturbance, as measured by the Midtown Psychiatric Impairment Scale, the Depression Scale, and the Unhappiness Scale. Espino (1991) analyzed migration from Central America to the United States and concluded that "migration is a stressful process challenging the resources of those who chose to undergo it" (Espino 1991:106). Valdes and Baxter (1976) carried out a study of stress among Cuban exiles in the United States using Holmes and

Rahe's (1967) Social Readjustment Rating Scale (SRRS). The respondents rated "migration" as the fourth most stressful event, similar to the death of a close relative and divorce. Williams (1991) notes that anxiety and depressive disorders have been shown to have a higher prevalence among immigrants during stages of final resettlement than in the general population. A similar trend was observed also among immigrant children. Littlewood and Lipsedge (1981) found that immigrants from the West Indies were most likely to be admitted to hospitalization two to five years after immigration, and immigrants from West Africa even later.

Still, it is not clear whether change per se is the cause of stress, or whether specific factors associated with immigration precipitate stress among immigrants. Several studies provide evidence relevant to this question. Schleifer and colleagues (1979), who applied the SRRS scale in a study of young Jewish American professionals who immigrated to Israel, reported that, overall, the respondents scored immigration as the ninth most stressful event, similar to feeling redundant, joining the armed forces, retirement, and marital reconciliation. Yet, the variance of responses was immense, with ratings ranging from 25 through 1500 (500 for marriage was used as a standard for comparison), suggesting that an array of factors, and not immigration per se, may underlie the immigrants' stress. Hiok-Boon and colleagues (1985), in their study of Vietnamese refugees in the United States, found that depression was most common among elderly and those with limited English. Westermeyer and colleagues (1983), in a study of refugees from Laos living in Minnesota, found high levels of depression among those who had been herbal healers prior to migration, among respondents with marital problems, and among those who had negative feelings about the United States. Having a job was also related to depression. However, contrary to the findings among nonimmigrants, the highest level of depression was found among women with a job, perhaps because employed women were exposed to more difficulties outside of their homes. Cheung and Dobkin de Rios, in their study of mental health problems among Chinese immigrants to the United States, assert that for many elderly Chinese, adjustment to Western culture is extremely difficult, if not impossible: "Often they are confused and bewildered as to what is correct and appropriate. . . . Many middle-aged Chinese who are more rigid in their thinking and rooted deeply in the traditional systems experience difficulties too. . . . Their psychological well-being is affected by the stress exerted upon them to adjust" (Cheung and Dobkin de Rios 1982:152–153).

Bavington and Majid (1986) show that lack of a supportive family is one of the main factors explaining depression among Asian women in the United Kingdom. Alma (1986) reports, on the basis of her experience as a health worker with migrant workers in Europe, that after thirty years many still suffer from unresolved psycho-social problems. She suggests an array of factors that can explain the migrants' distress, such as working conditions, housing, and financial conditions; unfortunately, her conclusions are not based on systematic investigation. In contrast to the above, Cochrane and Stopes-Roe (1977) suggest, based on their study of Asians in the United Kingdom, that the level of psychiatric symptoms among Indian and Pakistani immigrants is not higher than among age- and sex-matched British natives. Eitinger and Schwarz (1981) reach similar conclusions. Murphy (1973) discovered lower mental hospitalization rates among immigrants than among natives in both Canada and Singapore.

This brief review of studies, with their diversity of results, supports the conjecture that the change inherent in migration is not in itself the cause of stress. Mirowsky and Ross noted the lack of an empirically verified basis in approaches like those of Holmes and Rahe (1967) and their colleagues as well as in that of the numerous researchers who applied that approach, who "asserted the importance of change itself . . . [and] rejected the importance of the psychological and social meaning of events" (Mirowsky and Ross 1989:125–130). Rather, they argued, Holmes and Rahe's "emphasis on change per se, apart from its meaning and valence, [was] purely theoretical" (Mirowsky and Ross 1989:127; see also Kuo and Tsai 1986; Creed 1987).

One can gain insight into possible sources of stress in the change inherent in immigration from Pearlin's examination of the change-stress relationship from the perspective of loss and gain of roles:

A fairly substantial body of research . . . [regards] transitions as life events and views events, in turn, as . . . benchmarks of stress in the lives of people. Underlying this view is the implicit assumption that any life change is capable of arousing stress. . . . The major shortcoming of the assumption that any change is stressful in proportion to its magnitude is simply that it is not empirically correct. . . . Life events are important to stress not generally but selectively. This fact in turn, is directly relevant to the loss and acquisition of roles as sources of strain. Concretely, it is important to distinguish whether loss and gain are part of the scheduled progression of the individual through the family and occupational life cycle, or if they are eruptive, nonscheduled occurrences. There is no evidence that scheduled role transitions, those that are built into the life cycle, are particularly stressful. I am not saying that these transitions are unimportant. . . . But with limited exceptions, . . . they are not stressful . . . for the very reason that they are scheduled. . . . Not so the nonscheduled role changes. Shifts in roles and statuses, . . . particularly those involving loss, that are not tied to [the life cycle] . . . are capable of evoking considerable distress. . . . Partly perhaps, this results from the absence of anticipatory socialization. . . . [However,] the gains and losses of roles, whether scheduled or unscheduled, do not automatically generate stress simply because they involve life changes. Rather their connection to stress is largely indirect. . . . [For example, unscheduled role changes, such as involuntary job losses,] first act as levers for creating durable strains in economic, family, or other roles and these strains stimulate stress. (Pearlin 1983:21–22)

Similarly, Berry (1991) uses the term "acculturative stress" to refer to a situation in which the stressors originate in the process of immigrant acculturation. According to Weil, "[So] many factors affect the rate and mode of integration of immigrant groups into a new society—immigrants' expectations, structural conditions, individual preferences, societal sanctions, and prevailing ideologies—that it is often difficult to pinpoint any single societal factor which could be considered dominant in the integration of immigrants" (Weil 1988:150). Thus, understanding immigration-induced stress requires identifying factors— "stressors"—that are apt to disrupt the immigrants' emotional homeostasis. Application of the fundamentals of the current approaches to stress and coping can be useful in this regard.

In summary, though immigration aims at improving the immigrants' well-being, it is liable to have profound stress-precipitating, hence maladjustive, consequences, "even among the most motivated and well prepared individuals, and even among the most receptive circumstances" (Rumbaut 1991:56). Immigrants are confronted with unprecedented demands, which they may have difficulties in meeting. But immigration ordinarily succeeds in advancing the central goal that motivated that change. Why, then, do harmful effects of inadequately met demands nonetheless appear? To what extent could the differential in impetus for emigration explain the differential in success at readjustment? This topic will be explored in the following chapter.

2

Reasons for Migration and the Absorbing Society's Perspectives

Migration often, though not always, has stress-precipitating consequences for migrants. When and why does such stress occur? One possible explanation involves the reasons for migration. I turn now to an analysis of the differences between voluntary and forced migration.

VOLUNTARY MIGRATION

Postulates Regarding the Impetus for Migration

For the purposes of this book, "voluntary" migration refers to cases in which the decision to migrate is mainly in the hands of the prospective migrant, who wants to achieve positive goals in a new country. To what extent do these goals affect readjustment in the country of destination? Before answering this question, I shall summarize several theories of migration.

As early as the 1880s, Ravenstein (1885, 1886) suggested several "laws of migration." These "laws," which deal mainly with the volume of migration, streams, and counter-streams, emphasized economic motives. Postulates delineating the factors underlying migration have since then been developed to cover a wide range of causes, consequences, and patterns of migration. Some of these postulates follow.

a. *The theory of intervening opportunities* states that the number of persons migrating a given distance varies positively with the number of destinations and negatively with the number of intervening opportunities (United Nations 1973:210). A similar approach was developed by Lee (1966), who argued that the factors instigating migration may be grouped into those associated with the migrants' origin, those associated with their destination, intervening obstacles, and personal factors.

b. *The economic theory of migration* (Lowry 1966; Todaro 1969) states that individuals migrate mainly to take advantage of better economic conditions (employment and income). Zelinsky's (1971) mobility-transition theory may be viewed as an extension of the economic theory that focuses on the regularities characterizing migration in modern society and on the role of migration as an essential element in the process of modernization.

c. *Behavioral theories* include that of Wolpert (1965), who emphasized the behavioral factors influencing migration, as well as those of DeJong and Fawcett (1981), Haberkon (1981), and Pryor (1981), who focused mainly on the decision-making process in migration.

d. *Developmental and political factors* have been illuminated by Achanfuo-Yeboah (1993), who studied migratory movements in Africa, developing a comprehensive approach suggesting that migration is a product of: (1) socio-cultural changes, and particularly educational developments, which motivate rural-urban migration; (2) economic developments, which bring about increasing employment opportunities; and (3) psycho-social factors, including the search for status improvement.

e. *Ideological factors*, i.e., following the directives of an ideological or religious belief may be an important goal that can be realized only by migration. Zionist ideology is one major reason for immigration to Israel (Eisenstadt 1954; Ben-Sira 1993). Those who strongly adhere to such an ideology are likely to perceive realization of this goal in itself as extremely gratifying.

"Push" and "Pull" Factors in Studies of Migration

If the migrant wants to attain certain valued goals—no matter which ones—it seems likely that he/she will try to determine the extent to which conditions in the country of origin and the potential country (or countries) of destination facilitate or impede attainment of these goals. In principle, the decision to migrate involves factors that "push" prospective migrants out of their country of origin as well as those that "pull" them towards a particular destination. In practice, however, it is often difficult to distinguish and calculate the relative weight of each set of factors. According to Lobodzinska, in a study of emigration from Poland after World War II, many of these emigrés "made the decision to leave Poland hastily, impulsively and without any preparations for the great adventure" (Lobodzinska 1986:412). They mainly wanted to escape the political and economic turmoil, and the resultant hopelessness, prevailing in Poland at that time. They came to the United States, not because it was the "land of opportunity" but because they saw it as a country of peace, optimism, strength, and stability. In this case, though Lobodzinska stresses the "push" factor—the instability of Poland—there is also a "pull" factor—the presumed stability of the United States—which contributed to the immigrants' decision (even when this decision was made "hastily"). Because of its importance to these immigrants, stability was both a "push" and a "pull" factor.

Similarly, in an analysis of the factors motivating emigration from countries like Russia and Poland, Brym noted that "the major reasons identified were economic conditions in their respective countries, and political pessimism (prospects for dictatorship)" (Brym 1992:392). While he focuses explicitly on the "push" factor, he implicitly considers the "pull" factor as well. Similarly, too, in an analysis of Jewish immigrants to Israel from the Soviet Union and North America. Horowitz (1979) argued that immigration was strongly linked to alienation in their country of origin. Yet, she added, alienation can be either a result of real or perceived discrimination against Jews in the country of origin or identification of the immigrant with a society other than that from which he emigrated; that is, it can be either a "push" or a "pull" factor.

Does this mean that attainment of the immigrants' principal goal in the country of destination (stability for the Polish, better economic and political conditions for the Russian, and alleviation of the alienation for the Jewish immigrants) will have a stress-buffering effect? To answer this question, I probe further into the process of reaching the decision to emigrate.

The Decision to Emigrate: A "Social Exchange" Approach

In general, the decision to migrate is based on an evaluation of the conditions in both the country of origin and the country of destination. In terms of the analysis by Pryor (1981) and by DeJong and Gardener (1981), the decision to emigrate is the result of calculating the costs and benefits of staying and of moving. One of the costs of moving into a new environment is an inevitable confrontation with unprecedented demands. Presumably, migrants consider this cost in the process of reaching the decision to emigrate, decide that the value of the benefits exceeded the value of the costs, and are prepared to "pay" for these benefits by confronting the "costs" of these demands. Why, then, are they distressed when confronted by the demands of migration?

To answer this question, it is necessary to specify the concept of "value" that was included in the immigrants' calculation. Pryor's (1981) and DeJong and Fawcett's (1981) analyses are based on the approach of social exchange. In terms of the classic social exchange model (Homans 1974), individuals try to maximize their profits, that is, benefits (or rewards) minus costs. The decision to emigrate is based on a comparison of the subjectively assessed "profits" available in their country of origin and expected in the country of destination. The expected profit to be derived in the country of destination consists of the expected "rewards" to be obtained in that country minus the expected "costs" that will have to be invested—where these costs include both the expected hardships and the rewards currently secured in the migrants' home country, which will have to be foregone (Homans 1974:31–32). It should be apparent that this presumably "rational" calculation is, in fact, rather complex. In particular, there are three points that cast doubt on the usefulness of that calculation for moderating the stress-potential of confronting a new reality: the variability of subjectively assessed values, the problem of interpretation-based expectations, and the social dynamics in the absorbing society.

The Variability of Subjectively Assessed Values

Assessment of the values of both the rewards to be gained in the country of destination and the relative costs are based on the subjective perception of reality (Thomas and Thomas 1928). In terms of the classic social exchange model, the assessed values of rewards vary according to the abundance or scarcity of their supply.[1] Thus, subsequent to immigration, the desired rewards in the new country are likely to be devalued due to their abundance, while the costs of the rewards foregone in the old country are likely to be inflated due to their current scarcity. Subsequent to immigration, then, a "rational" calculation causes the change to be reassessed as "loss" rather than "profit."

The assessed loss in itself may impose stress-arousing demands, in addition to those of the unprecedented demands confronting the immigrant in the new environment. It follows that the immigrant's initial sense of well-being upon arrival in the new country is liable to be gradually transformed into a sense of stress. Mirsky and Kaushinsky's (1989) study of the transformation from euphoria to distress among American-Jewish students in Israel further illustrates this point. (For an analysis of the fluctuation in emotional homeostasis according to the length of stay in the new country, among immigrants from the former Soviet Union to Israel in 1990–1993, see Chapter 4.)

The Problem of Culturally Based Expectations

Not only the transformation in the assessments but also the ambiguous basis of the estimated value of the conditions in the country of destination can exacerbate the stress of immigration. The above-mentioned "calculation" is grounded on the immigrants' subjectively formed expectations about conditions in the country of destination. These expectations are derived from information gathered from various sources.

However, the understanding of, and the meaning attributed to, even the most reliable information is a product of interpretations based on the culturally infused frame of reference of the prospective immigrant. Thus, even when immigrants have relatively reliable information, the cultural bias of their interpretations means that they are likely to find reality in the country of immigration to be very different than they expected.[2] The following passage from Lobodzinska's study of Polish immigrants to the United States illustrates this point:

[The immigrants] bring with them illusionary stereotypes of the American life. . . . The aggregate image . . . boils down to a country of the ultimate affluence, full of job opportunities leading easily to upward mobility; a land of freedom for persecuted people. . . . The confrontation of the illusionary stereotype with reality is one of the causes for disappointment and confusion. The newcomers are unprepared for the extent of inflation, are surprised by the unemployment and competition in the labor market. They have to learn the value of the dollar, to learn about the "rat race." [They may] associate prosperity with liberalism, tolerance, progressive ideology. . . . The existing social conflicts and social distance between different groups in this pluralistic society are causes for consternation for individuals whose background is derived from a socially, ethnically, religiously homogenous society. (Lobodzinska 1986:426–27)

In short, erroneous expectations based on misinterpreting the available information are likely to distort the values of variables in the decision-making equation.

The Social Dynamics in the Absorbing Society

The attitudes of the absorbing society toward immigration are also apt to change. Though societies often initially welcome immigration, they may later come to see it as jeopardizing their social well-being (Brym 1992). Thus, for instance, a study by Brownstein and Simon (1993) of attitudes towards immigration in the United States reported that, in communities that had encouraged immigration, tensions and intergroup hostilities are mounting, and old timers feel that the changing composition of the population has lowered the quality of their lives and aggravated economic problems.

In her study of Jamaican immigrants to the United States, DaCosta-Bagot (1985) points to the stress-arousing effect of the absorbing society's attitudes toward them and concludes:

The relative deprivation of worth was most significantly related to psychological symptomatology among employed adults. . . . [It] represented a measure of respondents' perception of how they are perceived, evaluated, and treated by members of the mainstream culture, particularly with respect to racial matters. Participants reported experiences of racial discrimination in the work-place, indicated that they were often regarded as being less capable than members of the mainstream group and reported attendant feelings of insecurity and discomfort at work. It is noteworthy that the relative deprivation was significantly associated with stress among employed adults. (DaCosta-Bagot 1985:123)

Thus, even if the values introduced in the immigrants' decision-making process correspond with reality at the time of the assessment, this reality may change as a result of immigration. Moreover, to the extent that immigration upsets the homeostasis of members of the absorbing society, the interaction between both groups is liable to trigger, as indicated earlier, an escalating cycle of discord that may increase the stress immigrants feel and impede their adjustment.

Summary: The Frustrating Consequences of Preliminary Assessment of the Absorbing Society

The central question underlying this section is how to understand that while immigration is aimed at bettering the immigrants' well-being, it may in fact have stress-arousing consequences. I conclude that the preliminary assessment of the rewards and costs of immigration is an inadequate basis for predicting the readjustment process. It appears that, whatever the values of the "rewards" and "costs" assessed in the decision to emigrate, the social dynamics in the absorbing society will be the decisive starting point for the process of readjustment.

FORCED MIGRATION

Immigrants and Refugees

Until now, I have been discussing voluntary migration and its implications for immigrant absorption. I now turn to forced migration to see whether similar conclusions apply. A brief review of the magnitude of the problem is in order. In the introduction, I cited Westermeyer's (1991) estimate that, since the start of World War II, about one hundred million people have had to leave their native countries due to war, civil unrest, or political or religious persecution, as well as Aaronson's (1984) estimate that about sixteen million people were either in transit or had recently been granted asylum in foreign countries during the early 1980s. Achanfuo-Yeboah (1993) reported that in 1969 a decision of the government of Ghana resulted in the expulsion of millions of Nigerians from Ghana. Berry has asserted that, "The largest refugee dislocations at the present time are those due to military interventions (either direct or indirect) by major world powers and to the long and painful process of decolonization. . . . Within nation states, other more direct factors are evident: ethnic, racial, and religious conflict and persecution, political violence, imprisonment and deliberate torture" (Berry 1991:29–30).

It is not always easy to distinguish forced migration from voluntary migration. In the literature, "refugees" are commonly defined as involuntary migrants "pushed" by perceived threats to life and liberty and by coercive political conditions. "Immigrants," on the other hand, are conventionally defined as voluntary resettlers "pulled" by expectations of a better future and attractive economic opportunities (see David 1970; Stein 1986). The distinction between voluntary and forced migration seems to be more complex, however, since supposedly voluntary migrations are not always voluntary or planned, as claimed, and there are wide differences in the migration experiences of "acute flight" versus "anticipatory" refugees (see Kunz 1973). Thus, for instance, Jews in Germany at the earlier stages of the Nazi regime, when emigration was still possible, preferred to remain despite the persecutions, having decided that it was still more profitable to stay than to leave. Had they decided to emigrate, they would be defined as "anticipatory refugees," but they would still be "voluntary" migrants, since the decision to migrate was in their own hands.

In fact, the status of "refugee" is not determined necessarily by the migrants but rather by the host governments for a variety of ideological or political reasons. For example, the Vietnamese "boat people" were identified by the American government as "political refugees." while Central American escapees were classified as "illegal economic immigrants," even though both groups had experienced persecution and traumatic flight (Rumbaut 1991:56–57). Until 1990, Jews emigrating from the Soviet Union with an Israeli visa were defined by the American government as refugees and as such were permitted entry to, and support by, the United States. From 1990 on, their definition was changed, mainly due to political pressures ("Soviet Jews" 1990).

For the purposes of this analysis, I shall use the term "immigrant" for voluntary migration and "refugee" for forced migration, in which the migrants have no reasonable alternative to escaping the country of origin.

The Impact of Forced Migration

Can the social exchange model delineated above be applied usefully to refugees? In particular, will confrontation with unprecedented demands in the country of refuge have a distressing impact on persons escaping life-threatening persecution similar to that on voluntary immigrants, and will refugees have the same risk of stress due to frustrated expectations as do voluntary immigrants?

Evidence in the literature suggests that refugees are even more prone than are voluntary migrants to stress and maladjustment. Apparently, the impact of the trauma experienced in the country of origin is apt to make readjustment more difficult (see Berry 1991:29–30). Murphy reached a similar conclusion with regard to the long-term effect of the trauma of war and uprooting on the Vietnamese Binh Hoa evacuees:

In the five years after [their evacuation], . . . effort was made by governmental agencies to relieve the Binh Hoa evacuees from the acute disadvantages of what had happened to them. Despite these efforts and despite the passage of time, the Binh Hoa people were still suffering a psychological aftermath . . . [which] may well extend into the future. The fact that they did not recover from the depressed feelings which are understandably evoked by such traumatic circumstances is a mark of the seriousness of the effect. It may mean that they carry the scars of permanent despair. (J. M. Murphy, 1977:105)

Kinzie and Sack's case study of Cambodian refugee children from childhood to young adulthood suggests that Post-Traumatic Stress Disorder (PTSD) symptoms affected half of the students five years after the worst trauma had ended. Follow up of these students three years later indicated that PTSD symptoms were still present in about half, but the prevalence of depressed symptoms had diminished. Some students improved during this time, but others developed symptoms for the first time (Kinzie and Sack 1991:104).

Yet, the difficulties of readjustment of refugees cannot be attributed only to post-traumatic stress. A case study by Pollock of the readjustment problems of a South American refugee to the United States illustrates the effects of the assessed "loss" inherent in immigration. The refugee told him:

How much he missed his beautiful homeland, even with its tyrannies and risks. He dreamed in Spanish, even though he had been in the United States for some time and was a successful professional. He applied for United States citizenship and not long before it was formally conferred upon him he went into a fit of despair. "It is a final break with my motherland." He knew that if he returned as long as the existing political group was in power he was in great danger of either death or permanent incarceration. (Pollock 1989:148)

Leiper de Monchy reports that many refugees arrive in the United States with the scars of the traumatic destructive and lethal events of their tragic past yet with "hope for a bright new future, the dream that often sustained them during the hardship of their forced immigration. Unfortunately, arrival to this land of freedom does not in itself fulfill this dream. Rebuilding lives is a long, difficult process exacerbated by the new stresses and traumas of adjustment and acculturation" (Leiper de Monchy 1991:163).

Similarly, Espino's study of refugees from Central American conflict- and war-torn countries suggests that stress among refugees is attributable to both the trauma experienced in the country of origin and their condition in the absorbing society. She concludes:

Families from war-torn areas arrive with the scars of traumas experienced in their country of origin as a result of exposure to violence and poverty. On their arrival they become part of the inner city working poor with the added anxiety of illegal status. The children, living in overcrowded, high conflict homes experience neglect and abuse. Marked educational delays further inhibit their capacity to adapt, resulting in loss of self-esteem and depression. (Espino 1991:122)

It appears, then, that readjustment of refugees escaping is apt to be especially problematic, due not only to confrontation with unprecedented demands and unmet expectations in the absorbing society—as for voluntary migrants—but also due to the lingering effect of trauma in the country of origin. Traumatic experiences in the country of origin are likely to have an impact on the immigrants' emotional homeostasis. However, after immigration, the absorbing society inevitably becomes the locus of the immigrants' life, and both confrontation and coping with that society's perspectives become crucial in the immigrants' readjustment. The following quotation from the story of a young immigrant to the United States from Korea may illustrate this point:

By far the greatest challenge of my life has been adapting to American society, an experience that has not only dramatically changed my attitude but noticeably improved my character as well. In 1992, I came to the United States from Korea. Because Korea and the United States differ so immensely, it is impossible to describe all the nuances and peculiarities that distinguish the two nations. To me America seemed strange, chaotic and overwhelming. . . . [Despite my excellent knowledge of English,] I couldn't fully interact in my new surroundings, so I felt disabled. . . . I made few new friends and became increasingly isolated. I never thought that coming to America would be so disappointing. I eventually came to regret having moved to America and blamed my parents for my unwarranted suffering. But my faulting others in no way made my situation less grievous or more tolerable. . . . [Finally, I followed the advice of a friend, who] said that I could learn from my painful experiences. Instead of recoiling from my tribulations, he recommended that I meet these challenges head on. I skeptically accepted his advice. . . . Although this process was tedious and frustrating at times, it did eventually prove to be rewarding. . . . Communication helped me replace my groundless animosities with an appreciation for social cultures. (Oh 1994)

This quotation describes an immigrant who evidently has a strong sense of "potency" (Ben-Sira 1985, 1989, 1991; see discussion in Chapter 3) but also emphasizes the significance of coping with the demands in the absorbing society. Successfully meeting these demands depends both on the immigrant's capabilities and on the absorbing society's perspectives. Immigrants who lack appropriate resources and feel the absorbing society's perspectives to be unfavorable have a higher risk of maladjustment.

THE ABSORBING SOCIETY'S PERSPECTIVES

The Role of "Societal Perspectives"

Immigrants not only live in, but usually also become members of, a society that differs—often substantially—from their society of origin.   Unless they migrate again, they are committed to life in the absorbing society, and their continued well-being depends on successful interaction with members of that society. For this interaction to be gratifying and effective rather than frustrating and conflictual, at least a minimal common denominator among the members of a society is imperative (Coser 1964).

One major element that can serve as this common denominator is "societal perspectives," defined as the orientations and attitudes towards various areas of life that prevail in a society (Ben-Sira 1991:19). To the extent that there is a correspondence of societal perspectives among members of a society, interaction is likely to be successful, and immigrants are likely to have an easier readjustment to that society. (The role of societal perspectives in the readjustment process will be discussed further in Chapters 3 and 5.)

The decisive societal perspectives for the readjustment of immigrants are, naturally, those relating to immigration. These perspectives could favor immigration; alternatively, they could originally or subsequently discourage immigration. Moreover, groups in the absorbing society may differ in their perspectives on immigration, in which case it is important to determine what the prevailing perspectives are and how the opposing perspectives affect the immigrants. In general, a reasonable level of concomitant readjustment seems to require the prevalence of immigration-supporting perspectives in the absorbing society.

But while the societal perspectives are important, it is perhaps equally important to know how the immigrants perceive these perspectives and, in particular, discrepancies that exist between the prevailing societal perspectives and their perception by the immigrants. If there is a high correspondence and the prevailing perspectives are positive or even neutral, there is a good basis for successfully completing the process of readjustment.[3]

On the other hand, if there is a low correspondence, and especially if the prevailing societal perspectives discourage immigration, then it will be difficult to successfully initiate and complete this process.

*The Absorbing Society's Perspectives on Immigration: The Austrian
Experience*

Brym, in his study of migratory movements in Europe and particularly in
Austria at the time of the decline of the Soviet Union, underscores the increasing
threat of the influx of immigrants. He states that some 240,000 of Vienna's 1.8
million residents are immigrants from the former Soviet bloc countries, who arrived in 1989 or later. Presumably due to the influx of so many of immigrants,
the unemployment rate in Austria doubled. Competition from Czechs, Slovaks,
Hungarians, Poles and Russian Jews angered Austrian workers, strained Vienna's ability to provide social services, and challenged the tolerance of long-term
residents. Brym views the doubling of popular support for the right wing in the
1991 Viennese municipal elections as an indirect outcome of that influx. The
party's leader, Jorg Haider, campaigned on an anti-immigration platform, having
attained publicity earlier when, as governor of Corinthia, he praised Nazi labor
politics. At the time of Brym's study, no violent outbursts against foreigners
had occurred—as they did in France and Germany where 200,000 immigrants,
mainly from Eastern Europe, arrived in the first ten months of 1991 alone.
However, Brym argues, "in Austria and much of the rest of Western Europe a
simmering xenophobia is being fuelled by the threat of . . . mass-immigration
from the former Soviet bloc countries" (Brym 1992:387).

*The Absorbing Society's Perspectives on Immigration: The American
Experience*

The United States is composed almost entirely of many generations of immigrants. Immigration is the basis of its existence, and pluralism is often encouraged as a stimulus for progress (De Vos 1980). Yet the societal perspectives
regarding immigration are, nonetheless, characterized by fluctuations, varying
from supportive through overtly hostile.

Brownstein and Simon (1993), in their essay on the changing attitudes toward
immigration in California, maintain that, from its founding, the state has
followed a schizophrenic pattern of welcoming immigrants when there is economic need and then turning against them either when the economy sours or
when the ranks of newcomers reach critical mass. Brown and Warner (1992),
in their study of immigration to the United States in the 1890s, discussed the
intense labor conflicts and the depression, second only to the depression of the
1930s, that occurred in the wake of that wave of immigration. They described
the hostility, mass demonstrations, and strikes against immigrants, who represented a seemingly infinite supply of cheap labor. Immigrants were viewed as
the symbol of disorderliness, were blamed for city decay and for deteriorating
city life, and were perceived as a moral and cultural threat to American society.
Brown and Warner argue that no other social problem was seen as the source
of so many urban ills as was immigration.

Lobodzinska, in her study of immigration from Poland, noted many cases of
hostility toward these immigrants. For instance, the Immigration and Natural-

ization Service (INS) has denied asylum to more than seven thousand Solidarity activists, although many would be in danger if they returned to Poland. Poles have also been harassed by INS official in other ways: there have been street roundups of Polish speakers, and work permits have been arbitrarily denied or revoked (Lobodzinska 1986:420–421). Lobodzinska cites complaints published in the Polish-language press in the United States and presents numerous other examples of discrimination. She suggests that one reason for this antagonistic treatment of Poles fleeing martial law and its aftermath could be the general atmosphere of apprehension toward newcomers, who represent a potential threat on the labor market.

As indicated above, in the early 1990s the American media highlighted the mushrooming debate on the question of immigration. For instance, Impellizeri described the change in one city's attitude toward immigrants. While in 1987, its residents declared their city a sanctuary for immigrants and refugees, since 1990 there has been a growing rejection of and hostility toward immigrants:

There were racial conflicts in some neighborhoods and a brawl at . . . [a] high school between Haitian and white students. . . . Natives blamed [the immigrants] . . . for dilapidated private housing, for a rise in violent crime that was actually less dramatic than in any nearby city and for cuts in city services. "I think they cost in housing, subsidized housing," said . . . a lifelong resident. "They have welfare, they have food stamps, they eat better than I do. They take up space in schools, the bilingual program. They have special teachers; we never had that." (Impellizeri 1993:A5)

Impellizeri indicates that this change was related to growing levels of immigration, which raised the Latino and non-white population of the city from 4 percent in 1980 to 16 percent in 1990.

The hostile attitudes toward the immigrants are not unanimous. In fact, there is an ongoing debate between those who advocate restricting immigration and those who oppose such restrictions and emphasize the essence of the American society as a country of immigration and refuge. The ambivalence toward immigration in a society that is entirely grounded on generations of immigrants can be seen in a statement released by the Federation for Immigration Reform, a national public interest organization that is currently pushing for a three-year moratorium on legal immigration: "We acknowledge that immigrants are part of our heritage. But people don't realize the Statue of Liberty is a symbol of liberty and justice, not immigration" (Turner 1993:16).

Summary: The Dynamics of Frustration

In conclusion, preliminary assessments of societal perspectives are undoubtedly critical in the decision to immigrate to a certain country. However, after the immigrants settle in the new country, interaction with members of the absorbing society provides them with newer and more accurate data. Their revised perception of societal perspectives relating to their immigration and the place of immigrants in the new society is likely to serve as a significant starting point for their readjustment. Moreover, since they must now live in that society, the role of these perspectives will probably be more salient than that of the factors that motivated immigration. Even in societies characterized by immigration-favoring perspectives, some groups may hold unfavorable attitudes toward immigration or may change their attitudes after encountering the social change instigated by the influx of immigrants. But also crucial is the extent to which these attitudes affect the immigrants' perception of the prevailing societal perspectives in that society. In the rest of this chapter, I consider these issues with respect to the mass immigration to Israel from the Soviet Union between 1990 and 1993.

ISRAEL: AN ABSORBING SOCIETY'S PERSPECTIVES

Societal Perspectives: Declared Ideologies

Shortly after the State of Israel was established in 1948, Ben Gurion, the first prime minister, stated (as noted above): "Ingathering of the exiles is the purpose of our existence" (Ben Gurion 1969:386). *Aliya* (immigration to Israel) is a principal tenet of Zionist ideology, the realization of the dream of returning to Zion shared by Jews all over the world for the nearly two thousand years of Diaspora (Gottesman 1988:7). Legally, the "Law of Return" entitles virtually every Jew to move to Israel at any time and become a citizen of Israel. In addition, the belief that Israel is the homeland of every Jew implies the right of immigrants to feel at home in Israel.

Absorption of immigrants as a national goal is not confined to the Law of Return. It also implies that the onus of immigrant absorption falls, to a great extent, on the State of Israel. As part of its Zionist ideology, Israel is characterized by a collectivity orientation that places the interests of the society as a whole—in this case, the absorption of immigrants—over the self-interests of individual members of the society. Ahad ha'Am, for instance, felt that "each individual Jew would place national existence above his private interests and personal status" (Rotenstreich 1972:81). In the pre-State period, the *halutz* (pioneer), who placed national goals above his self-interests, was an ideal-typical representative of the collectivity orientation.

Societal Perspectives: Waning Ideologies and Reality

To the extent that *aliya* and the collectivity orientation reflect the "societal perspectives" of Israeli society, they ought to facilitate the readjustment of both the immigrants and the members of the absorbing society to the changes inherent in immigration. However, four developments challenge the claim that *aliya* and collectivity orientation constitute predominant societal perspectives in Israel at the close of the twentieth century: the erosion of the dominant ideological basis of Israel's existence; the waning of *aliya* as a fundamental tenet of Zionism; the dilemma of the conception of Zionism; and a sectoral sense of deprivation.

Erosion of the Dominant Ideological Basis of Israel's Existence

Eisenstadt discusses the deterioration of Zionist ideology over time. The *Yishuv* (Jewish national entity in Palestine before 1948), he says, "was an ideological society, and its collective identity was couched in ideological tenets" (Eisenstadt 1967:117). However, even during the time of the *Yishuv*, contradictions arose between Zionist ideology and other goals. "The major potential contradiction was between the general diffuse ideal of the pioneer and the orientation toward a differentiated economic and political structure entailing a high degree of specialization and individualism" (Eisenstadt 1967:120).

A further erosion of the ideological foundations accompanied the maturation of the State. Writing in the 1960s, Eisenstadt already noted:

Ideology is now only a part of the overall cultural universe of Israel, and its place and meaning within the total setting has been greatly changed. . . . These developments . . . have posed some grave problems for its collective identity. . . . The central problem . . . [has been] the extent to which the orientations and commitments to broader values and to collective responsibility could be maintained in the face of the weakening of the specific ideological commitments and orientations. (Eisenstadt 1967:121–122)

Apparently, an important transformation has occurred. Though in principle the central purpose of the Jewish state as the homeland of all Jews has not changed, in reality *aliya* has lost its centrality for most Jews, both in Israel and in the Diaspora. Eisenstadt emphasizes the changing place of *aliya* in the relationship between Israel and the Jewish communities in the Diaspora and in its very motivation:

Immigration to Israel . . . was no longer the most important . . . [event, and many of the] elements binding Jews together . . . did not necessarily give rise to Aliya. . . . Even when it took place, Aliya was rarely conceived as a revolutionary experience. It was rather an act of . . . seeking some framework for living among Jews, of expressing Jewish solidarity or an attachment to Jewish tradition; or . . . of being able to live a fuller religious or religious-national life. . . . It was only among themselves, within the more extremist political movements in Israel, that some ingredients of a revolutionary experience could be identified—and even they were probably a small part of this Aliya. . . . Whatever the composition and orientation of these Aliyoth [plural of *aliya*], . . . [they moved] into the natural direction of most immigrant countries. . . . [But] no less important . . . was the fact that for many Jews in search of security, Israel was not even the natural first place of refuge. . . . From the mid-1970's—most of the Jews who left Russia with an Israeli visa, officially proclaiming their intention to go to Israel, in fact opted to go not to Israel but to other countries in the West—above all to the United States. (Eisenstadt 1985:484)

One would expect the waning of both the ideological tenets underlying immigration to Israel and the centrality of Israel as the homeland for every Jew to be reflected in the prevailing societal perspectives.

The Dilemma of the Conception of Zionism

In the past decade, there has been a widening gap between contradictory ideological streams in the conception of Zionism, namely, the particularistic and the universalistic. The particularistic conception focuses on the Jewishness of the State, redemption of the soil, and settlement in all parts of *Eretz Yisrael* (the Land of Israel). The universalistic conception envisions the development of a pluralistic, humanistic, and tolerant society. It is in this context that Smooha predicts a trend towards "decolonization, de-Zionization and de-Judaization" of Israeli society (Smooha 1978:264).

Evidence suggests that the split between these two extreme views is becoming unbridgeable, with devotees of each identifying themselves as supporters of the authentic Zionist ideology and insisting that adherents of the other ideology are subverting the Zionist idea—are even perhaps "traitors" (Ben-Sira 1993). The split clearly has implications not just for Zionism in general but for the place of immigration within Zionist ideology.

Sectorial Sense of Deprivation

I mentioned earlier the gap between "Western" and "Eastern" Jews in Israel. Western Jews have long had a dominant position in Israel, in terms of both socioeconomic status (SES) and political power. This gap predates the State of Israel and is partly due to the fact that most Western Jews come from relatively modern industrialized societies, whereas most Eastern Jews come from more traditional societies. In addition, according to Eisenstadt, during the mass immigration of Eastern Jews during the early years of the State, the stronger, more skilled, more intellectual Jews opted to go to Europe, while the weaker ones went to Israel, where they would be assured of being taken care of, at least minimally (Eisenstadt 1985:485). Then, continues Smooha, the Ashkenazim (Westerners) were worried that:

The "backward" Orientals would dilute the Western culture and upset political democracy of the newly founded state. To forestall dangers, the dominant Ashkenazi group has taken the countermeasures of providing minimal services for the Oriental arrivals in order to prevent destitution, admitting them into the lower and middle rungs of society and neutralizing them as an independent force. Over the years a conflict-laden uneven development of ethnic pluralism and inequality has transpired. . . . Significant headway has been made in assimilating Orientals into Ashkenazi lifestyles and social frameworks. At the same time, considerable ethnic disparities have persisted despite appreciable improvements in the Oriental's living conditions. . . . [Although, over time,] class is superseding ethnicity, . . . ethnic stratification has nevertheless remained a sticky problem. (Smooha 1978:260–61)

It is not within the scope of this work to discuss the origins and persistence of interethnic tension in Israel. Whatever they are, it seems that the mass immigration of "Western" Jews from the former Soviet Union may have added fuel to a previously simmering fire. Eastern Jews see more aid than they received given to these immigrants and assert that, once again, the Western-dominated government is discriminating against them and in favor of their fellow Westerners. This is likely to create further tension within the absorbing society as well as between parts of that society and the immigrants.

Based on the above, it is clear that actual societal perspectives may not reflect declared ideologies. But, what are the societal perspectives, and how are they perceived by the immigrants? It is to these questions that I now turn.

SOCIETAL PERSPECTIVES IN THE EYES OF ISRAELI SOCIETY AND THE IMMIGRANTS: EMPIRICAL EVIDENCE

Immigration of Jews from the Former Soviet Union

As indicated earlier, the focus of the empirical study is on the immigration of Jews from the former Soviet Union to Israel between 1990 and 1993. It is important to reiterate that for many of these Jews, the United States was the preferred destination with Israel a second choice that gained in popularity only after the American government stopped defining them as "refugees":

[In the past,] the Jewish immigrants [to the United States] were people who got as far as the way-station outside Rome on an Israeli visa. . . . [Now,] Russians who want to make America rather than Israel as their place of refuge must apply directly to the American consulate in Moscow. Given the flood of people who want to get out, and the relative smallness of the American quota, most have to abandon their American dream and set off for an open-armed Israel. ("Soviet Jews" 1990:52)

Thus, most immigrants seem to have been motivated mainly by the "push" to leave Russia. To the extent that there was a "pull," it was mainly an economic one to industrialized Western countries and rarely an ideological one to the Jewish homeland. In that sense, this immigration to Israel does not differ from many other migratory movements. At the same time, however, those immigrating to Israel are likely to be aware of the declared societal perspectives that underlie the legitimization of the State of Israel. The presumption that their immigration accords with Israel's national goals may result in their putting the onus of their successful adjustment on Israeli society.

Prevailing Societal Perspectives: Perception and Reality

As indicated earlier, the immigrants' perception of the prevailing societal perspectives relating to immigration is an important starting point for their readjustment. However, one must also consider to what extent the immigrants' perception conforms with perspectives actually held by members of the absorbing society. A large discrepancy between immigrants' perceptions and the reality is apt to provoke frustration and intergroup conflicts and may lead to long-term maladjustment.

What, then, are the prevailing perspectives in Israel relating to immigration? I have noted that societal perspectives comprise two elements, orientations and attitudes. It is suggested, then, that the societal perspectives relating to immigration include an orientation viewing immigration as a fundamental element in the Zionist ideology, and a favorable attitude toward immigration. How prevalent are these in Israel in the 1990s?

Immigration-Supporting Perspectives

Data in Tables 1 and 3 suggest that immigrants from the former Soviet Union have a higher degree of immigration-supporting perspectives than do veteran Israelis: 21 percent of the immigrants but only 7 percent of the veterans view immigration as most essential to Zionism. Similarly, 56 percent of the immigrants and 15 percent of the veterans hold immigration-favoring attitudes.

Table 1
Immigrant Absorption as the Most Essential Characteristic of Zionism[a] by Population Group

Rank	Veterans (%)	Immigrants (%)	Total (%)
High	7	21	12
Medium	13	17	14
Low	80	62	74
(N)	(853)	(454)	(1307)

a. A scale based on two questions. Respondents were given a list of nine topics and asked which one best defined Zionism. They were then asked, "And what else?" The nine topics were: economic independence, Israel's security, settlement within the "Green Line" (Israel's border until the Six-Day War), settlement beyond the Green Line, Jewish labor, immigration, integration of all Jewish ethnic groups, peace treaty with Arab countries, and industrial development. The topic chosen first was ranked high; the one chosen second was ranked medium; all others were ranked low. For factor loadings, see Appendix B.

If we analyze the veterans by country of origin and the immigrants by year of arrival (Tables 2 and 4), several other points emerge. As hypothesized, Westerners hold a higher degree of immigration-supporting perspectives than do Easterners (11% and 5%, respectively, view immigration as most essential to Zionism; 24% and 11%, respectively, have a high level of immigration-favoring attitudes). Second-generation Israelis are in between but are more similar to Easterners. The latest (1993) arrivals also seem most skeptical about the centrality of immigration to Zionism, while the 1992 immigrants are most optimistic (13% v. 29%, respectively, rate it high). The earliest (1990–91) immigrants are in the middle (20% rank immigration as highly central). It is not clear whether this is a change over time of each group or a cohort effect with immigrants of different years having different preconceptions. Moreover, there is no obvious trend with regard to immigration-favoring perspectives (Table 4).

Table 2
Immigrant Absorption as the Most Essential Characteristic of Zionism[a] by Veterans' Origin and Immigrants' Year of Immigration

	Veterans			Immigrants			
	East	Israel	West	1993	1992	1991	1990
Rank	(%)	(%)	(%)	(%)	(%)	(%)	(%)
Highest	5	6	11	13	29	21	19
Next highest	10	14	15	17	16	15	19
Other	85	80	75	70	55	64	62
(N)	(378)	(197)	(259)	(46)	(73)	(150)	(182)

a. See Table 1, footnote a.

Table 3
Immigration-Favoring Attitudes[a] by Population Group

Level of Favoring	Veterans (%)	Immigrants (%)	Total (%)
High	15	56	30
Medium	32	39	34
Low	53	5	36
(N)	(890)	(485)	(1375)

a. A scale based on the extent of agreement with eight statements referring to Israeli society's responsibility to immigrants and other citizens: "The State should ensure that all immigrants have housing" (agree); "The government should ensure housing first for young couples and soldiers and only then for immigrants" (disagree); "Immigrants should have priority in finding appropriate employment" (agree); "Immigrants are a burden on the State" (disagree); "Ex-soldiers should have preference over immigrants in finding jobs" (disagree); "Immigration contributes to the economic development of the State" (agree); "Every immigrant should take care of him/herself. The State has no obligation to do so" (disagree); and "Immigrant absorption justifies raising taxes" (agree). Factor analysis confirmed the relation of these statements to the same content universe. For factor loadings, see Appendix B. Each level comprises two categories out of six.

Table 4
Immigration-Favoring Attitudes[a] by Veterans' Origin and Immigrants' Year of
Immigration

| | Veterans | | | Immigrants | | | |
| Level of | East Israel | West | 1993 | 1992 | 1991 | 1990 |
Favoring	(%) (%)	(%)	(%)	(%)	(%)	(%)
High	11 12	24	57	49	59	55
Medium	30 33	35	39	46	36	40
Low	59 55	41	4	5	5	5
(N)	(397) (204)	(272)	(47)	(77)	(165)	(194)

a. See Table 3, footnote a.

Table 5
Collectivity Orientation[a] by Population Group

| Degree of | Veterans | Immigrants | Total |
Agreement	(%)	(%)	(%)
High	30	28	29
Medium	39	44	41
Low	31	28	30
(N)	(890)	(485)	(1375)

a. A scale based on the extent of agreement with five statements regarding the responsibility of
the State and of the citizens: "The State is responsible for everyone having what he needs to live"
(agree); "Citizens should first worry for the needs of their families and only then contribute to the
State" (disagree); "Every citizen is responsible for him/herself, and the State does not have to help
anyone" (disagree); "As matters stand today, citizens should first contribute to the State and only
then worry about the needs of their families" (agree); and "The State should use taxes to transfer
money from the wealthy to the needy" (agree). For factor loadings, see Appendix B. Each level
comprises two categories out of six.

Collectivity Orientation

There are no significant differences between veterans and immigrants regarding this perspective (Table 5). Less than one-third of both groups feel that
obligations to the State take precedence over individual and familial obligations.
This provides some evidence for Eisenstadt's contention regarding the waning
of the collectivity orientation. However, analysis by region of origin of the veterans (Table 6) suggests that Easterners tend to expect a higher degree of collectivity orientation than do Westerners (38% v. 26%). Second-generation Israelis

are the least convinced of the importance of that orientation (22%). With regard to the immigrants, the latest (1993) arrivals are least convinced of the importance of a collectivity orientation in Israel (21% v. 27%–30% for other cohorts).

Table 6
Collectivity Orientation[a] by Veterans' Origin and Immigrants' Year of Immigration

Degree of Agreement	Veterans			Immigrants			
	East (%)	Israel (%)	West (%)	1993 (%)	1992 (%)	1991 (%)	1990 (%)
High	38	22	26	21	30	29	27
Medium	37	39	41	53	38	45	43
Low	27	38	33	26	32	26	30
(N)	(397)	(204)	(272)	(47)	(76)	(165)	(194)

a. See Table 5, footnote a.

Sense of Deprivation

Immigrants feel more deprived than veterans (Table 7): 46 percent of the immigrants compared to 29 percent of the veterans have a "high" or "medium" sense of deprivation. Among the veterans, the second-generation Israelis seem to feel most deprived (36%), Westerners least (22%) (Table 8). Among the immigrants, there is no consistent trend, but there is some indication that the earliest immigrants feel less deprived than the others (13% v. 21%–23%).

Table 7
Sense of Deprivation[a] by Population Group

Degree of Felt Deprivation	Veterans (%)	Immigrants (%)	Total (%)
Low	71	54	65
Medium	21	28	23
High	8	18	12
(N)	(889)	(485)	(1374)

a. Based on the question, "How often do you feel that Israeli society deprives you?" The response categories ranged from "Never" to "Very frequently." Each level in the table combines the responses to two categories.

Table 8
Sense of Deprivation[a] by Veterans' Origin and Immigrants' Year of Immigration

Degree of Felt Deprivation	Veterans			Immigrants			
	East (%)	Israel (%)	West (%)	1993 (%)	1992 (%)	1991 (%)	1990 (%)
Low	70	64	78	51	54	49	57
Medium	21	30	14	26	25	28	30
High	9	6	8	23	21	23	13
(N)	(395)	(203)	(272)	(47)	(77)	(164)	(194)

a. See Table 7, footnote a.

Sense of Deprivation and Immigration-Supporting Perspectives

Among the veterans, having immigration-supporting perspectives is negatively related to feeling deprived (20% of those feeling least deprived v. 11% of those feeling most deprived view immigration as fundamental to Zionism; 16% v. 8% hold immigration-favoring attitudes; Table 9). Among the immigrants, conversely, holding immigration-favoring attitudes is positively related to feeling deprived (50% of those feeling most deprived v. 69% of those feeling most deprived hold immigration-favoring attitudes). There is no clear relationship between seeing Zionism as fundamental and feeling deprived among immigrants.

Table 9
Immigration-Supporting Perspectives by Sense of Deprivation[a]

Immigration-Supporting Perspective	Veterans' Sense of Deprivation			Immigrants' Sense of Deprivation		
	Low (%)	Medium (%)	High (%)	Low (%)	Medium (%)	High (%)
A. Percent supporting immigration by population and level of deprivation						
Zionism[b]	20	21	11	36	39	40
Favoring[c]	16	11	8	50	57	69
B. Percent expressing collectivism by population and level of deprivation						
Collectivism[d]	29	31	35	26	28	34

a. See Table 7, footnote a.
b. Percentage ranking immigrant absorption as most essential characteristic of Zionism—see Table 1, footnote a.
c. Percentage expressing the most favorable attitude to immigration—see Table 3, footnote a.
d. Percentage supporting the highest level of collectivism—see Table 5, footnote a.

Sense of Deprivation and Collectivity Orientation

The last line in Table 9 indicates that the "collectivity orientation" scale, as defined in Table 5, is consistently, though weakly, related to sense of deprivation among both veterans and immigrants. If "collectivity orientation" measures the sense of obligation of the citizen to the state, one might expect it to be negatively related to sense of deprivation. Perhaps, then, this scale is more a measure of the citizens' sense of the society's obligations towards its members; indeed, two of the five questions making up this scale refer to these obligations. If this is so, then a positive correlation with sense of deprivation makes sense; individuals who feel deprived may also feel that the society has obligations towards its members, which it is not fulfilling.

Immigration-Supporting Perspectives: Veterans and Immigrants

Overall, the data support the contention in the literature that immigration-supporting perspectives are not very strong in Israeli society. This is evident in the small percentages viewing immigration as a fundamental tenet of Zionism and holding favorable attitudes towards immigrants. The fact that Easterners score lowest on both scales provides some evidence that they feel most threatened by the mass immigration. Among the immigrants, there is some tendency for those in Israel longer to be slightly more similar to the veterans, but even the earliest immigrants (1990) see immigration as more central than do any of the veteran groups (Tables 1 and 2).

Also noteworthy is the discrepancy between the relatively high level of immigration-favoring attitudes that the immigrants consider normative and the much lower level held by veterans (Table 2). These immigration-favoring attitudes could reflect an unrealistic optimism among the immigrants that veteran Israelis will welcome and help them. Alternatively, they could be a assertion of their eligibility for assistance, in the name of the declared values of Israeli society.

There is some evidence for the latter in Table 10. The data indicate that levels of felt deprivation increase, albeit weakly, with the level of immigration-favoring attitudes. If the immigration-favoring attitudes reflect the norms held by immigrants, then perhaps immigrants who believe that Israeli society ought to help them (in the name of Zionist ideology or for other reasons) are more likely to sense that they have not received their due and thus to feel deprived. Believing that Israeli society ought to help immigrants is more likely to intensify disappointment with that society than to contribute to readjustment when the reality does not conform to these beliefs. In terms of the veterans, the tendency of both types of immigration-supporting perspectives to decrease with felt deprivation (Table 9) suggests that the willingness to support immigrants depends on the veterans' own needs being satisfied first.

Finally, the data suggest that the collectivity orientation of Zionist ideology is interpreted in self-serving terms by both immigrants and veterans. To take Shuval's argument that the pioneer ethic has become a myth (Shuval 1992:10) one step further, it seems that this myth is often interpreted by members of various groups so as to legitimize their own self-serving needs.

Table 10
Immigrants' Sense of Deprivation[a] by Immigration-Favoring Attitudes[b]

Sense of Deprivation	Immigration-Favoring Attitudes		
	High (%)	Medium (%)	Low (%)
Low	48	56	62
Medium	29	20	27
High	23	24	11
(N)	(271)	(189)	(25)

a. See Table 7, footnote a.
b. See Table 3, footnote a.

CONCLUSION: THE EFFECT OF THE INTERPRETATION OF SOCIETAL PERSPECTIVES ON READJUSTMENT

The main argument in this chapter is that the immigrants' perception of the dominant societal perspectives relating to immigration is likely to constitute a significant starting point for their readjustment process. Since they are now living in a new society, the perspectives held in this society will be more salient than the factors that originally prompted their immigration. The analysis in the preceding section referred to the role of the perceived societal perspectives.

I must emphasize that, so far, the analysis refers only to the prevalence of societal perspectives and their interpretation by both immigrants and veteran society. No direct relationship between societal perspectives and readjustment has been hypothesized. The specific role of these perspectives will be discussed in the next chapter.

NOTES

1. This interpretation is derived from Homans's (1974) deprivation-satiation proposition, according to which: "The more often in the recent past a person has received a particular reward, the less valuable any further unit of that reward becomes for him" (Homans 1974:29).

2. By reality, we mean the "societal perspectives" prevailing in a society, as developed later in this chapter.

3. The hypothesis does not suggest a direct relationship between perceived societal perspectives and readjustment. Rather, the hypothesized relationship refers to the process of readjustment, in which societal perspectives are likely to serve as an important starting point. This topic will be discussed further in the next chapter.

3

Immigration and Stress:
A General Overview

THE STRESS-POTENTIAL OF IMMIGRATION

The immigrants' confrontation with significant changes in many areas of their lives, their interpretation of these changes, and their the perception of societal perspectives about immigration impose severe pressures on them. These pressures challenge their available resources (Espino 1991:106) and may to set into motion an escalating cycle of discord which could harm their well-being and obstruct their adjustment (see Antonovsky 1979; Ben-Sira 1985, 1991; Monat and Lazarus 1991).

The literature on stress often connects migration to stress. In Palinkas' words, inherent in migration is "psychological stress and disorders that accompany the process of leaving a familiar environment and moving into an unfamiliar one" (Palinkas 1982:235). There is some evidence that the risk of stress increases over time. Williams (1991), for instance, suggests a higher prevalence of anxiety and depressive disorders among refugees during the final stages of their resettlement. Similarly, Mirsky and Kaushinsky's (1989) study of American Jewish students in Israel concludes that, over time, the euphoria that dominated the initial stages of their immigration in Israel decreases, while stress increases. Successful culmination of the immigration process requires alleviation of stress, hence restoration of emotional homeostasis—which we shall call "readjustment" (see Ben-Sira 1981, 1983a, 1985, 1991; Berry 1991; Dohrenwend and Dohrenwend 1970; Kuo and Tsai 1986; Pollock 1989; Rumbaut 1991). However, the changes resulting from immigration may also affect the absorbing society or certain groups in that society, requiring their readjustment as well. Thus, successful culmination of the process of immigration may require concomitant readjustment of both the immigrants and the absorbing society.

I emphasize again that it is not the change in itself but rather ingredients inherent in that change that should be regarded as causal factors in stress (Menaghan 1983; Mirowsky and Ross 1989; Pearlin 1983). In Mirowsky and Ross's words, "The misery, demoralization, or distress a person feels are not the problem. They are the consequences of the problem. . . . Suffering contains a message about the causes of suffering; a message that can be understood and acted upon" (Mirowsky and Ross 1989:5-6). In this chapter, I shall outline the components of a stress-coping-readjustment paradigm (see also Ben-Sira 1991) which can help us understand the factors underlying the stress-potential of immigration and the process of readjustment and may be instrumental in developing a systematic, comprehensive paradigm of immigration-related stress and readjustment.

THE COMPONENTS OF THE STRESS PROCESS AND THEIR IMPLICATIONS FOR IMMIGRATION

Stress and Tension

Much theoretical and empirical work has been devoted to the study of stress. According to Monat and Lazarus: "The concept of stress has received considerable attention in the recent years, yet much confusion and controversy remain. Attempts have been made to integrate various points of view, and further efforts along these lines may be forthcoming. Nevertheless, finding consensus among definitions of stress and related concepts . . . is still likely to remain a difficult endeavor" (Monat and Lazarus 1991:5). Dohrenwend and Dohrenwend contend: "'Stress' is a term that has been linked to varied concepts and operations. For some researchers it is a stimulus, sometimes more, sometimes less complex; for others it is an inferred inner state; and for still others it is an observable response to a stimulus or situation" (Dohrenwend and Dohrenwend 1974:1-2).

Broadly speaking, then, the term "stress" in the literature may be classified according to the three approaches referred to in this quote (see T. Cox 1978; Coyne and Holroyd 1982; Lazarus and Folkman 1984; Mechanic 1976; Pearlin et al. 1981; Sarafino 1990; Stotland 1987). The first approach views stress as stimulus. In this approach, the reference is to the source of the discomfort or tension such as events or circumstances that are perceived as threatening or harmful (e.g., a high-stress job), thereby arousing feelings of tension. The second approach views stress as a state of tension, "feeling nervous." It also includes a physiological component, such as heart palpitations. The third approach views to stress as a process that includes stressors and strains emphasizing continuous interaction with the environment and adjustments—called transactions—between the person and the environment reciprocally affecting each other. Stress, then, is a perceived discrepancy between the demands of a situation and the resources that are at the affected person's disposal for meeting these demands.

The concept of stress employed here is based on Antonovsky's (1979) conceptualization, according to which stress is a prolonged disturbance of an individual's emotional homeostasis, similar to what is often called "chronic stress" (Budzynski and Peffer 1980:414) or "continuing role strain" (Pearlin and Schooler 1978), and distinct from tension, which is a passing disturbance. Disturbance of emotional homeostasis refers to a non-specific response of an individual confronting a situation that exceeds his/her resources (see Barret and Campos 1991). This response may include a subjective state of depression and anxiety, which has both emotional and physiological manifestations.[1]

Demands: Their Nature, Stress-Potential, and Salience

The essence of the stress process may be summarized as follows: individuals are regularly confronted by demands, that is, stimuli requiring some response. Some of these are from the external environment: for instance, having to answer a question, being confused in a bureaucratic maze, having to make a phone call to an unknown person, or even passing a person whose behavior or appearance is unconventional. Others are from the internal environment (that is, from the individual him/herself): for instance, experiencing pain, remembering something that must be done, or thinking about a person. While almost any demand disturbs the individual's emotional homeostasis to some degree, individuals are generally capable of responding to most such demands, often automatically, with the help of resources they have at their disposal. However, there are also demands that are not so easy to meet.

In order to understand the conditions that make a demand problematic, we must distinguish among three concepts. First is the stress-potential of a demand, namely, the likelihood that it will disturb the individual's emotional homeostasis. In Lazarus and Cohen's words, demands with high stress-potential are those "that tax or exceed the resources of the system or to which there are no readily available responses" (Lazarus and Cohen 1977:109). Such demands are likely to become "stressors" (Kessler 1983). Second is the salience of a demand, namely, the extent to which it occupies the individual's mind. The more salient a demand, the more likely it is to realize its stress-potential. Indeed, the literature indicates that the subjective appraisal of the insurmountability of a demand is more important than the objective demand itself in determining its stress-potential (Kaplan 1983). In Thoits's words, "Psychological symptoms may be the result of the meanings people attach to, or the cognitive interpretations people make of, events and their aftermaths with respect to self" (Thoits 1983:83). Third is the demand's likelihood to constitute an acute threat to an individual's emotional homeostasis. This depends on both its stress-potential and its salience. For a demand to constitute an acute threat to emotional homeostasis, it must both have a relatively strong stress-potential and be fairly salient. In Chapter 6, I discuss the topic further and test it with empirical data.

Demands, then, may vary in the level of both their stress-potential and salience. An individual may encounter a problem characterized by a high degree of stress-potential (that is, of becoming a stressor if not adequately met), yet with low salience, in that it can be overcome without difficulty. For instance, he/she may feel pressure in the chest, which may indicate an imminent heart attack, and thus have strong stress-potential, yet if he/she does not feel the pressure, it has low salience and is not problematic. On the other hand, the individual could encounter a problem having high salience and requiring the investment of much effort to overcome it, but which nonetheless has low stress-potential. For instance, if one is trying to find a parking space for one's car, the need may be highly salient (in Lazarus's words, a "hassle"), but it may have low stress-potential and again not be very problematic.

Catalysts

Why do individuals become attentive to specific objective circumstances, that is, phenomena, events, or others' verbal or non-verbal behavior, in a way that they become salient demands? Underlying an individual's cognizance of objective circumstances—making them into demands and determining their salience—is the individual's perception of reality, which I call "individual perspectives," and his/her perception of the prevailing societal perspectives (see Chapter 2).

Thus, for stimuli to become salient demands, there must be not only objective circumstances but also appropriate individual perspectives and societal perspectives affecting their interpretation. These three elements, which together compose what I refer to as "catalysts" (Ben-Sira 1991:19), tend to be interrelated. Most obviously, individual perspectives are likely to be affected by perception of the prevailing societal perspectives. To illustrate, occasionally an empathetic person (that is, one with an empathetic individual perspective) may not "see" a homeless person sprawled on the street because he/she has internalized a societal perspective holding the homeless responsible for their own situation. In addition, objective circumstances may be affected by individual and societal perspectives. To illustrate, car accidents may be a product of the individual perspective of competitiveness and societal perspectives downplaying the significance of speed limits.

This interrelationship among objective circumstances, individual perspectives, and societal perspectives may be seen as the cornerstone of the stress process. According to Kaplan:

The mutually influential processes that together are intimately involved in the genesis of psychological distress are variously influenced by still other factors. That is, less directly, the frequency, intensity, course, and duration of experiences of psychological distress are a function of those factors that influence: (1) the nature of and changes in the person's need-value system; (2) the frequency and continuity of disvalued circumstances; and (3) the fact and changes in the subject's perception, recall, anticipation, or imagination of such circumstances. . . . From a diachronic point of view, . . . the system of concepts that gives structure to personal awareness and appropriate behavioral responses [is] learned in the course of the socialization process.[2] From a synchronic point of view, the perceptual and evaluative significance of a person's behavior and attributes varies according to the social context.[3] Further, within any given social context the discrete responses of the interacting parties . . . are the stimuli for the subject's cognitive, evaluative and further behavioral responses. (Kaplan 1983:198)

The Salience-Provoking Nature of the Demands Inherent in Immigration

The basic premise underlying the present work is that the process of immigration exposes both the immigrants and the absorbing society to the risk of stress. The following passage from Rumbaut's work on refugees illustrates the risk of stress inherent in immigration. Though the passage refers to refugees, I posit that it also applies to immigrants, specifically since, as indicated earlier, the distinction between refugee and immigrant is often vague and open to political and ideological interpretation. Rumbaut maintains that:

Psychologically, the refugee's experience may be conceived as a dialectic loss and trans-cendence, entailing a prolonged inner conflict or agony. In the process of acting to re-construct a meaningful social world in a new country, the resettled refugee is challenged to resolve dual crises: a "crisis of loss"—coming to terms with the past—and a "crisis of load"—coming to terms with the present and immediate future. On the one hand, . . . the refugee loses or is separated from home and homeland, family and friends, work and social status, material possessions, and meaningful sources of identity and self-validation. . . . On the other hand, the refugee is overloaded by the compelling pressures to sur-vive, find shelter and work, learn a different language, and adjust to a radically changed environment, often amid conditions of poverty, prejudice, minority status, pervasive uncertainty and "culture shock." (Rumbaut 1991:57)

Immigrants are confronted by many demands brought about by the often-ex-treme change in almost all areas of their life. The demands aroused by these changes may include the following: inadequate provision of basic sustenance needs; unemployment; types of employment requiring know-how and skills dif-ferent from those acquired in the country of origin; lack of acceptable housing and other amenities; unfamiliar political processes, legal system, and bureau-cratic procedures; cultural problems, such as unfamiliar language, children's education, approach to religion and leisure; changes in social relationships, including intergroup and interpersonal relations, as well as different types of dominance; behavioral problems, such as conduct in public places; and health-care problems, including dissimilar approaches to nutrition (Berry 1991:22).

Similarly, certain groups in the absorbing society are likely to confront demands resulting from the influx of immigrants. These include: unemployment and wage cuts due to the provision of cheap labor by immigrants; feelings of being compelled to carry the financial burden of immigration; feelings of disc-rimination and deprivation (see Table 9); changes in the social composition of neighborhoods; disorderliness and decay of city life; and confrontation with cultural differences in public places (Brown and Warner 1992; Brownstein 1993; Brym 1992; Impellizeri 1993). The stress-arousing impact of the demands instigated by immigration is liable to be particularly salient for the weaker groups in the absorbing society (Ben-Sira 1988a; Bernstein 1979; Cohen 1980; Lawson 1993). Demands confronting the veterans are not necessarily an outcome of face-to-face interaction between them and the immigrants. Rather, they are primarily a consequence of social changes brought about by the coexistence of distinct cultural groups in the same social system. Thus, for instance, mere knowledge of the construction of housing projects for immigrants may become a stressor for deprived segments of the absorbing society.

Thus, both the immigrants and certain groups in the absorbing society confront demands that are evoked by the immigration-instigated changes in their life situation and/or the social structure. However, there is an important difference between the two groups. For the immigrants, whatever the incentive for their immigration, the change is usually an outcome of their own initiative; therefore, they may accept at least partial responsibility for these demands. Members of the absorbing society, and in particular disadvantaged groups in that society, on the other hand, may feel that they are being subjected to demands for which they have no responsibility.

Initial Demand-Rejecting Defense: A Stress-Aggravating Response

The literature emphasizes that both immigrants and members of the absorbing society may respond to such demands by placing the blame for their difficulties on the other group.

The Immigrants' Viewpoint

As suggested in Chapter 2, immigrants may, in the initial period after immigration, accept responsibility for the change itself, along with elation at having attained at least some of their aspired goals. Subsequently, however, and faced with unprecedented demands, they may not necessarily accept the onus for their difficulties or even for their failure in meeting them. Grove and Torbiorn note that immigrants may insist that their own behavior standards are correct and thus resist changing them, while viewing the standards of the absorbing society as aberrant. Some immigrants "might even struggle to preserve those standards intact at all costs; in their view, allowing the standards to 'slip' would undermine their self-esteem by presaging their ultimate personal degradation under the influence of the hostile values in the new environment. . . . From [the immigrant's] ethnocentric point of view it is 'they' who are acting strangely or even unnatural, not 'me'" (Grove and Torbiorn 1985:211–212). In other words, a possible initial defense against the difficulties in meeting unprecedented demands is to blame the absorbing society. This may help alleviate dissonance in the wake of the hardships resulting from immigration that they themselves initiated.

The Veterans' Viewpoint

Similarly, some members of the absorbing society may blame the immigrants for the demands to which they are subjected. I have cited expressions of this kind of response in the form of unfriendly newspaper articles, hostility against immigrant children (Lawson 1993), mass demonstrations against immigration (Brown and Warner 1992), and even riots accusing the authorities of favoring immigrants and disregarding the deprived sectors in the absorbing society (Bernstein 1979; Cohen 1980). Studies on immigration also reveal cases of bias against immigrants by representatives of the authorities. In the United States, for instance, such bias has sometimes found expression in a greater likelihood both of persecution by the police for petty delinquencies and of harassment by immigration officials (Lobodzinska 1986; see also Brown and Warner 1992).

An Escalating Cycle of Discord

Immigration-instigated change affecting the lives of both immigrants and members of the absorbing society can thus arouse reciprocal hostile reactions. Immigrants are apt to feel rejected, exploited, and perhaps even harassed by the absorbing society. Even when members of the absorbing society do not overtly express hostility but simply avoid social contact with immigrants, the latter may perceive this behavior as indifference and lack of concern. Conversely, members of the absorbing society are apt to feel offended by the immigrants' seeming disdain regarding the nature of their society and resentful that they must bear much of the expense of absorption. On top of this, members of the absorbing society may expect the immigrants to be grateful, impressed, excited, and happy, while in reality many of them are merely confused (Lobodzinska 1986). This may be interpreted as ingratitude and lack of appreciation of the "sacrifices" made for immigrant absorption.

Again, there is no need for face-to-face interaction between the groups to evoke immigration-related stressors. The knowledge of, or belief in, deprivation is sufficient to evoke these stressors. In the case of wage cuts, for instance, the tendency to employ immigrants for less than the minimum wage standard is apt to be perceived by the immigrants as exploitation by the absorbing society. Yet workers in the absorbing society are apt to feel that, by accepting lower wages, the immigrants are depriving them of employment or forcing them to accept lower wages as well (Brownstein 1993). These reciprocal, subjective perceptions of the attitudes, reactions, and behaviors of members of the other group are apt to impose stress-arousing demands, over and above those resulting from the change itself, setting into motion an escalating cycle of discord. Concomitant readjustment, then, implies successfully meeting the demands evoked by both the change in itself and the damaging cycle, thus breaking out of that cycle.

Some effects of immigration are not viewed as demands. For example, immigrants may be unaware of certain behavioral expressions of the absorbing society toward them, while members of the absorbing society, in turn, are likely to be unaware of all the economic implications of immigration. On the other hand, a long-prevailing condition may become a salient demand following immigration. To illustrate, unsanitary conditions that prevailed in a neighborhood even prior to a wave of immigration may subsequently become salient and be attributed to immigration. Treating an event as a salient demand depends on both the individual perspectives held and the societal perspectives perceived by individuals, while the stress-potential of a demand depends on the subjective interpretation of its threat. Demands characterized by overload (such as the need to acquire a new language) or underload (inadequate utilization of one's professional skills) may be stressors and have the potential to cause tension. Yet these demands may not necessarily be salient. For example, underutilization of an immigrant's skills may be a potential stressor but not necessarily salient in view of the immigrant's capacity to cope cognitively (though perhaps not instrumentally) with it.[4]

Coping

In the literature, coping is defined as an individual's effort to master a demand, hence to reduce the likelihood that the demand will disrupt his/her emotional homeostasis (see, for instance, Monat and Lazarus 1991:5-6; Menaghan 1983:159). Underlying the notion of coping is the assumption that the stress process should be understood in terms of constant transactions between individuals and their environment, each influencing and being influenced by the other. It is a process in which the individual can affect the impact of a demand through instrumental, cognitive, and affective techniques (see Cox 1978; Lazarus and Folkman 1984; Mechanic 1976). In Pearlin's words, "Coping can be seen as having three functions: (1) the modification of the circumstances giving rise to stress; (2) the cognitive and perceptual management of the meaning of the circumstances in a way that minimizes their potency as stressors; and (3) the control and relief of symptoms of distress that result from the stressors" (Pearlin 1991b:267).

In terms of the analysis above, since the stress-potential of demands is often objective (that is, externally determined), the main strategy in coping is moderating the salience of these demands. This does not mean merely going through the motions of "instrumental" behavior but creating the subjective perception of having successfully overcome the demand (Ben-Sira 1981, 1983a; Ben-Sira and Eliezer 1990; Lazarus and Folkman 1991:200),[5] either by devaluing the significance of the demand or by believing in the effectiveness of the invested behavior. As suggested elsewhere (Ben-Sira 1985, 1989, 1991), coping can best be understood as a two-stage process: an initial stage of responding to a demand and a second stage of restoring emotional homeostasis, if it was disrupted due to inadequate coping in the initial stage. The initial stage of coping implies: (a) determining the salience of a demand that the individual assesses to have a significant degree of stress-potential; (b) taking action to meet it; and (c) assessing the effectiveness of that action. The assessment of having successfully met a demand determines whether emotional homeostasis is restored.

Consider an individual who has a physical symptom with a strong stress-potential (say, associated with a chronic disease). One way to reduce its salience is to assess it as sporadic and occasional. If the symptom recurs, this may not be effective. However, if a physician conducts a through examination and a series of tests and assures the individual that no pathogenic condition is involved, he/she may again be able to reduce the salience of the demand and cope effectively. Note that it is the individual's own assessment of the validity of the examinations and test results, and not the examination and the tests per se, that moderates the salience of the demand and restores emotional homeostasis. If the individual doubted the validity of the examination and tests, his/her emotional homeostasis would not be restored.

Resources

Coping is carried out with the help of resources that individuals have at their disposal (Wheaton 1985). These resources can be of various sorts and include "innate or achieved traits or properties of an individual (such as physical stamina, self-esteem, education, skills, knowledge, experience, cultural characteristics and wealth) as well as environmental support (such as primary social support and professional assistance), that have the potential of facilitating effective coping with demands" (Ben-Sira 1985:397; see also Menaghan 1983:159). Some demands can be met with the resources at the individual's own disposal; however, there are likely to be demands for which these resources are inadequate. Under such circumstances, individuals must resort to resources (that is, support) from the environment.

Evidence suggests that environmental resources are usually less effective than the individual's own resources. One of the explanations offered is the fact that eventually the individual him/herself must respond to the demand (see also the section on resources in Chapter 7). Moreover, reliance on environmental resources is likely to further diminish the individual's belief in his/her own "control" (Thoits 1991:236), that is, ability to change stressful situations and can lead to dependency, which further exacerbates coping limitations and increases the risk of maladjustment (Ben-Sira 1981, 1983a, 1985; Ben-Sira and Eliezer 1990). Secondary environmental assistance (e.g., bureaucratic or professional) is likely to be even less effective than primary environmental assistance (e.g., friends and relatives) in coping with demands and also arouses suspicion that the assisting agent is pursuing his/her own self-interests (e.g., power or money) (Ben-Sira 1986a).

Potency

Individuals are often confronted with demands which initially they are unable to meet. In this case, these demands may disrupt the individual's emotional homeostasis. Most of these disturbances are of a passing nature; they cause tension but do not lead to stress. Individuals normally succeed in alleviating tensions caused by inadequate initial coping. Indeed, many individuals derive satisfaction from overcoming challenging demands. Rumbaut illustrates this point, noting: "Mastery of . . . challenges may deepen a personal sense of efficacy and purpose, enhance a person's energies and productive capacities. . . . Successful refugees often state that their hardships have made them stronger and built up their sense of self-confidence and self-reliance (Rumbaut 1991:58).

What are the forces that can restore homeostasis? A more crucial question is: "If resources initially were inadequate for maintaining homeostasis, how can they become efficacious in restoring it, considering the considerably greater effort needed for restoring [homeostasis] than for maintaining it?" (Ben-Sira 1991:23). Taking Rumbaut's line of reasoning a step further, it stands to reason that successful readjustment may augment the immigrants' capacity to cope with new demands. Similarly, Thoits argues that "It is possible that the self-denigrating impacts of events and continuing strains are mitigated to the extent that individuals' coping strategies or supportive contacts aid them in sustaining perceptions of mastery, self-worth or both" (Thoits 1983:83).

As suggested in earlier work, individuals may have at their disposal a mechanism that functions over and above their resources and enables them to moderate the impact of inadequate coping and thus prevent occasional disturbances of emotional homeostasis from developing into stress. We shall call this mechanism "potency." Potency refers to a person's enduring confidence in his/her own capacities, as well as his/her commitment to a social environment that is perceived as being characterized by a basically meaningful order and by a reliable and just distribution of rewards (Ben-Sira 1985, 1991). Potency is an experience-based product of both an accumulation of successful coping outcomes and an aggregate of gratifying encounters fostering trust in the social environment. The stress-moderating faculty of potency finds its expression in facilitating re-equilibration, following a failure successfully to meet a demand, either by calling forth an experience-based confidence that a solution is bound to come up or by reassessing the stress-potential of that demand. Pearlin and his colleagues approach the position of the accumulation of coping failures from a similar angle, indirectly corroborating the stress-buffering potential of an aggregate of successes. They maintain that, "Persistent role strains can confront people with dogged evidence of their own failures—or lack of success—and with inescapable proof of their inability to alter the unwanted circumstances of their lives. Under these conditions people become vulnerable to the loss of self-esteem and to the erosion of [a sense] of mastery" (Pearlin et al. 1981:340). It should be emphasized that since a crucial element in potency is commitment to one's social environment, potency is contingent on that individual's integration into society.

To what extent is potency an adequate mechanism for re-equilibration in the wake of an extreme life change? The issue is particularly significant when dealing with immigration, when immigrants confront immense, unprecedented demands, often perceived to be insurmountable. Gitelman suggests:

Fundamental beliefs about human nature and the ways of the world are so deeply imbedded in an individual that even a change in physical and social environment will not alter them. The "primacy principle" . . . is assumed to be so powerful as to cancel the effects of situational and personal change in later life. Thus, a person who, for example, develops a cynical and suspicious outlook early in life is unlikely to alter it, even if his later experiences do not reinforce his outlook. (Gitelman 1989:259)

Indeed, a three-year study carried out by Gitelman with regard to political orientations among immigrants from the Soviet Union and the United States to Israel ascertained that "The fundamental orientations relevant to politics do not change very much over the first years in Israel, and [we] suspect that they have not changed greatly from what they had been in the Soviet Union and the United States. These may be so firmly embedded as a result of socialization, or of 'imprinting' at critical stages of life, that they function like personality characteristics, not easily shaped by changing environments" (Gitelman 1989:259). On the other hand, it stands to reason that, since potency implies commitment to one's social environment, the immigrants' feeling of potency depends, at least in part, on their integration into the new society.

Societal Integration and Readjustment

From the discussion above, the significance of a person's conception of society emerges as a crucial factor in the coping process and, in particular, in his/her feeling of potency. Individuals are exposed to a social environment that is a source of both demands and rewards. It stands to reason, then, that a critical precondition for readjustment—restoration of the emotional homeostasis that has been disrupted due to inadequate coping—lies in the individual's ability to communicate, to express his/her needs in societally acceptable terms, to view the responses of the society as intelligible, and to know what is appropriate, in that society, to obtain the desired responses. Presumably, then, individuals must attain a reasonable degree of integration into the social system in order to maintain meaningful interaction with their social environment. In the words of Shuval and her colleagues, "An immigrant is integrated in a society when he himself . . . thinks that he can perform adequately, believes that he has dealt competently with everyday problems of living and thinks that he is interacting with others as much as he himself deems it desirable" (Shuval et al. 1975:155). Taking this a step further, I suggest that integration into a society refers to a sense of identification with and feeling part of a reasonably balanced (in contrast to conflict-split) and just social system and its problems (Ben-Sira 1988a).

It should be pointed out that integration does not mean foregoing the entire cultural universe individuals have internalized in the course of their socialization. In Berry's words, "The option taken is to retain cultural identity and move to join with the dominant society" (Berry 1991:23–25). Instead, integration leads to readjustment and a reasonable feeling of potency by enhancing the capacity to maintain an effective interactional relationship with the social environment, which is perceived as being characterized by a reasonable level of order and distributive justice.

Maladjustment, Breakdown and Disease

Readjustment is often particularly problematic for immigrants, due to their exposure to unprecedented demands and the limited effectiveness of available resources for the meeting these demands. Moreover, considering the unfamiliarity of the social environment, the primary and secondary social environment are less likely to furnish the appropriate "environmental resources." Prolonged failure to restore homeostasis, indicating "maladjustment," may result in breakdown. Dohrenwend and Dohrenwend (1970), who translated Selye's (1976) model of physiological stress into psychosocial terms, regard disease as a consequence of "maladjustment" due to ineffective coping with stressors.

Accumulating evidence suggests that stress may contribute to the onset and seriousness of heart disease (Cooper 1983; Lundberg et al. 1975), infectious diseases (Jensen 1981), diabetes (Grant et al. 1974), and complications in pregnancy (Norbek and Tilden 1983). Considerable work has been devoted to the role of stress in cancer (Cohen and Cordoba 1982; Cooper 1984; Sklar and Anisman 1981). Bieliauskas concludes, by inference from numerous studies on the stress-cancer relationship, that the most significant relationship between stress and cancer appears to be the inability to cope with stressors effectively, not exposure to stressors per se. He finds this true for the effect both on tumor growth and on immune system-related hormonal changes which can effect neoplasms (Bieliauskas 1982). There is further corroboration for this in Murphy and Brown's (1980) finding that individuals with psychiatric disorders have a significantly higher rate of organic diseases.

In light of the central theme of this study, Hinkle's observations, though subject to considerable criticism, still may be noteworthy. On the basis of studies of the relationship between social or cultural change and disease, he suggests that "Exposure to culture change, social change, and change in interpersonal relations may lead to a significant change in health if (a) a person has pre-experienced illness or susceptibility to illness, and he perceives the change as important to him, or (b) there is a significant change in his activities, habits, ingestants, exposure to disease-causing agents, or in the physical characteristics of his environment" (Hinkle 1970:42). Hinkle's work thus alludes to the contributory role of stress resulting from extreme social change in the onset of disease.

CONCLUSION

In this chapter, I presented an augmented paradigm of the stress-coping-re-adjustment relationship that initially was developed in an earlier work (Ben-Sira 1991). The essentials of this paradigm may be summarized as follows (see also Figure 1): Individuals are constantly confronted with demands from their internal and external environment. Underlying the perceived salience of demands are catalysts, comprising objective circumstances, individual perspectives, and perceived societal perspectives. Almost all demands are characterized by a certain degree of stress-potential, hence a potential to disrupt the individual's emotional homeostasis. Demands that are inadequately met are likely to realize their potential as stressors, hence to disrupt the individual's emotional homeostasis. Coping is aimed at moderating the salience of demands. It is carried out with the help of resources that individuals have at their disposal or which are allocated by the primary (relatives or friends) or secondary (society at large, formal agencies, or professionals) environment. Maintenance or restoration of emotional homeostasis depends on coping successfully with demands. Societal integration contributes to that process, fostering readjustment and, to a great extent, potency. Potency is a stress-buffering mechanism facilitating restoration of the emotional homeostasis by moderating the stress-potential of a demand, if initially disturbed due to insufficiency of the resources for coping with that demand. A prolonged failure to restore homeostasis is apt to result in breakdown, disease being one of its expressions.

Figure 1
Schematic Display of the Stress-Coping-Readjustment Relationship

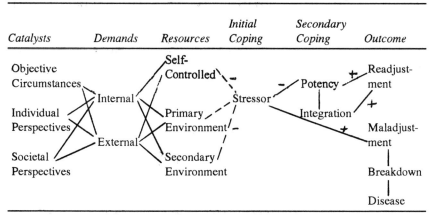

NOTES

1. This definition relates to what is often conceptualized as "distress" (see Mirowsky and Ross 1989).

2. These are similar to what we have called "individual perspectives."

3. This is somewhat similar to what we have called "societal perspectives."

4. Instrumental coping could mean working in a job that utilizes one's skills. Cognitive coping could mean understanding that utilization of one's skills is not a realistic expectation.

5. There is an ongoing debate regarding the extent to which it is possible to identify stressor-specific coping strategies. Some scholars think that this is necessary in order to "get a clear fix on the effects of coping" (Pearlin 1991b:268). However, "considerable evidence [suggests] that different modes of coping are used in dealing with different sub-areas of a stressful situation, and at different stages in a stressful encounter; . . . [hence,] a dispositional measure of coping will not be able to characterize the array of coping strategies used in dealing with a complex stressful event" (Cohen 1991:230). There may also be a "high degree of variability [in coping strategies] among and within persons" (Folkman and Lazarus 1991:212).

4

Immigration and Readjustment

ACCULTURATION AND THE COMPLEXITY OF IMMIGRANT READJUSTMENT

Culture, Enculturation, and Acculturation

In Tylor's (1874) classic definition, culture encompasses a complex whole including knowledge, belief, art, morals, law, custom, and other capabilities and habits that man acquires as a member of society. Keesing adds an ideational aspect to his definition of culture, which he views as comprising "systems of shared ideas, systems of concepts and rules and meanings that underlie and are expressed in the ways of human life" (Keesing 1981:68). Thus, culture is a set of explicit and implicit guidelines steering individuals as to how to view the world, how to experience it, and how to behave in it. In terms of this work, the culture of immigrants is the basis of the salience and stress-potential of the demands confronting them, the catalysts underlying the demands, and the availability and effectiveness of the resources for coping with them.

Growing up in a society involves enculturation, namely, internalization of its culture. Internalization means that the above-mentioned properties of culture become inherent traits of the cognitive, affective, and instrumental facets of the individual's personality. These traits are decisive in the perception of and response to the demands inherent in the life of a society. In the course of acculturation to a new society, immigrants may need to internalize cultural elements that differ from those internalized in the society of origin. In Parkes's (1971) terminology, these individuals must pass "psychosocial transitions" with respect to those parts of the environment with which they interact and in relation to which they organize their behavior—namely, other persons, material possessions, the familiar world of home and workplace, and the individual's body and mind. Parkes maintains that psycho-social transitions which have the most powerful potential to cause stress are those which take place over a relatively short period of time, are lasting in their effects, and affect many assumptions that individuals make about their "worlds." As we saw, immigration meets all three of these criteria and therefore is particularly stressful.

We can appreciate the significance of readjustment as a crucial indicator of successful culmination of the immigration process if we understand that an immigrant must undergo a process of acculturation. "Acculturation" refers to the internalization of cultural attributes of another society, resulting from continuous contact between two distinct cultural groups (see Redfield et al. 1936). Acculturation is currently recognized as not merely a social phenomenon but also an individual-level phenomenon, which Berry (1991) calls "psychological acculturation." At this level, acculturation refers to changes in the life of individuals whose cultural group is collectively experiencing cultural change. It implies confrontation by the immigrants with demands instigated by the cultural change.

Acculturation and Stress

The magnitude of stress precipitated by leaving a familiar environment and resettling in alien surroundings is partly expressed by the terminology used to describe immigration. Marris (1980), for instance, chose the term "uprooting of meaning" in order to underscore the stress associated with the reintegration into an alien environment. Handlin (1951), too, referred to the European immigrants to the United States at the turn of the century as "the uprooted." Eisenbruch (1988) went even further, referring to the permanent and traumatic loss of familiar land and culture as "cultural bereavement." He maintained that the collective grief of groups undergoing a stressful migration-related change in the wake of war or persecution is parallel to that of an individual who has lost a loved one.

According to Creed, the degree of acculturation and, consequently, the risk of stress depend on the cultural gap between the country of origin and the host country. He maintains that, "Certainly, the experience of the Vietnamese refugee who is suddenly uprooted from his farm and flown to a large city in the United States is quite different from the planned move of a professional person within the EEC (European Economic Community) because of an advantageous career" (Creed 1987:186).

Evidence of a relationship between the cultural gap and various emotional problems, such as regression, withdrawal, and psychosomatic complaints may be found in Gold's (1989) study of Russian-Jewish and Vietnamese refugees in the United States. Gold reports that social workers with refugee clients commented that self-destructive, violent, psychosomatic, or antisocial reactions occurred as a result of family role reversals (for instance, inability of the husband to fulfill the traditional breadwinner role). Westermeyer (1991:137) also suggests that refugee parents who could not fulfill their parental responsibilities effectively (that is, had inadequate acculturation to parental roles in the new society) often suffered from major depression, substance abuse, schizophrenia, or other disorders. The most extreme problems were experienced by fathers who were unable to fulfill traditional responsibilities and resented their loss of power (Cohon 1981:263-65). Frustration of immigrants who cannot find appropriate work (another indicator of unsuccessful acculturation—see Ben-Barak 1989) as an additional illustration of this relationship.

The Meaning of Readjustment in the Process of Immigration

The literature on immigration emphasizes the significance of readjustment as a critical indicator of successful culmination of the immigration process. Thus, Berry (1991:22-23) refers to adjustment as the decisive outcome of successful acculturation, where adjustment is viewed as the result of changes in the organism in a direction that increases the harmony between the organism and its environment. Grove and Torbiorn maintain that "A well adjusted and socially adept person . . . feels confident that his understanding of the way the world works is accurate, complete, clearly perceived, and positively useful in guiding his behavior. He recognizes (perhaps implicitly) that his habitual pattern of activity is consistent with his mental model of the functioning of society" (Grove and Torbiorn 1985:206-7). Similarly, Adler contends, "Adjustment, then, can be seen as a recovery process in which the immigrant gradually moves back up the hierarchy toward self-actualization. Progress up the hierarchy involves overcoming self-confusion, in other words, recovering from the state of disability known as culture shock" (Adler 1977:446). In a study of Asian immigrants to the United States, Kuo and Tsai (1986) focus on the immigrants' effort to "actively reroot," emphasizing the importance of the immigrants' motivation and initiative in restoring disrupted social networks in the new society. They maintain that, by taking the initiative to reroot, immigrants become more likely to attain success in transplanting their lives—or, in the terms of this work, readjusting—from their homelands to the countries of destination.

Concomitant Readjustment

As indicated earlier, immigration is likely to constitute a demand-imposing change not only for the immigrants but also for certain groups in the absorbing society. They may regard immigration as imposing "instrumental" demands, such as consuming resources that have been accumulated by the efforts of the absorbing society, depriving certain members of the society of jobs, and imposing financial demands. They may also incur "affective" demands; for instance, if social relationships are disrupted due to changes in the composition of neighborhoods. As stated above, they may react with discrimination, overt and covert hostility, and even expulsion. Mutual misunderstanding and hostility may set into motion an escalating cycle of discord that makes it very difficult for immigrants to achieve a reasonable level of adaptation (Gordon 1964). Breaking that cycle requires, in Gordon's terminology, structural assimilation or, in the terms of this work, concomitant readjustment.

READJUSTMENT IN ISRAELI SOCIETY

The Immigrants' Perspective

I now turn to the readjustment of the recent wave of Jews from the former Soviet Union in Israeli society. This issue is of interest both as a study of acculturation and because of the particular dynamics in this case. On the one hand, the immigrants must acculturate from a socialist system into a basically capitalist one. In her study of Polish immigrants to the United States in the 1960s and 1970s, Lobodzinska raises the question of how such immigrants can become absorbed into American life, since the socialist system in which they were socialized "accustoms people to centralized power, to state institutions offering health care, jobs, retirement benefits, etc. A democratic society, with its free enterprise, competition and individualism presents an unknown territory" (Lobodzinska 1986:421–23).

On the other hand, they must confront the ambiguous nature of Israeli society. Though Israel is, at present, primarily capitalist, Zionist ideology contains elements of immigrant absorption, collectivity orientation, and a welfare state—elements that still find expression in Israeli policy and, to at least some degree, public opinion. The declared ideology may lead immigrants to expect solutions to their personal problems (see Chapter 2), but in fact, these expectations are likely to be unmet. Thus, they are likely to feel deprived (see Tables 7 and 8).

The Absorbing Society's Perspective

From the viewpoint of a society characterized by "alienated identification" (Ben-Sira 1988a), the declared values of collectivity orientation and equality may lead to immigration becoming a stressor, especially for members of the society who already regard themselves as disadvantaged. In Israel, the sense of deprivation is negatively related both to viewing immigration as a cardinal tenet of Zionism and to supporting immigration (see Table 9).

Measuring Readjustment

In order to compare the emotional homeostasis of the immigrants from the former Soviet Union to Israel in the 1990–1993 period and that of the absorbing society, I used the six-item Scale of Psychological Distress (SPD) (Ben-Sira 1979, 1982a; for a discussion on the use of this scale see Appendix B, section 3). Note that while the scale allows one to compare the relative emotional homeostasis of groups, it cannot be used to measure absolute level of homeostasis.

Results

Immigrants and Veterans

The data in Table 11 clearly demonstrate the lower level of emotional homeostasis of the immigrants compared to that of the veterans: 47 percent of the veterans have high homeostasis, compared with only 28 percent of the immigrants. Contrary to expectations, there is no meaningful difference among the veteran groups in their level of emotional homeostasis (Table 12): the proportion of veterans with high homeostasis varies between 46 percent and 49 percent for all three groups.

Table 11
Level of Emotional Homeostasis Based on Scale of Psychological Distress (SPD)[a] by Population Group

Level of Homeostasis		Veterans (%)	Immigrants (%)	Total (%)
High	5	30	18	26
	4	17	10	14
	3	22	20	21
	2	20	31	24
Low	1	11	21	14
(N)		(892)	(486)	(1378)

a. A scale containing six items, each of which contained a symptom the respondent may have experience in the past year. The symptoms were: "Headaches that bothered you noticeably"; "Problems sleeping"; "Trembling hands"; "Fainting"; "Strong heart pounding"; "Feeling that you are about to have a nervous breakdown." The response categories for each item were "often," "sometimes," "occasionally," and "never."

Immigrants by Length of Stay in Israel

There seemed to be no overall improvement in the emotional homeostasis of immigrants during the four-year range of this study. Nonetheless, the immigrants from all four years are not the same. Fewer immigrants arriving two years before the study (in 1992) had high emotional homeostasis than those in the other three cohorts (21% v. 28% to 30%, respectively). This suggests that perhaps the second year in the new country is most problematic. Such a suggestion fits in nicely with the theoretical framework developed in this work. Upon arrival in Israel, immigrants may feel that they have achieved many of the rewards they aspired to obtain by immigration (see discussion of motivation to emigrate in Chapter 2). However, following the initial satisfaction, the "value" of these rewards decreases due to their very availability. At the same time, the salience of the demands increases in the wake of the earlier-discussed pressure of acculturation. This development may explain the decline in homeostasis among the second-year immigrants. Apparently, as more time passes, the pressure subsides and some stabilization occurs.

Table 12
Level of Emotional Homeostasis Based on SPD by Veterans' Origin and Immigrants' Year of Immigration

Level of Homeostasis		Veterans			Immigrants			
		East (%)	Israel (%)	West (%)	1993 (%)	1992 (%)	1991 (%)	1990 (%)
High	5	31	32	27	22	14	21	14
	4	16	17	19	6	7	9	14
	3	23	19	24	23	22	21	19
	2	19	20	22	23	40	29	30
Low	1	12	12	8	26	17	20	23
(N)		(397)	(204)	(272)	(47)	(77)	(165)	(194)

STRESS, MALADJUSTMENT AND HEALTH

Immigration and Health

As indicated in Chapter 3, the literature on the coping-health relationship refers to disease as an expression of breakdown resulting from maladjustment (Antonovsky 1972; Dohrenwend and Dohrenwend 1970). Prior to probing into the question of the stress-disease relationship from the viewpoint of immigration, I briefly review some of the literature on the effects of immigration on health.

Numerous studies suggest a causal relationship between immigration and disease. Thus, for instance, several studies use health-care-utilization patterns to suggest that immigrants may have a poorer level of health than members of the absorbing society. Kiev (1965), in a study in the United Kingdom, revealed a significantly higher consultation rate with general practitioners among West Indians than among native English males. A similar trend was observed by Creed and Carstairs (1982) with regard to Asian immigrants in the United Kingdom who were separated from their wives. Similarly, Magnusson and Aurelius (1980) report that, in Sweden, the proportion of immigrants who turned to the emergency department of a general hospital and were subsequently admitted for ill-defined symptoms was higher than that of the native population. However, utilization patterns approached that of native Swedes after three to five years in the country. Cassel (1975) in his review of studies on the migration-hypertension relationship showed that, controlling for age, immigrants from the Cape Verde Islands (West Africa) to the United States had a higher average blood pressure than their compatriots who remained in their native country. Similarly, a higher level of hypertension was found among Irish immigrants to the United States than among their brothers living in Ireland.

Several researchers attribute the immigration-disease relationship to the fact that in certain cultures there is a greater likelihood of somatization of stress (Beiser 1985; Bridges and Goldberg 1985; Kleinman and Kleinman 1985; Zborowski 1969). According to this approach, one explanation of the higher disease rate among immigrants is culturally specific responses to stress. Other studies try to find intervening variables to explain the relationship between migration and disease. Cassel (1975), for instance, attributes the relatively higher blood pressure levels among immigrants to both physical factors (such as changes in food consumption) and psychosocial factors (in particular, the disappearance of a coherent value system), so that the migrant's traditional way of coping with life became ineffective. Hiok-Boon and colleagues (1985) report that Vietnamese refugees who turned to primary health clinics for physical symptoms were likely to show depressive symptoms. Kiev (1965), in his above-mentioned study, found that many of the West Indian immigrants consulting physicians had psychiatric symptoms as well as somatic ones. Portes and his colleagues (1992), in their study of mental health among Cuban and Haitian refugees to the United States, attribute the higher level of mental disease among these immigrants to factors related to the problems involved in their emigration. On the other hand, Oodegaard (1932) explains the higher rate of schizophrenia among Norwegian immigrants to the United States, compared to that of veteran Americans, by the selective emigration of the most susceptible to that disturbance. This interpretation gained support in other studies (see Leff et al. 1976).

Carpenter and Brockington (1980) explain the higher incidence of mental diseases (in particular, schizophrenia) among Asian, West-Indian, and African immigrants in Manchester, compared to that of native-born British, by the former's social and linguistic isolation, and by the attitudes toward them by the latter. Cochrane (1985), however, explains the higher admission rates to mental hospitalization of Asian immigrants in the United Kingdom by differences in age and SES. Controlling for these factors, Cochrane found that Asians had similar hospitalization rates to the native British. Several studies suggesting a higher incidence of mental disease among West Indian immigrants in the United Kingdom (see Dean et al. 1981; Leff et al. 1976) have been criticized because their authors did not control for demographic factors. Eitinger (1960), in his study on mental health among refugees in Norway, suggests that the higher incidence of mental disease among them may be explained by the exposure of immigrants to isolation, helplessness, language difficulties, hostility, or indifference from the host population.

Creed (1987), in her comprehensive review of the immigration-disease relationship, tends to attribute the higher rates of disease among immigrants to stress. However, she challenges many of the conclusions reached in these works, arguing that studies concerned with severe or definite psychiatric illness "have mostly used hospital admission rates, which may not provide a reliable indicator of psychiatric illness in the community. In addition, these studies rarely give any indication of the environmental stresses involved. Community surveys of immigrants should overcome both of these difficulties. . . . There are numerous studies which have described the social stresses that are facing immigrants; but few studies have identified those environmental factors which are associated with the onset of psychiatric illness" (Creed 1987:186).

Health and Immigration to Israel

Prior to analyzing Soviet immigrants to Israel as an example of the stress-disease relationship, it seems worthwhile to compare the state of health of these immigrants to that of veterans. The data in Table 13 suggest that immigrants are characterized by a poorer state of health than veterans: 46 percent of immigrants, compared to 70 percent of immigrants, report the highest state of health (labeled "very good"), while 17 percent of immigrants, compared to only 4 percent of veterans, report the lowest ("very poor") state of health. The data in Table 14 suggest that the longer the immigrants stay in Israel, the better their reported health. The percentage of immigrants who report the highest state of health increases from 32 percent of those who arrived in the year of the study (1993) to 53 percent of those who immigrated three years earlier (1990). But the reported health of even the earliest immigrants is worse than that of any of the veteran groups.

Table 13
State of Health Based on Disease Score[a] by Population Group

State of Health		Veterans (%)	Immigrants (%)	Total (%)
Very good	5	70	46	61
	4	21	25	22
	3	5	12	8
	2	2	10	5
Very poor	1	2	7	4
(N)		(882)	(486)	(1368)

a. State of health was measured by a composite "Disease Score" comprising the respondents' reporting any of fifteen physician-diagnosed prolonged or chronic health problems (Ben-Sira 1982b, 1985, 1987, 1988b; see Appendix B). The score can vary from 5 (no diagnosed condition) through 1 (four or more conditions).

Table 14
State of Health Based on Disease Score by Veterans' Origin and Immigrants' Year
of Immigration

| State of Health | | Veterans | | | Immigrants | | | |
		East (%)	Israel (%)	West (%)	1993 (%)	1992 (%)	1991 (%)	1990 (%)
Very good	5	62	73	73	32	40	45	53
	4	25	21	19	36	23	27	21
	3	8	3	4	15	10	11	13
	2	2	2	2	8	14	10	7
Very poor	1	2	2	2	9	12	6	6
(N)		(393)	(201)	(269)	(47)	(77)	(165)	(194)

Examination of the Readjustment-Health Relationship

While stress may lead to disease, disease is a stressor as well. Given this, is there some way to determine which is the cause and which the effect? In order to resolve this question, I used a simple technique devised by Levy and Guttman (1976), who show how one can draw conclusions from asymmetry in the relationships between a pair of variables in two-way cross tabulations. Table 15 contains cross-tabulations between the immigrants' state of health and their emotional homeostasis (a similar table, not presented here, applies to veterans). In sub-table A, I control for state of health (row-wise); in sub-table B, I control for emotional homeostasis (column-wise). In the top row of sub-table A, we see that only 32 percent of the respondents with the highest reported state of health have the highest level of emotional homeostasis. In the left column of sub-table B, we see that 84 percent of those who have the highest level of emotional homeostasis report the highest state of health. This suggests that individuals with high emotional homeostasis are more likely to have good health than are people with good health to have high emotional homeostasis. The opposite holds with respect to poor health and low emotional homeostasis. In the bottom row of sub-table A, we see that 63 percent of the respondents with the worse reported state of health have the lowest level of emotional homeostasis. In the right column of sub-table B, we see that only 22 percent of those who have the lowest level of emotional homeostasis have the worst reported state of health. Interpretation of these data suggests, then, that the likelihood of a sick person to suffer from disrupted emotional homeostasis is greater than the likelihood of a distressed person to be sick.

We can conclude first, that high emotional homeostasis predicts good health better than good health predicts high emotional homeostasis; second, and contrary to what one might expect, poor health predicts low emotional homeostasis better than low emotional homeostasis predicts poor health (see also Hinkle 1970; Ben-Sira 1982b). This suggests that stress (low emotional homeostasis) contributes to disease (poor health) only indirectly, by depriving the individual of the health-protecting function of high emotional homeostasis.

Table 15
Conditional Distribution of State of Health and Emotional Homeostasis among Immigrants

| | | Emotional Homeostasis | | | | | |
| | | High | | | | Low | |
State of Health		5	4	3	2	1	(N)
A. Controlling for State of Health[a]							
Very good	5	32	14	19	25	10	(25)
	4	8	11	23	38	20	(20)
	3	3	3	27	40	27	(60)
	2	7	2	15	41	35	(46)
Very poor	1	0	3	14	20	63	(35)
(N)		(18)	(10)	(20)	(31)	(21)	(86)
B. Controlling for Emotional Homeostasis							
Very good	5	84	65	43	37	23	(46)
	4	11	27	29	30	23	(25)
	3	2	4	16	16	16	(12)
	2	3	2	7	12	16	(10)
Very poor	1	0	2	5	5	22	(7)
(N)		(88)	(48)	(98)	(151)	(101)	(486)

a. Percentages add up to 100 by row rather than by column.

SUMMARY

The theory and data presented in this chapter indicate the arduous path that immigrants must traverse in order to cope with the changes inherent in immigration, changes that require the immigrants to confront unprecedented demands. Their difficulties in doing so with inadequate resources may lead to low emotional homeostasis, which indirectly increases their risk of poor health. Over time, the health of immigrants improves, but not to the level of veterans. What, then, are the factors that promote or impede readjustment? The following chapters will probe into this question.

5

Integration

INTEGRATION AND READJUSTMENT

Integration

Integration into a society means being part of that society. As stated in Chapter 3, integration is a crucial element in the coping process. In Pearlin's words, "Societies have a dominant part in individual change and adaptation by being the source of challenges and hardships, by providing the contexts that give meaning to and determine the consequences of these hardships, and by allocating resources—both social and psychological—that help people fend off the harmful emotional distress that may otherwise result" (Pearlin 1993:321). According to the functional approach to sociology, interaction among the members of a society is the building-block unit of social systems (Parsons 1951). In classical exchange theory (Homans 1974), society is an important source of rewards and is, thus, a critical motivator of human behavior. To function effectively in a society, the individual must be able to express his or her needs in socially acceptable terms, understand the responses of the society, and have trust in its basic order and in the prevalence of distributive justice.

Yet interacting and satisfactorily coping with the demands imposed by a social environment are not sufficient for integration into a society. For instance, a visitor may be able to cope with demands and maintain effective interactions with others during his or her stay in a country and yet not be integrated into the society. Kuo and Tsai, who use the term "rerooting" in speaking of integration, argue that the essence of such rerooting is creating social networks in the new society. They underscore the importance of rerooting for successful immigrant readjustment, pointing to the "excessive amount of social stress among immigrants resulting from social isolation, cultural conflicts [and] poor social integration" (Kuo and Tsai 1986:133). Similarly, Brody (1970:14) contends that adaptation is the capacity to establish and maintain a relative stable reciprocal relationship with the environment. In short, by creating an effective basis for, and enhancing the capacity of, maintaining enduring, effective, meaningful, and gratifying relationships within the social environment, integration contributes to readjustment and, to some extent, to a feeling of potency. In this chapter, I explore the relationship between integration on the one hand and readjustment and potency on the other.

For conceptual clarity, I note that, in this work, successful culmination of the immigration process is referred to not as integration but as readjustment. This is based on the assumption that immigration forces the immigrant to confront unprecedented demands—demands that are likely to become stressors—and that readjustment means acquiring the capacity to cope with these demands and restore emotional homeostasis.

INTEGRATION: A MULTIFACETED CONCEPT

The Facets of Integration

Although integration requires that the individual identify as a member of society, such one-sided identification is inadequate for him or her to be a full member of the society (see Merton 1968:95). Rather, integration includes four crucial facets: the individual's identification as a member of society, the society's acknowledgement of that identity, the individual's awareness of society's acknowledgement, and the absorbing society's becoming a positive reference object for the individual's integration, which requires that the society be seen to have a basic social order. I now consider each of these facets in greater detail.

Identity as a Member of the Reference Society

Underlying the concept of "society"—and distinguishing if from a casual aggregate of individuals—is a basic sense of identification of the individuals as members of that society (see Weber 1968:16; Blau 1977:129-32). Such collective identity "cuts through" the boundaries of the great variety of indigenous groups that compose the society (Blau 1977:85-86) and defines the meaning of "we" and "they" (Barth 1969). "We" are individuals who share common values, sentiments, language, and behavior patterns, and "they" are those who do not. Collective identity is also an important component of "ego identity" (Erikson 1968) or "self identity" (Hallowell 1955).

For the immigrant, identification as a member of the new society requires acculturation to its overall cultural framework, which, as I showed in Chapter 4, can be very problematic. Palinkas (1982:242) maintains that immigration may precipitate an "identity crisis." Based on the work of David (1970:80), he asserts that migration involves complete disorganization of the individual's role system. The environment has changed, and familiar patterns of behavior no longer enable the individual to deal with people, places, or activities around him. As a result, some disturbance of identity is to be expected. Berry (1991) contends that integration need not mean renouncing one's entire cultural universe; rather, the immigrant group may maintain its own cultural identity while simultaneously creating significant relationships with members of the absorbing society (Berry 1991:24).

Taking Berry's point into account, I view identity as a member of a society as feeling "at home" in that society, recognizing the implications of that membership, and having an explicit intention to remain in that society (see also Ben-Sira 1988a:13–15). Note that identity as member of society is defined in terms of "affective" (feeling at home), "cognitive" (recognition of implications), and "instrumental" (intention to remain) modalities.

Acknowledgement as a Member of Society

I stated earlier that an individual's integration into a society is contingent on that society's acknowledgement. In a slightly different context, Barth focuses on the significance of that acknowledgement:

The identification of another person as a fellow member of an ethnic group implies a sharing of criteria for evaluation and judgment. It thus entails the assumption that the two are fundamentally "playing the same game," and this means that there is between them a potential for diversification and expansion of their social relationship to cover eventually all different sectors and domains of activity. On the other hand, a dichotomization of others as strangers, as members of another ethnic group, implies a recognition of limitations for judgment of value and performance, and a restriction of interactions to sectors of assumed common understanding and mutual interest. (Barth 1969:15)

Berry, on the other hand, points to the limits of the absorbing society's tolerance and some of the problems that may result:

There are clear variations in the degree to which the maintenance of cultural diversity is tolerated. . . . Tolerant (pluralist, multicultural) societies do not generally force individuals to change their ways of life, and they usually have viable ethnic support groups to assist individuals in the acculturation process. In contrast, monistic societies place more pressures on acculturating individuals to change, and often lack social supports for them. Both of these factors have clear implications for the social and mental health of acculturating individuals. Even in relatively pluralistic and tolerant societies, all ethnic groups are not equally accepted; variations in ethnic attitudes in the larger society (including levels of prejudice and acts of discrimination) are well documented. (Berry 1991: 26–27)

Even when a certain degree of cultural diversity is acceptable, an individual or group differing significantly from the cultural mainstream of a society is likely to suffer prejudice and discrimination. Berry's emphasis on immigrants joining the dominant society and Kuo and Tsai's focus on the restoration of social networks as essential for the successful transplantation of the immigrants' lives in the new society point to the importance of the immigrants' acknowledgement as members of a society, for their integration into that society.

Perceived Acknowledgement as a Member of Society

Although acknowledgement by the absorbing society is critical, the immigrant's perception of being acknowledged as a member of the absorbing society is also essential for his/her integration. This is because there must be a mutually recognized and accepted common denominator for a stable, meaningful, and rewarding transactional relationship between the members of a society to develop (see Burke 1969; Homans 1974). In Burke's words: "You persuade a man only insofar as you talk his language by speech, gesture, tonality, order, image, attitude, idea—identifying your ways with his" (Burke 1969:55).

Positiveness of the Reference Society

Integration into a society, by definition, implies that the society, specifically the "dominant group" in that society, serves as a reference group for the immigrants. Therefore, a positive image of the society in the eyes of the immigrants is imperative (Merton 1968). The inclination to become a member of an unbalanced, problem-ridden, unjust society torn apart by intergroup conflict is apt to be rather low, and integration is likely to be limited or nonexistent.

INTEGRATION IN A HETEROGENEOUS SOCIETY: THE CASE OF ISRAEL

The Complexity of Integration into Israeli Society

A study of Israel may further our understanding of integration into a heterogeneous society. Farago (1978, 1979) views the assumption of Israeli identity as the most significant element of integration into Israeli society. Identity formation may be problematic, however, because of several aspects of Israeli Jewish society: the ambiguity of Jewish Israeli identity in a culturally heterogeneous society (Ben-Sira 1988a); the ambivalent role of Zionism as a central tenet underlying Israel's existence (Ben-Sira 1993); and the discrepancy between perceived and prevailing immigration-supporting perspectives (Tables 1 and 3).

These issues raise questions as to what type of society would serve as a reference group for integration, and if, indeed, the immigrants are welcomed as "kinsmen" who have returned to their "homeland." If integration is partly a result of viewing the "dominant group" in a society as the reference for the formation of a new identity (Berry 1991), it is not clear who is the "dominant group" in Israeli society. Moreover, in view of the ambiguity regarding the desirability of their "homecoming," the need of immigrants to undergo the arduous process of acculturation may be questioned.

Measuring Integration

To what extent, then, have the immigrants from the former Soviet Union who arrived in Israel from 1991 to 1993 been integrated into Israeli society? To answer this question, I collected data on the facets of integration just discussed and compared the answers of the immigrants to those of veteran Israelis.

Identity as a member of the reference society was measured, as in an earlier study (Ben-Sira 1988a), by five questions. A composite measure, which I called the "Israeli Identity Scale" (IIS), was constructed from these items. Factor analysis ascertained that the items belong to the same content universe (see Appendix B).

Acknowledgement as a member of society was measured by one question, which dealt with the integration of Soviet immigrants and was aimed at elucidating the respondents' position with regard to this issue.

Perceived acknowledgement as a member of society was probed by three questions eliciting the respondents' sense of being accepted by Israeli society. They dealt with the affective, cognitive, and instrumental domains. A composite measure, which I called the "Societal Acknowledgement Scale" (SAS), was constructed from these items. Factor analysis ascertained that the items belonged to the same content universe (see Appendix B).

Positiveness of the reference society was measured by four questions. A composite measure, which I called the "Reference Positivity Scale" (RPS), was constructed from these items. Factor analysis ascertained that the items belonged to the same content universe (see Appendix B).

A caveat is in order: the scores on the scales refer to relative position with regard to the topic in question and thus facilitate intergroup comparisons. They cannot be viewed as absolute indicators of the respondents' positions.

Results

For each facet of integration, I shall present first the percentage of positive responses for each item and then the results of the scales.

Identity as Members of the Reference Society

The data in Table 16 indicate that immigrants identify as Israeli less than do veterans. The difference between the groups is particularly striking for the affective modality: only 38 percent of the immigrants, compared to 86 percent of the veterans, "feel at home in Israel." If they had a choice, the immigrants would prefer less than the veterans to live in Israel (36% v. 68%) and to have their children stay in this country (44% v. 83%). However, their inclination to remain in Israel themselves is similar to that of the veterans (76% v. 85%).

The data in Table 17 suggest a curvilinear pattern of Israeli identification over time. Following an increase among the second- and third-year immigrants, there is a slight decrease in the fourth year, leaving a rather wide gap between the earliest immigrants and the veterans. The position of the most recent immigrants (1993) on these crucial topics is particularly noteworthy: Only 19 percent feel at home in Israel, only 21 percent would prefer to stay in Israel if they had choice, and only 26 percent would like their children to stay in Israel.

Table 16
Israeli Identity Based on Five Items[a] by Population Group

Item of Identity	Veterans (%)	Immigrants (%)	Total (%)
At home in Israel	86	38	69
Part of Israeli society	74	40	62
Prefer living in Israel	68	36	57
Remain in Israel	85	76	82
Children stay in Israel	83	44	69

a. The items were: "To what extent do you feel yourself part of the State of Israel and its problems?"; "To what extent do you feel at home in Israel?"; "If you could, would you prefer to live outside of Israel?"; "Are you sure you will stay in Israel?"; and "Do you want your children to live permanently in Israel?" There were five or six response categories for each question; reported percentages are those at the two most positive levels.

Table 17
Israeli Identity[a] by Veterans Origin and Immigrants' Year of Immigration

| Item of Identity | Veterans | | | Immigrants | | | |
	East (%)	Israel (%)	West (%)	1993 (%)	1992 (%)	1991 (%)	1990 (%)
At home in Israel	88	86	83	19	41	38	34
Part of Israeli society	74	71	78	28	37	33	33
Prefers living in Israel	69	59	73	21	35	39	32
Remain in Israel	87	80	86	55	78	78	66
Children stay in Israel	87	81	79	26	51	46	44

a. See Table 16, footnote a.

The overall gap between the relative levels of Israeli identity of the veterans and the immigrants is evident from the combined data on the IIS (Table 18). Compared to 53 percent of the veterans whose relative Israeli identity is at the three highest levels, only 10 percent of the immigrants reached that level. The curvilinear trend in the relative identity with the duration of their stay in Israel is interesting (Table 19): The percentage of immigrants identifying as Israelis increases from 4 percent among first-year immigrants (1993) to 13 percent among second year immigrants. After that, however, the percentage decreases to only 8 percent of fourth-year immigrants. The relatively lower level of Israeli identification among second-generation Israelis is also striking: 44 percent of second-generation Israelis, compared with 51 percent of Westerners and 57 percent of Easterners, are at the three highest levels of the IIS.

Table 18
Israeli Identity Based on Israeli Identity Scale (IIS)[a] by Population Group

Level of Identity		Veterans (%)	Immigrants (%)	Total (%)
High	6	16	2	11
	5	25	4	18
	4	12	4	9
	3	27	24	26
	2	14	35	21
Low	1	6	31	15
(N)		(892)	(486)	(1378)

a. A scale based on the five questions listed in Table 16, footnote a.

Table 19
Israeli Identity Based on Israeli Identity Scale (IIS)[a] by Veterans' Origin and Immigrants' Year of Immigration

Level of Identity		Veterans			Immigrants			
		East (%)	Israel (%)	West (%)	1993 (%)	1992 (%)	1991 (%)	1990 (%)
High	6	15	15	17	0	1	1	2
	5	30	17	24	2	4	5	3
	4	12	12	10	2	8	6	3
	3	25	29	29	15	23	22	28
	2	13	21	10	38	29	37	35
Low	1	5	6	10	43	35	29	28
(N)		(397)	(204)	(272)	(47)	(77)	(165)	(194)

a. A scale based on the five questions listed in Table 16, footnote a.

Acknowledgement of Immigrants as Members of Society

The data in Table 20 suggest that the veterans are by far more optimistic than are the immigrants as to the acknowledgement of the immigrants' membership in Israeli society: 65 percent of the veterans, compared to 36 percent of the immigrants, say that the immigrants are "definitely" or "somewhat" integrated into Israeli society. Twenty-seven percent of the immigrants, compared with only 12 percent of the veterans, think that they are "greatly" or "entirely" a foreign body in Israel.

Table 20
Acknowledgement of Immigrants as Members of Israeli Society[a] by Population Group

Level of Acknowledgement	Veterans (%)	Immigrants (%)	Total (%)
Definitely integrated	18	3	12
Somewhat integrated	47	33	42
Somewhat foreign body	23	37	28
Greatly foreign body	9	22	14
Entirely foreign body	3	5	4
(N)	(876)	(479)	(1358)

a. Based on the question: "Have the immigrants who have come recently from the former Soviet Union been integrated into Israeli society, or are they still a foreign body in this society?"

The data in Table 21 show no consistent relationships between length of time in Israel and the immigrants' assessment of their being acknowledged members of Israeli society. But, while 38 percent of second-year immigrants and 40 percent of fourth-year immigrants feel at least somewhat integrated, only 30 percent of third-year immigrants do. As to the veterans, Westerners are somewhat more likely than Easterners and second-generation Israelis to see the immigrants as integrated into Israeli society (the figures are 71% for Westerners and 61% for both Easterners and second-generation Israelis).

Table 21
Acknowledgement of Immigrants as Members of Israeli Society[a] by Veterans' Origin and Immigrants' Year of Immigration

Level of Acknowledgement	Veterans			Immigrants			
	East (%)	Israel (%)	West (%)	1993 (%)	1992 (%)	1991 (%)	1990 (%)
Definitely integrated	15	16	21	0	7	2	3
Somewhat integrated	46	45	50	37	31	28	37
Somewhat foreign body	24	26	19	39	38	35	37
Greatly foreign body	13	10	7	22	22	26	19
Entirely foreign body	3	3	3	2	3	8	4
(N)	(388)	(199)	(271)	(46)	(77)	(164)	(192)

a. See Table 20, footnote a.

Perceived Acknowledgement as Members of Society

Whatever the indicator of perceived acknowledgement, immigrants are less likely than veterans to feel that they are acknowledged members of Israeli society (Table 22): The widest gap between the veterans and the immigrants is with respect to their acceptance as members of Israeli society (only 44% of the immigrants v. 73% of the veterans do not feel rejected by society). Immigrants also feel more deprived by the society (71% v. 54% do not feel deprived), hence acknowledge less than the veterans the application of the rules of distributive justice toward them, and only half the immigrants (50% v. 65% of the veterans) feel that they understand Israeli society.

Table 22
Perceived Acknowledgement of Immigrants as Members of Israeli Society[a] by Population Group

Item of Perceived Acknowledgement	Veterans (%)	Immigrants (%)	Total (%)
(Non-) Rejection	63	73	44
(Non-) Incomprehensibility	60	65	50
(Non-) Deprivation	65	71	54

a. The items were: "How often do you feel that Israeli society rejects you; that Israeli society deprives you; and that you do not understand this society at all?" The response categories ranged from "Never" to "Very frequently"; reported percentages are those at the two most positive levels, in which respondent does not feel rejected or deprived and feels he/she understands Israeli society.

The data in Table 23 suggest that an improvement occurs over time in the comprehensibility of society, from 36 percent up to 55 percent. Yet even fourth-year immigrants are much less likely than veterans to feel that they understand Israeli society. Moreover, the increase in their feeling of being accepted and not being deprived by Israeli society is rather slight (from 42% to 49% and from 51% to 57%, respectively).

The immigrants' overall feeling of acknowledgement as members of Israeli society seems much lower than that of the veterans (Table 24): 42 percent of the immigrants compared to 62 percent of the veterans were in the upper three levels of the SAS. Among immigrants, there is almost no increase, over the period covered by the study, in perception of being acknowledged as members of society (Table 25): 43 percent of those who arrived in 1993 compared to 47 percent of those who arrived in 1990 feel that they are acknowledged members of Israeli society. As in the case of actual acknowledgement (Table 21), perceived acknowledgement also seems to undergo a crisis roughly at the third year in Israel (Table 25). Only 34 percent of third-year immigrants, compared with 43–47 percent of others, are in the highest three levels of the SAS.

Table 23
Perceived Acknowledgement of Immigrants as Members of Israeli Society[a] Based on Three Items by Veterans' Origin and Immigrants' Year of Immigration

Item of Perceived Acknowledgement	Veterans			Immigrants			
	East (%)	Israel (%)	West (%)	1993 (%)	1992 (%)	1991 (%)	1990 (%)
(Non-) Rejection	74	70	75	42	44	39	49
(Non-) Incomprehensibility	65	63	69	36	49	48	55
(Non-) Deprivation	70	64	78	51	54	49	57

a. See Table 22, footnote a.

Table 24
Perceived Acknowledgement Based on Societal Acknowledgement Scale (SAS)[a] by Population Group

Level of Perceived Acknowledgement		Veterans (%)	Immigrants (%)	Total (%)
High	6	38	18	31
	5	16	16	16
	4	10	8	9
	3	20	27	22
	2	6	12	8
Low	1	10	19	13
(N)		(891)	(486)	1377)

a. A scale based on the three questions listed in Table 22, footnote a.

Positiveness of Reference Society

Veterans have a more positive image of Israeli society than do immigrants (Table 26: 40% v. 28%, respectively, think conditions in Israel are good). Similarly, veterans perceive Ashkenazi-Sephardi relations to be much better than do immigrants (68% v. 22% think they are good). However, there is no difference between the groups in terms of overall evaluation of the social situation (38% v. 39% consider it good). Similarly, veterans and immigrants have similar evaluations of the relations between themselves (37% v. 31% consider them good).

Table 25
Perceived Acknowledgement Based on Societal Acknowledgement Scale (SAS)[a] by Veterans' Origin and Immigrants' Year of Immigration

Level of Perceived Acknowledgement		Veterans			Immigrants			
		East (%)	Israel (%)	West (%)	1993 (%)	1992 (%)	1991 (%)	1990 (%)
High	6	39	32	40	13	16	13	23
	5	14	17	19	15	22	11	19
	4	11	11	8	15	6	10	5
	3	20	19	21	17	22	29	29
	2	5	10	3	13	10	15	11
Low	1	10	11	9	28	23	22	13
(N)		(396)	(204)	(272)	(47)	(77)	(165)	(194)

a. A scale based on the three questions listed in Table 22, footnote a.

Table 26
Perception of Positiveness of Israeli Society Based on Four Items[a] by Population Group

Item of Image	Veterans (%)	Immigrants (%)	Total (%)
Conditions in general	40	28	35
Social situation in general	38	39	38
Ashkenazi-Sephardi relations	68	22	52
Veteran-immigrants relations	37	31	35

a. The items were: "What is the situation in Israel in general?"; 2. What is the social situation in Israel?"; "How are relations among Ashkenazim (Westerners) and Sephardim (Easterners)?"; "How are relations between new immigrants and veterans?" The response categories ranged from "Very good" to "Not at all good"; reported percentages are those at the two most positive levels.

The positive image by the immigrants of Israeli society diminishes over time on all four questions (Table 27). The trend of the general evaluation of social conditions in Israel is particularly interesting: first-year immigrants evaluate of social conditions better than do veterans (50% v. 37–39% think them good), but among others there is no difference. In terms of Ashkenazi-Sephardi and veteran-Soviet immigrant relations, there is a fairly noticeable decrease from 30–38 percent of first and second-year immigrants who rate these relations good, to only 18–19 percent of third- and fourth-year immigrants who do so.

Table 27

Perception of Positiveness of Israeli Society[a] Based on Four Items by Veterans' Origin and Immigrants' Year of Immigration

Item of Image	Veterans			Immigrants			
	East (%)	Israel (%)	West (%)	1993 (%)	1992 (%)	1991 (%)	1990 (%)
Conditions in general	37	42	42	26	32	26	27
Social situation in general	37	39	37	50	38	36	39
Ashkenazi-Sephardi relations	67	72	64	30	32	18	19
Veteran-immigrant relations	38	39	34	38	31	18	19

a. See Table 22, footnote a.

The gap between the veterans and the immigrants in the overall perception of the positiveness of Israeli society is clearer from the data on the RPS (Table 28). Compared with 51 percent of the veterans whose perception of the relative positiveness of Israeli society is at the three upper levels, only 34 percent of the immigrants assessed Israel's positiveness at that level. The decrease in values of the RPS over length of time in Israel can be seen in Table 29. Forty-four percent of first-year immigrants, but only 30–32 percent of third and fourth-year immigrants, have high RPS scores. As to veterans, second-generation Israelis assess the society slightly more positively than do either Easterners or Westerns (55% v. 49–50% in the top three levels of the RPS).

Table 28

Overall Level of Positiveness of Israeli Society Based on Reference Positivity Scale (RPS)[a] by Population Group

Level of Positiveness		Veterans (%)	Immigrants (%)	Total (%)
High	6	14	7	12
	5	17	10	15
	4	20	17	19
	3	17	22	19
	2	14	26	18
Low	1	18	18	18
(N)		(892)	(486)	(1378)

a. A scale based on the four questions listed in Table 26, footnote a.

Table 29
Overall Level of Positiveness of Israeli Society Based on Reference Positivity Scale
(RPS)[a] by Veterans' Origin and Immigrants' Year of Immigration

Level of Acknowledgement		Veterans			Immigrants			
		East (%)	Israel (%)	West (%)	1993 (%)	1992 (%)	1991 (%)	1990 (%)
High	6	14	13	14	13	10	6	5
	5	17	21	15	8	8	8	12
	4	19	21	20	23	19	16	15
	3	16	18	18	15	25	22	22
	2	16	11	14	23	27	27	27
Low	1	18	17	19	17	10	21	19
(N)		(397)	(204)	(272)	(47)	(77)	(165)	(194)

a. A scale based on the four questions listed in Table 26, footnote a.

THE INTERCORRELATION OF FACETS

The Dynamics of the Integration Process

As a first step towards better understanding these trends, let us compare the dynamics of the four facets of integration over the period of close to four years covered in this study. The data in Table 30 show the following: Assumption of Israeli identity rises among second-year immigrants but then decreases slightly among third and fourth-year immigrants. Acknowledgment and perceived acknowledgment as a member of society both decrease during the third year in Israel and increase somewhat during the fourth. Positiveness of society consistently decreases from the year of arrival to the third year, remaining at this level in the fourth year.

Table 30
The Dynamics of the Facets of Integration 1990–1993 Based on Percentages at the
Highest Levels of Tables 19, 21, 25 and 29: Immigrants

Facet	Source Table	Categories	1993 (%)	1992 (%)	1991 (%)	1990 (%)
Israeli identity	19	4–6	4	13	12	8
Acknowledgement by society	21	3–4	37	38	30	40
Perceived acknowledgement	25	4–6	43	44	34	47
Positiveness of society	29	4–6	44	37	30	32

In summary, perceived positiveness of society is the first to decrease, followed by assessed acknowledgement, and then Israeli identity. This suggests that integration into Israeli society reflects a sequential interdependence among the facets. The correlations among these facets (Tables 31 and 32) and their schematic display (Figures 2 and 3) provide some support for this hypothesis (for an explanation of μ_2, see Appendix C).

Table 31
Correlations (μ_2) Among the Facets of Integration: Immigrants

Facet	#	1 (μ_2)	2 (μ_2)	3 (μ_2)	4 (μ_2)
Israeli identity	1	-	.67	.59	.32
Acknowledgement by society	2	.67	-	.60	.49
Perceived acknowledgement	3	.59	.60	-	.55
Positiveness of society	4	.32	.49	.57	-

Figure 2
Schematic Display of the Correlations Among the Facets of Integration: Immigrants[a]

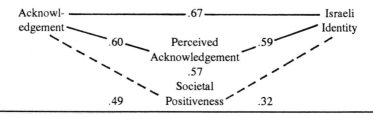

a. Based on the data in Table 31.

Table 32
Correlations (μ_2) Among the Facets of Integration: Veterans

Facet	#	1 (μ_2)	2 (μ_2)	3 (μ_2)	4 (μ_2)
Israeli identity	1	-	.39	.23	.12
Acknowledgement by society	2	.39	-	.28	.32
Perceived acknowledgement	3	.23	.28	-	.24
Positiveness of society	4	.12	.32	.24	-

Figure 3
Schematic Display of the Correlations Among the Facets of Integration: Veterans[a]

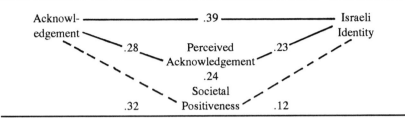

a. Based on the data in Table 32.

We note the similarity of the "structures" generated by the correlations among facets but also the much stronger correlations among facets for the immigrants compared to the veterans. For instance, the correlation (μ_2) of Israeli identity with perceived acknowledgement is .59 for immigrants but only .23 for veterans. This suggests that among the new immigrants, a change in one facet is more likely to lead to changes in the others than it is among the veterans. We also see that the Israeli identity of immigrants is quite highly correlated with their assessment of being acknowledged ($\mu_2 = .67$) and their perceived acknowledgement by the absorbing society ($\mu_2 = .59$), and fairly highly correlated with the positiveness of society ($\mu_2 = .32$). Perceived positiveness of the society and perceived acknowledgement are also highly correlated ($\mu_2 = .57$).

A Sequential Process of Integration

How can these correlations help us understand the immigrants' integration into Israeli society? Let us study this process over time.

The First Year

The initial low level of Israeli identity in the first year seems quite reasonable and is consistent with other findings (see Farago 1979). The first year is also characterized by an optimistic perception of Israeli society (see Table 30), as suggested by the relatively high level of perceived positiveness of society (44%), as well as perceived acknowledgement by society (43%).

The Second Year

The effect of the positive perceptions of Israeli society expresses itself in an increase in Israeli identity in the second year (from 4% to 13%). The strong correlation between Israeli identity and both the perceived acknowledgement by the society ($\mu_2 = .67$) and the positiveness of society ($\mu_2 = .59$) could explain the continued high levels of these latter variables, though there is a decrease in the perceived positiveness of society (from 44% to 37%).

The Third Year

Presumably, the effect of the decrease in positiveness, together with the stability in perceived acknowledgement in the second year, is felt in the third year in the stability of Israeli identity (13% and 12%) and the fairly sharp decrease in perceived acknowledgement (from 44% to 34%). The perceived positiveness of society further decreases (from 37% to 30%).

The Fourth Year

The decrease in both the positiveness of society and perceived acknowledgement may explain the decrease in Israeli identity in the fourth year (8%). The increase in the perceived acknowledgement and the rather small improvement in the perceived positiveness of society in the fourth year may point to the beginning of recovery; however, I do not have data to test this possibility.

Do these findings allude to the exposure of the immigrants to an "escalating cycle of discord"? What we can say for now is that the majority of veteran Israelis (65%—see Table 20) acknowledge the immigrants' integration into Israeli society. Thus, the problem is evidently in the feeling of the immigrants, a feeling that may be connected to their relatively poor overall perception of the positiveness of the society. In summary, then, the data suggest that the perceived positiveness of the society may have a pivotal function in the immigrants' integration into the absorbing society. The extent to which that may propel the immigrants into an "escalating cycle of discord" that may hamper their adjustment must still be explored (see also Chapter 8).

Corroboration of Trends

My interpretation of the meaning of the trends in the questions relating to the immigrants' integration can be understood in terms of the approach which is based on the exchange model described in Chapter 2. According to this approach, we can explain the decrease in the immigrants' assessment of the positivity of the absorbing society as an outcome of both the increasing costs (salience of the demands incurred by life in Israeli society) and a gradual decrease in the rewards (advantages of living in that society). The costs increase as the immigrants increasingly become aware of the rewards they have foregone in the society of origin (e.g., better utilization of skills, better dwelling conditions, culture), while the rewards (e.g., freedom, political stability) are devalued due to their relative availability.

The decrease in the positive assessment of the absorbing society is fairly typical of immigrant movements and parallels the trends observed in other migration studies (see Espino 1991; Leiper de Monchy 1991; Lobodzinska 1986; Pollock 1989). It also corroborates data from a study by Mirsky and Kaushinsky (1989) describing the transformation from euphoria to distress among American Jewish students in Israel. In terms of the integration of Soviet Jews into another society (the United States), the following passage is instructive:

The culture shock may be especially hard for Soviet Jews. The very word "acculturation" has derogatory overtones when translated into Russian. They come expecting an idyllic society, having dismissed the negative American image of drugs, crime and homelessness as propaganda. But on arrival they stay in cheap Manhattan hotels, and some begin to wonder if they made the right decision. Soviet Jews, accustomed to intense friendships with relative few people, tend to see Americans as superficial and materialistic. In turn, they themselves may be perceived as aggressive, demanding and sometimes lazy. . . . NYANA [New York Association for New Americans], for example, is a non-profit organization. But since there is no equivalent in the Soviet Union, immigrants think of it as an arm of the government, to be milked as far as possible. They are used to cheating and lying to manipulate an unfriendly system, so they often give misleading information. ("Soviet Jews" 1990:51)

Finally, it appears that the strong interrelationships among the facets of integration and, in particular, the pivotal role of acknowledgement as Israeli by the absorbing society and of the assessed positivity of the absorbing society corroborates Horowitz's (1979) conclusions, according to which immigrants from the Soviet Union are more likely than are those from North America to have an external locus of control with regard to political and societal issues. If these interpretations are reasonable, then the data allude to the importance of the perceived attitudes of the absorbing society in the immigrants' integration and to the harmful consequences of the cycle emerging from the perceived cues derived from interaction with that society.

INTEGRATION AND READJUSTMENT

Integration and Segregation

The literature on immigration refers to the significance of the integration of immigrants into the host society as an important factor in their psycho-social well-being (see Kuo and Tsai 1986). For instance, collective identity (the first facet of integration) may promote a feeling of equality with the members of that collectivity. There has also been research on the implications of segregation for the well-being of immigrants. On the one hand, several studies have emphasized the advantage of "ethnic enclaves" (a type of self-segregation). Portes (1981), for instance, notes the importance of ethnic enclaves in permitting the immigrant to escape from economic exploitation. Several studies (Banchevska 1981; Koranyi 1981; H. B. M. Murphy 1973) have suggested that the ethnic subculture and community are vital for sheltering the immigrant from adaptation stress, either by serving as a social support system or by functioning as an "escape hatch" from psychiatric problems.

On the other hand, other studies imply that certain types of indigenous social networks among immigrants may impede the immigrants' social mobility and psychological well-being. Granovetter (1973) suggests that strong ties among ethnic groups lead to political powerlessness. Wilcox (1981) and Hirsch (1979) report that among women undergoing major life transitions, a weaker density of indigenous networks was associated with positive adjustment. Palinkas cites three cases of immigrants from China and Vietnam who suffered from a lack of integration into the absorbing society and consequent identity crisis. In Palinkas' words: "In all three cases, the symptoms of some form of psychological disorder were associated with a series of cultural conflicts. . . . In each case there was . . . an element of what is referred to . . . as identity disorder. Associated with this disorder is a severe subjective distress" (Palinkas 1982:245).

Integration and Readjustment in Israel

Israeli studies of the period of mass immigration in the 1950s point to the deleterious impact on the immigrants' well-being of the melting-pot ideology and the culturally heterogeneous settlements thought to promote integration (Eisenstadt 1967). There is accumulating evidence of the intergroup conflicts and hostilities prevailing in culturally heterogeneous neighborhoods and settlements (Shumsky 1955), which created, on a national basis, a "mosaic of segregated people" (Klaff 1980). On the other hand, ethnic enclaves may be a deliberate attempt to preserve the minority status of certain immigrant groups (Smooha 1978). What is the role of integration in the immigrants' readjustment and in their sense of potency? What is the weight of each of the four facets of integration in readjustment? It is to these questions that I turn next.

Findings Referring to New Immigrants

The data in Table 33 suggest that integration into the society has a small correlation with readjustment for both immigrants and veterans ($\mu_2 = .16$ and $.15$, respectively). It has a much larger correlation with potency for both groups, the correlation being even higher for immigrants than for veterans ($\mu_2 = .54$ and $.34$, respectively). For immigrants, perceived positiveness of society is most highly correlated with readjustment ($\mu_2 = .30$); perceived acknowledgement as a member of Israeli society is second in importance for both readjustment and potency ($\mu_2 = .57$ and $.20$). For the veterans, this latter facet is most highly correlated with both ($\mu_2 = .28$ and $.50$). Assuming Israeli identity and perceived positiveness of society are more important for the potency of immigrants than of veterans (identity: $\mu_2 = .59$ v. $.33$; positiveness: $\mu_2 = .52$ v. $.36$). The former has a relatively low correlation with readjustment for both immigrants and veterans ($\mu_2 = .12$ and $.10$, respectively). Interestingly, acknowledgement of the immigrants' integration into Israeli society is virtually unrelated to the readjustment of either group and has the weakest relationship with their potency.

Table 33

Correlations (μ_2) Among Readjustment, Potency and the Facets of Integration by Population Group

Facet of Integration	μ_2 with Integration		μ_2 with Potency	
	Immigrants	Veterans	Immigrants	Veterans
Israeli identity	.12	.10	.59	.33
Perceived acknowledgement	.20	.28	.57	.50
Acknowledgement by society	.00	.09	.46	.15
Positiveness of society	.30	.11	.52	.36
Average μ_2	.16	.15	.54	.34

CONCLUSION: THE ROLE OF INTEGRATION IN READJUSTMENT AND POTENCY

The central premise underlying this work is that readjustment indicates a successful culmination of the process of immigration for both immigrants and the absorbing society. The rationale for this premise is that since immigration-instigated life-change confronts both immigrants and members of the absorbing society with unprecedented demands that can disrupt their emotional homeostasis, readjustment is the most important factor to study. However, since integration is seen as critical to readjustment and sense of potency, this chapter has addressed the role of integration.

With regard to the role of each facet of integration in readjustment, the perceived positiveness of the absorbing society seems most salient for readjustment of immigrants. This conclusion corresponds with the findings regarding the interdependence of the facets of integration (Tables 31 and 32; Figures 2 and 3), which pointed to the pivotal role of the perceived positiveness of society in shaping a person's collective identity. Particularly for immigrants, a decrease in the perceived positiveness of a society is likely to have a negative effect on integration. Combining the data from the two tables, we conclude that assessment of the positiveness of the absorbing society is more likely than the other facets to promote the immigrants' readjustment, though even this has a fairly low correlation with readjustment.

The relationship between potency and integration is more striking. This finding underscores the complexity in the immigrants' capacity to overcome the difficulties of coping with unprecedented demands. As hypothesized in Chapter 3, potency has a pivotal role in restoring a person's emotional homeostasis, when that is disturbed due to inadequate coping with demands. From a theoretical point of view, the relationship between potency and integration into a social system supports the contention regarding the societal component of potency (see Chapter 3).

The relationship between potency and integration also emphasizes the complexity of the immigrants' readjustment. Immigrants are confronted with an array of stress-precipitating demands and are likely to be in need of stress-buffering mechanisms, such as potency. Yet the rather strong relationship between potency and integration suggests that, with inadequate integration, they may have a low level of potency. As we shall see in Chapter 7, the immigrants' sense of potency is indeed weaker than that of the veterans.

These conclusions conform with the extensively discussed function of the social environment in a person's coping and eventual well-being (Chapter 3 and this chapter). At this stage, I note the readjustment-conditioning function of evaluating the society as positive, particularly for immigrants (Tables 31 and 32, Figures 2 and 3). This relationship can be explained in terms of the classic approaches to reference groups and to the social exchange approach, according to which, the appreciation of the status or expected profit to be derived from a group increases the desire to join it. Moreover, it reflects the confidence in the society that is essential for the individual's potency. It also corroborates the earlier-mentioned conclusions of Horowitz (1979) that immigrants from the Soviet Union are more likely than immigrants from the United States to have an external locus of control. Finally, the conclusion regarding the importance of the perceived positiveness of the absorbing society for the immigrants' readjustment and feeling of potency conforms with the trends in numerous migration studies discussed earlier. However, as we saw, there is a decrease over time in the assessment of the positiveness of the absorbing society. This may be due to the devaluation of the "rewards" that now are abundant and the increasing value of those that were given up by leaving the society of origin.

The lack of correlation between the absorbing society's emotional homeostasis and the acknowledged integration of the immigrants may, at a first glance, seem rather odd. However, I have pointed to the possibly distressing effect of immigration on the members of the absorbing society (Chapter 2). Specifically, with regard to Israel, the ambivalence and the rather limited immigration-favoring perspectives of Israeli society (Tables 1 and 3) may have led to the expectation that the emotional homeostasis of the veterans depends, to some extent at least, on the integration of the immigrants. There are at least two possible interpretations of this independence. On the one hand, immigration per se may not affect the members of the absorbing society. On the other hand, for those members of Israeli society who feel distressed by immigration, integration of the immigrants may be inadequate for maintaining their emotional homeostasis. Finally, I would stress that these suggestions are, obviously, no more than plausible interpretations of findings and that further research is necessary for arriving at more substantial conclusions.

6

Demands, Stressors, and Catalysts

IMMIGRATION-SPECIFIC DEMANDS

Demands Facing the Immigrants

In this chapter, I discuss the demands inherent in immigration and their effects on readjustment. A systematic categorization of typical immigration-related demands may contribute to an understanding of the factors that can impede readjustment. One way of defining demands is according to their source, that is, demands coming from the individual's internal or external environment (Antonovsky 1979, Ben-Sira 1991). Yet, in the case of immigration, most demands are those that are evoked by the changes in the individual's external environment. Therefore, it seems more relevant to categorize of these demands according to three modalities: instrumental, affective, and cognitive.

Instrumental Demands

Economic problems and problems of employment are among the most salient instrumental problems of immigrants. To the extent that immigrants obtain employment, it is often in peripheral, low-ranking jobs. There is evidence of the disproportional representation of immigrants in peripheral sectors (Bouvier and Gardner 1986; Bach and Bach 1980). Reasons for the immigrants' difficulties in obtaining employment in suitable occupations or positions according to their self-assessed proficiency include cultural differences, inadequacy of their occupational proficiency in the eyes of the absorbing society, and coming too late into the labor-market (Chiswick 1978).

Gold, in his study on Jewish immigrants from the Soviet Union to the United States, emphasizes the difficulties men face in trying to find employment: "Economic necessity often required the women or children . . . to enter the labor force . . . because women's jobs such as house cleaner, hotel maid, and food-service worker were much more readily available than the male-oriented un-skilled occupations" (Gold 1989:423–425).

Ben-Barak (1989), in her study of Jewish immigrants from the Soviet Union to Israel, reports a similar trend and suggests that women were more willing than men to accept lower positions than they qualified for on the basis of their education and previous professional experience. Gold points out that because immigrants "had a prestigious occupation in their country of origin, . . . [they] were [often] reluctant to accept a less desirable job in the United States, and so remained unemployed" (Gold 1989:426).

In a similar vein, Shuval and her colleagues report that "In 1971, 40% of the Russian immigrants to Israel who were 55 years or over at the time of the inter-view were fully employed. Of the 60% not fully employed, almost half said that they wanted to work and had sought employment unsuccessfully; three quar-ters of these stated that they had looked for jobs for over a year" (Shuval et al. 1975:156–57). They particularly emphasize the immigrants' difficulties in finding suitable positions, concluding:

The immigrants are frequently confronted with the need for readjustment to somewhat different job requirements and at times to retrainment programs. Since they have long-established work habits, the old are more likely to find such requirements difficult to meet. It is not only a matter of finding employment for workers whose skills are not en-tirely appropriate to the Israeli labor market, but also of absorbing older immigrant workers in the face of competition by younger candidates. In a tight job market the problem can be especially acute. (Shuval et al. 1975:156–57)

Burawoy (1976), who studied immigration to the United States from a differ-ent angle, argues that peripheral minority immigrants bolster the American econ-omy. Indeed, a study by Stevens and others suggests that immigrant physicians apparently fulfill low-status and unattractive positions and "fulfill a residual role in the American employment market" (Stevens et al. 1978:131). According to Stevens: "Foreign medical graduates, entering hospitals, because of job avail-ability obtain the least sought-after training positions. The resulting patterns of entry are thus quite different for [American] medical graduates and foreign med-ical graduates" (Stevens et al. 1978:125).

A large-scale study by Shin and Chang compared the positions filled by Korean physicians who graduated from Yonsei University Medical School in 1953–1972 and immigrated to the United States, with those filled by physicians who remained in Korea. The study revealed that 54 percent of the immigrants to the United States filled peripheral positions, as opposed to only 24 percent of those who remained in Korea. These data were compared with the distribution of positions filled by the entire population of American graduates (born and practicing in the United States), of whom only 40 percent fill peripheral positions. The authors conclude that "immigrant physicians are peripherized as compared to both their homeland-staying cohort physicians and the native physi-cians of the host society" (Shin and Chang 1988:622).

Cognitive Demands

In the category of cognitive demands, the literature underscores problems relating to a lack of basic understanding of the way of life in the new society, including different bureaucratic and political approaches to the satisfaction of basic needs and language problems (see Furnham and Bochner 1986; Lin 1986). Lobodzinska's report on the areas of cultural problems that confront immigrants (including, but not limited to, Polish immigrants) may be instructive:

A questionnaire distributed among displaced persons in Minnesota in 1952 identified the resettlement problems as the language barrier, misunderstandings between sponsors and immigrants and "sponsors expecting too much before there was an understanding of the American way of life." In the first phase of getting acquainted with the new environment, behavioral and cultural differences become the most annoying sources of misunderstandings that contribute to confusion and frustration. (Lobodzinska 1986:428–429)

Grove and Torbiorn highlight the cognitive problems evoked by cultural incongruence in the advanced stages of acculturation of immigrants. They suggest that "as experiences in the host-culture are accumulated and applicability improves, host culture elements enter the frame [of reference] at an increasing rate. In most cases, the home- and host-based elements are mutually contradictory, so that the frame increasingly becomes a repository of cognitive elements that give conflicting advice regarding behavior, thus reducing a person's confidence or (as we termed it) clarity" (Grove and Torbiorn 1985:213).

Affective Demands

Affective demands are often viewed as the most pressing. In this category, the literature focuses on family relations, including inter-generational strains, social isolation, and social relations. Thus, for instance, Gold reports on the social isolation of Russian Jewish immigrant children. One explanation offered by Gold is the parents' rejection of the American customs and values, preferring their children's segregation from contact with American children, which sometimes leads to "depressing loneliness" for the children (Gold 1989:422).

Inter-generational conflict in immigrant families is a frequently reported affective demand. Gold reports that in order to protect their children from "alien influences," some Russian Jewish and Vietnamese immigrant adults fostered excessive dependence and thus limited the ability of their children to adopt American customs, adjust to American life, and develop American-style individualism. Another problem, besides social isolation, was that conflicts sometimes erupted when the children rejected their parents' attempts to plan their lives. Finally, much inter-generational conflict resulted from the inappropriateness of parental advice, since parents' experiences growing up in Vietnam or the Soviet Union provided few insights helpful to their children who were living in the United States (Gold 1989).

Westermeyer focuses on the inter-generational conflict in refugee families which occurs when the children acculturate more rapidly than their parents:

[Adolescents] are trying to establish their own identities, court, and enter mainstream social recreation and work-roles. Dating and marriage are often focal issues. . . . Refugee parents who fail to learn English, to understand the American social institutions, or to enter the world of work are less effective in preparing their children for life in the United States than those who do. Parental liabilities range from inability to cooperate with the school system in the education of their children, to inability to serve as role models or to teach relevant social survival skills to their children. In addition, such non-acculturating parents put themselves at risk [of] crises precipitated by unfamiliar behavior among their acculturating children. (Westermeyer 1991:136)

Gold reports on the difficulties of Russian Jewish immigrants in furnishing a proper education to their children. For instance, one immigrant woman said: "Right now with the kids we have a lot of dropouts. Some of our kids cannot get into the good program in school because they have a problem with language. . . . The parents are not satisfied with the public education, and they cannot afford anything else, so . . . [they] decide it is better off that they not go to school" (Gold 1989:421–22).

The need for establishing meaningful social relations may be regarded as an affective demand confronting immigrants in the new country (Kuo and Tsai 1986:134). Mirsky and Kaushinsky's (1989) study of American Jewish students in Israel emphasizes the students' frustrations due to obstacles to establishing affective ties with their Israeli peers—obstacles resulting from the wide cultural gap between Israel and their country of origin.

Perceived complexity of life in the new society may be regarded as another affective demand. Lobodzinska quotes a teacher from an English as a Second Language (ESL) school: "People who come to us often are burdened with complications of matters they have to deal with. Besides they worry about the families, . . . are over-worked, and [are] physically and psychologically exhausted" (Lobodzinska 1986:428).

Demands Facing the Absorbing Society

As indicated throughout this work, immigration may also impose demands on the absorbing society or on certain groups within that society. Some illustrations are in order.

Instrumental Demands

One of the central demands is the immigrants' competition in the labor market, offering cheaper labor and being less demanding as to working conditions than the veterans. As a result, immigration may be regarded by certain groups in the absorbing society as a threat to their employment, income, or working conditions. Brown and Warner (1992) describe the intense labor conflicts in the

United States of the 1890s caused by the threat of unemployment and wage cuts due to the cheap labor offered by immigrants. Similarly, Brownstein (1993), in his analysis of the illegal immigration from Central and South American countries to the United States in the 1990s, emphasizes the employers' inclination to hire immigrants, stating that many Americans resisted being forced to work in terrible conditions for less than the minimum wage. Lawson (1993) shows that even American citizens migrating from other states to California in the 1930s were accused of shiftlessness, lack of ambition, and stealing jobs from native Californians. Lobodzinska underscores the "general atmosphere of apprehension toward newcomers who represent a potential threat on the labor market during the time of unemployment and inflation. . . . Gallup polls taken in 1983 and in 1985 indicated that the public strongly opposed admitting illegal aliens," adding that, according to the 1985 Gallup poll, "the hard-line attitude of the public undoubtedly stems in considerable measure from the fear that illegal aliens will take jobs from [American] citizens" (Lobodzinska 1986:420–21).

Affective Demands

One example an affective demand confronting the veteran population is a fear that immigrants constitute a health hazard. Over the years, Americans have accused Irish immigrants of bringing cholera, Italians of importing polio, Chinese of being carriers of the bubonic plague, Jews of spreading tuberculosis, and Haitians of bringing AIDS (Kraut 1994). Immigration may cause change in the ethnic composition of neighborhoods, affecting the quality of social relations and evoking intergroup clashes (Impellizeri 1993). Immigration of Jews from the West in the 1970s aggravated feelings of deprivation among disadvantaged sectors in Israeli society, inciting such protest movements as the "Black Panthers" (Bernstein 1979; Cohen 1980).

Measuring the Salience of Demands

In this section, I discuss my findings regarding the salience of demands confronting the immigrants and the veterans in the empirical study. I measured salience of demands by questions which probed the respondents' problems in various life-areas (see Ben-Sira 1981, 1983a, 1986a, 1986b). The percentage of respondents claiming to confront severe problems in a specific life area was taken as an indicator of the salience of the demand.

Results

The data in Table 34 indicate that the salience of the demands confronting the immigrants is much higher than for the veterans. The most salient demands confronting the immigrants are in the areas of dwelling, ignorance of their entitlements and obligations, and economic condition. In the area of dwelling, 65 percent of immigrants, compared to 11 percent of the veterans, report serious problems. For 64 percent of the immigrants, but only 20 percent of the veterans, ignorance of their entitlements and obligations constitutes a highly salient demand. In addition, 60 percent of the immigrants, compared to 17 percent of the veterans, report highly salient demands in the areas of underutilization of their skills (51%), employment (46%), and unfamiliarity with bureaucracy (42%). The least salient demands confronting the immigrants are in the areas of social relations (3%) and education of their children (9%). Interestingly, the salience of demands in the areas of economic helplessness and problems with bureaucracy is similar for the immigrants and for the veterans (25% v. 23% and 12% v. 11%, respectively).

Table 34
Salience of Demands by Population Group

Mode of Demand Demand	Veterans (%)	Immigrants (%)	Total (%)
Instrumental			
Economic condition	17	60	32
Economic helplessness[a]	23	25	24
Job/employment	15	48	28
Dwelling	11	65	32
Contact with bureaucracy	11	12	11
Affective			
Family relations	6	11	7
Future of children	12	41	23
Education for children	2	9	5
Social relations	2	3	2
Emotional isolation[b]	27	36	30
Leisure	4	22	11
Cognitive			
Know obligations & entitlements	20	64	25
Unfamiliar with bureaucracy[c]	26	42	33
Underutilization of skills	15	51	25

a. The question was: "Did it ever happen that you needed monetary or other economic help, and there was simply nobody to help you?" There were six response categories, ranging from "Very often" to "Never"; reported percentages are those at the three highest levels.

b. The question was: "Did it ever happen that you felt bad, or were tense and nervous, and felt that you had no one to speak with about your troubles and problems?" There were six response categories, ranging from "Very often" to "Never"; reported percentages are those at the three highest levels.

c. There were only four response categories; reported percentages are those at the two highest levels.

The data in Table 35 suggest that the salience of demands decreases for longer-term immigrants. There is most improvement in the areas of employment problems, underutilization of skills and unfamiliarity with bureaucracy. In the area of employment problems, 67 percent of first-year immigrants, compared with 40 percent of fourth-year immigrants, report severe problems. With regard to under-utilization of skills, 69 percent of first-year immigrants and 41 percent of fourth-year immigrants define this problem as severe. As to unfamiliarity with bureaucracy, the figures are 64 percent and 35 percent, respectively. Yet, despite the overall weakening of the salience of the demands, dwelling problems (61%), ignorance of their obligations and entitlements (59%), and economic conditions (54%) are still quite salient demands even among fourth-year immigrants. The salience of most demands still exceeds that of the veteran population. There are no meaningful differences among the three veteran groups analyzed in the study.

Table 35
Salience of Demands by Veterans' Origin and Immigrants' Year of Immigration

Mode of Demand / Demand	Veterans[a]			Immigrants			
	East (%)	Israel (%)	West (%)	1993 (%)	1992 (%)	1991 (%)	1990 (%)
Instrumental							
Economic condition	16	13	16	70	61	65	54
Economic helplessness	26	26	18	28	24	29	26
Job/Employment	16	13	16	67	61	51	40
Dwelling	15	15	11	77	73	64	61
Contact with bureaucracy	12	9	9	11	13	11	12
Affective							
Family relations	7	6	6	13	9	11	11
Future of children	12	8	13	41	51	41	36
Education for children	2	1	2	9	8	9	8
Social relations	2	1	4	4	3	1	3
Emotional isolation	26	26	28	47	41	34	31
Leisure	4	3	5	32	31	22	15
Cognitive							
Know oblig's & entit's	20	16	21	74	71	65	59
Unfamiliar w. bureauc.	27	25	26	64	44	43	35
Underutilization of skills	16	18	11	69	72	45	41

CATALYSTS

Catalysts as Decoders of Demands

In Chapter 3, I defined three kinds of catalysts that generate demands and affect their salience, namely, objective circumstances, individual perspectives, and societal perspectives. These catalysts are interrelated, in that a person's awareness of objective circumstances and their salience will be affected by his/her individual perspectives, and both are likely to be affected by perceptions of prevailing societal perspectives. According to Gold, for instance, "the process by which children and/or mother rather than father become the primary source of a refugee family's income . . . often yielded hostility and resentment. . . . The most extreme problems were experienced by fathers who felt they had been unable to fulfill traditional responsibilities and resented their loss of power" (Gold 1989:423–425). The passage illustrates how an individual perspective (males should be the major breadwinners) can turn an objective circumstance (work, income) into a demand.

A catalyst may also prevent an objective circumstance from becoming a demand. Grove and Torbiorn, in their description of the immigrants' confrontation with a cultural universe differing extremely from that of their country of origin, maintain that:

At the moment the person arrives in the new environment his or her habitual pattern of activity is both socially unacceptable and interpersonally ineffective, . . . [yet] at first his confidence in the correctness of his [indigenous] frame of reference is not shaken. From his ethnocentric point of view it is "they" who are acting strangely or even unnatural, not "me." . . . At first home-culture elements completely dominate [that] frame of reference. (Grove and Torbiorn 1985:211–12)

In this case, an individual perspective (ethnocentric point of view) enhanced by an internalized societal perspective (home culture) means that objective circumstances (ineffectiveness of habitual patterns of behavior) may not be viewed as demands. As we shall see, this relationship is inherent in the nature of catalysts, depending on the relevance of the type of catalyst to specific areas of life.

Immigration-Related Catalysts

The literature on immigration suggests the significance of certain factors that may be considered catalysts in the framework I have developed. Some illustrations are in order.

Objective Circumstances

The "antecedent variables" which Rumbaut (1991) lists in his model of migration may be considered objective circumstances. These include family loss (in the country of origin), time in refugee camps, time lapse between leaving the country of origin and arrival at destination, length of time since immigration, and the "social distance" between country of origin and country of destination.

Many scholars view time in the country of destination as a significant factor in the successful culmination of the immigration process. Thus, for instance, Grove and Torbiorn (1985) view lapse of time since arrival as a crucial factor in creating a workable balance between the immigrants' indigenous cultural elements and the internalization of the absorbing society's relevant cultural elements. Writing of social distance, Rumbaut states, "less educated refugees from rural Southeast Asia clearly have much more difficulty managing the transition to post-industrial American cities than do middle class migrants of urban origin" (Rumbaut 1991:57–58).

Individual Perspectives

Following Berry's (1991) approach, immigrants' "ethnic identity" may be viewed as an important attribute, due to its incorporating an array of internalized beliefs, convictions, and life views that are likely to affect the individual's perception of reality. Similarly, Palinkas (1982) emphasizes the function of ethnic identity as providing guidelines for sentiments and forms of behavior.

Societal Perspectives

As stated above, perception of the societal perspectives prevailing in a society constitutes an important component in the characterization of that society and serves as a starting point for readjustment. In Chapter 2, I presented several illustrations of the prevailing societal perspectives in immigration countries and their effect on immigrants.

Measuring the Catalysts

Several questions addresses specific catalysts of demands. I consider them according to the threefold division just presented.

Objective Circumstances

Length of stay of an immigrant in the absorbing society is evidently a central catalyst. Indeed, as we saw in Table 35, the salience of many demands declines with time in Israel. Age may be another relevant objective circumstance affecting the perceived salience of demands. The literature suggests that the salience of demands increases with age, partly due to the difficulties of older immigrants in finding employment and their reduced capacity to acculturate (see Cohon 1981; Gold 1989; Shuval et al. 1975). As far as the veteran society is concerned, region of origin is an important "objective circumstance" in the literature, though it has not emerged as particularly significant in my data so far.

Individual Perspectives

Jewish identity may be regarded as encompassing a wide range of beliefs, convictions, and life views affecting the immigrants' perception of the salience of the demands facing them. In their study on immigration from North America to Israel, Antonovsky and Katz (1979) emphasize the significance of Jewish identification as motivating immigration. Farago, in his study of immigrant students from the Soviet Union, asserts that "their Jewish identity was intensified during the process of immigration as part of their preparation of establishing a common Jewish bond with their new country" (Farago 1979:37–38). Furthermore, "[Although] Jewish identity weakened at the second stage, [it] still remained the strongest element in the ethnic identity of the majority of the students" (Farago 1979:49). Jewish identity may be regarded as a belief of the sort that behavior according to its ruling is rewarding for its adherents (Ben-Sira 1993). The "rewards" derived from adhering to that identification may reduce the "costs" of demands, so that we may expect a negative relationship between Jewish identity and the salience of the demands.

Identification as a Zionist may be regarded as an additional individual perspective affecting the salience of demands. Despite the wide diversity of conceptions of Zionism (Ben-Sira 1993), the belief that Israel is the homeland of every Jew and that every Jew has the right to immigrate to Israel and view this country as his/her home, is the fulcrum of Zionist ideology. Zionist identification, like Jewish identity, may thus reduce the salience of the demands.

Finally, religiosity is likely to affect the salience of the demands. As suggested by various studies (Antonovsky and Katz 1979; Ben-Sira 1988a, 1993), religiosity is central to both Jewish identity and identification as a Zionist. Tables 36 and 37 show that immigrants are much less likely than veterans to view themselves part of the Jewish people in the world, identify as Zionists, and observe religious traditions.

Table 36
Identification as Jewish and Zionist by Population Group

| Intensity of Identification | Identify as Jewish among: | | | Identify as Zionist among: | | |
	Veterans (%)	Immigrants (%)	Total (%)	Veterans (%)	Immigrants (%)	Total (%)
Definitely yes	59	27	48	54	7	37
Yes	35	53	41	37	25	33
No	5	19	10	8	62	27
Definitely no	1	1	1	1	6	3
(N)	(882)	(484)	(1366)	(885)	(478)	(1363)

Table 37
Observance of Religious Tradition by Population Group

Extent of Observance	Veterans (%)	Immigrants (%)	Total (%)
Strictly	14	1	10
Greatly	20	6	16
Somewhat	45	58	49
Not at all	21	35	25
(N)	(885)	(485)	(1370)

Societal Perspectives

As indicated in Chapter 2, two societal perspectives may affect immigration and readjustment, namely, support of immigration, and collectivity orientation. It may be recalled that the immigrants accepted immigration-supporting perspectives more than did the veterans (Tables 1 and 2).

Catalysts and the Salience of Demands

In order to estimate the extent to which catalysts affect the perceived salience of the demands, I calculated correlations (μ_2) between them (Tables 38 and 39). In operational terms, the stress-potential of a demand can be defined in terms of the strength of the negative correlation between the salience of the demand and the disturbance of emotional homeostasis, since a strong negative correlation between the two implies that the chance that the demand will disrupt emotional homeostasis increase with its salience. Overall, the stronger the negative correlation, the stronger the demand's stress-potential.

Most generally, four patterns emerge from the data. First, the correlations between the catalysts and the perceived salience of the demands were stronger for the immigrants than for the veterans. Second, for the immigrants, length of stay in Israel and the individual perspectives seem to be the most decisive salience-moderating factors (that is, they had the strongest negative correlations with the demands). Third, immigration-supporting societal perspectives seem to exacerbate the salience of the demands (that is, they had the strongest positive correlations with these demands). Fourth, age and collectivity orientation seem to have no consistent correlation with the demands.

Looking at the pattern of correlations, we see that for the immigrants (Table 38), religiosity has a correlation of $\mu_2 \leq -.20$ with nine demand variables,[1] and time in Israel with seven variables. The correlation between time in Israel and lower salience of the demands in the area of employment and underutilization of skills is particularly striking ($\mu_2 = -.34$ and $-.46$ respectively). A similar effect may be observed with regard to Jewish identity ($\mu_2 = -.46$ and $-.38$). Employment problems and demands in the area of social relations are more salient for younger immigrants ($\mu_2 = .29$ and $.23$, respectively). However, demands in the areas of dwelling and of knowledge of obligations and entitlements are more salient for older immigrants ($\mu_2 = -.25$ for both demands). No relationship between the immigrants' region of origin and salience of demands was found (data not shown). As to the effect of the societal perspectives, the data suggests that immigration-supporting perspectives are positively correlated with the salience of demands, particularly those in the areas of economic conditions and dwelling. For the veterans (Table 39), the data suggest that the individual perspectives are not too helpful for understanding the perceived salience of the demands investigated. The inconsistent, somewhat scattered, distribution of the few large correlations does not reveal a discernable pattern.

Table 38
Correlations (μ_2) Between Catalysts and Salience of Demands:[a] Immigrants

Mode of Demand	Catalysts:							
	Circumstances		Individual Perspective			Societal Perspective		
Demand	Stay	Age	Jew	Zionist	Relig.	Coll.	Pro-Im.	Zi.→Im.
(High–Low)	(4–1)	(Y–O)	(H–L)	(H–L)	(H–L)	(H–L)	(H–L)	(H–L)
Instrumental								
Economic conditions	-.21	.03	-.23	-.30	-.25	.08	.23	.09
Economic helplessness	-.06	.09	-.13	-.11	-.10	.01	.15	-.00
Job/Employment	-.34	.29	-.46	-.29	-.20	.07	.09	.01
Dwelling	-.27	-.25	-.22	-.22	-.12	.12	.29	.40
Contact with bureaucracy	-.11	.00	-.07	.05	-.18	.03	.15	.13
Affective								
Family relations	-.03	.16	-.11	-.04	-.33	-.15	.04	.19
Future children	-.09	.11	-.26	-.11	-.28	.08	.11	.04
Education for children	.00	.09	-.05	.14	-.21	-.13	.01	.16
Social relations	-.20	.23	-.18	-.05	-.24	-.26	.18	.14
Emotional isolation	-.19	.17	-.23	-.20	-.21	.01	.15	-.11
Leisure	-.29	.02	-.24	-.41	-.32	.09	.06	.11
Cognitive								
Know oblig's & entit's	-.26	-.25	-.13	-.25	-.13	.23	.18	.19
Unfamiliar w. bureauc.	-.31	.00	-.13	-.24	-.22	.04	.21	.17
Underutilization of skills	-.46	-.01	-.38	-.14	.09	.17	.01	.08
Average μ_2	-.20	.06	-.20	-.16	-.19	.03	.12	.11

a. Negative correlation means: the stronger the catalyst, the weaker the salience of the demand.

Table 39
Correlations (μ_2) Between Catalysts and Salience of Demands:[a] Veterans

Mode of Demand	Circumstances		Individual Perspective			Societal Perspective		
Demand	Stay	Age	Jew	Zionist	Relig.	Coll.	Pro-Im.	Zi.→Im.
(High–Low)	(4–1)	(Y–O)	(H–L)	(H–L)	(H–L)	H–L)	(H–L)	(H–L)
Instrumental								
Economic conditions	.01	.04	.04	-.03	.00	.07	-.08	-.06
Economic helplessness	-.16	-.07	-.02	-.07	.06	.06	-.09	-.03
Job/Employment	-.05	.04	.01	-.12	-.07	.04	-.07	-.02
Dwelling	-.17	.39	-.05	-.10	-.05	.00	-.16	-.12
Contact with bureaucracy	-.13	.14	.05	-.03	.04	.19	.06	.03
Affective								
Family relations	.02	.10	-.13	-.12	-.25	.19	.08	-.07
Future children	.05	-.34	.04	.00	-.02	.02	-.04	.06
Education for children	-.08	-.23	.12	.01	-.01	.02	-.06	-.06
Social relations	.15	-.08	-.23	-.21	-.17	.12	.17	.15
Emotional isolation	.04	-.08	-.13	-.17	-.06	.12	.03	-.04
Leisure	.03	-.14	-.11	-.16	-.08	.13	.11	.08
Cognitive								
Know oblig's & entit's	.02	.05	-.10	-.22	.08	-.04	-.02	.02
Unfamiliar w. bureauc.	.04	.19	-.18	-.14	-.08	.05	-.04	-.03
Underutilization of skills	-.08	.19	-.29	-.22	.02	-.05	-.18	-.17
Average μ_2	-.02	.01	-.07	-.11	-.04	.06	-.02	-.01

a. Negative correlation means: the stronger the catalyst, the weaker the salience of the demand.

Comparison of the data from the immigrants and from the veterans underscores the population-specific nature of the correlations between catalysts and the salience of specific demands. Jewish identity, Zionist identity, and religiosity are correlated with the salience of most of the investigated demands for the immigrants, but not for the veterans. For instance, Jewish identity is negatively correlated with the salience of employment problems for the immigrants, but not for the veterans (μ_2 = -.46 v. .01). Religiosity is negatively correlated with salience of demands in the area of family relations for both immigrants and veterans (μ_2 = -.25 and -.33, respectively). In addition, age is correlated with salience of demands in the area of dwelling for both immigrants and veterans, but in opposite directions. Dwelling problems seem to be more salient for older immigrants and younger veterans (μ_2 = -.25 v. .39).

The population-specific nature of these correlations may reflect different experiences. For immigrants, the fact of immigration to Israel, especially if related to ideological convictions, may in itself serve as a "reward," thus moderating the salience of specific demands such as unsatisfactory employment. For veterans, on the other hand, such convictions are less likely to affect the salience of the demands of daily life. This finding corroborates the theory according to which internalized beliefs, convictions, and life views affect one's perception of reality (Berry 1991; Palinkas 1982), as well as the theory emphasizing the rewarding function of behavior according to one's convictions (Ben-Sira 1988a, 1993). Nonetheless, we must remember that immigrants identify as Jewish and as Zionist (Table 36) less than do veterans and also report much less observance of religious traditions (Table 37). Thus, the salience-moderating function of these convictions applies to only a small portion of immigrants.

The data also suggest that immigration-supporting perspectives may exacerbate the salience of the immigrants' demands, perhaps because such perspectives tend to legitimize these demands, thus leading to disappointment when the immigrants realize that Israeli society does not live up to their expectations. Under these circumstances, the negative effect of belief in the prevalence of immigration-supporting perspectives (Table 40) is understandable. The data pointing to the decline over time in the perceived positiveness of Israeli society (Table 21) may allude to the consequences of such disappointment. This conclusion seems to conform with the extensively documented disappointment of immigrants with the prevailing perspectives in host countries (see Espino 1991; Leiper de Monchy 1991; Lobodzinska 1986; Mirsky and Kaushinsky 1989; Pollock 1989).

Catalysts and Readjustment

To what extent are the catalysts correlated with readjustment? From a theoretical standpoint, no such direct relationship should be expected; and, generally, the data in Table 40 support the hypothesis that the catalysts are correlated mainly with the salience of the demands and not directly with emotional homeostasis. Thus, for instance, neither adherence to Zionist ideology nor religiosity is correlated with readjustment. Two exceptions should be mentioned: the strong positive relationship ($\mu_2 = .28$) between immigration-supporting perspectives and emotional homeostasis among the veterans, as contrasted with weak negative correlation ($\mu_2 = -.17$) among the immigrants; and the strong positive correlation ($\mu_2 = .47$) between age and emotional homeostasis among the immigrants, contrasted with the weak negative correlation ($\mu_2 = .14$) among the veterans.

Interpretation of the data suggests that, following the wave of immigration to Israel, maintenance of the veterans' emotional homeostasis is to some extent related to their immigration-supporting perspectives. Reservations regarding immigration are likely, under these circumstances, to have some stress-arousing effect. On the other hand, for immigrants, the belief in immigration-supporting perspectives may have a negative effect on readjustment. The data thus weakly corroborate the hypothesis that the immigrants' belief in immigration-supporting perspectives may have frustrating consequences. The data further suggest the critical role of age in the immigrants' readjustment: the younger the immigrant, the more likely is his/her readjustment. The role of age in the veterans' homeostasis is much less critical.

Table 40
Catalysts and Readjustment: Correlations (μ_2) Between Catalysts and Emotional Homeostasis Based on SPD by Population Group

Type of Catalyst Catalyst	Veterans (μ_2 with homeostasis)	Immigrants (μ_2 with homeostasis)
Objective Circumstances		
Age (Young–Old)	.14	.47
Veterans' Origin (West–East)	.00	—
Immigrants' Length of Stay (4–1 years)	—	.03
Individual Perspective		
Jewish	-.03	.06
Zionist	-.02	.09
Religious	-.01	.08
Societal Perspective		
Collectivity orientation	-.02	-.03
Immigrant-favoring attitudes	.28	-.17
Immigration as component of Zionism	.08	-.07

In summary, the data suggest that reservations against immigration may have a homeostasis-disturbing effect on veterans (Table 40). As we saw (Table 4), veteran Israelis of "Eastern" origin and second-generation Israelis are less supportive of immigration, hence are more apt be distressed by the recent wave of immigration from the former Soviet Union. These data corroborate the responses to, and consequent distressing consequences of, immigration for disadvantaged groups in the absorbing society (see Bernstein 1979; Brown and Warner 1992; Brownstein 1993; Brownstein and Simon 1993; Brym 1992; Cohen 1980; Impellizeri 1993; Kraut 1994; Lawson 1993; Lobodzinska 1986).

Relationship between Individual and Societal Perspectives

Contrary to expectations, the data do not reveal a meaningful relationship between the individual and societal perspectives investigated in this study (μ_2 varies between -.05 and +.05 and therefore is not included). These results suggest that Jewish, Zionist, and religious convictions are independent of perceptions of society's immigration-supporting perspectives and collectivity orientation. The lack of relationship with regard to immigrants may be explained by the finding that only a minority of immigrants define themselves as feeling attached to the Jewish nation throughout the world, as Zionist, or as religious (Tables 36 and 37), although the majority support immigration-supporting perspectives (Tables 1 and 3). From the veterans' point of view, the data suggest that feeling part of the Jewish nation throughout the world and defining oneself as Zionist does not necessarily imply holding immigration-supporting perspectives.

STRESSORS

Immigration-Related Stressors

As stated above, immigrants coming to a new society are likely to face numerous new demands, any of which may tax or exceed their capacities or resources, even disrupt their emotional homeostasis (see Watson 1977). Considerable work has been devoted to the stressors confronting immigrants. One of the common stressors alluded to in the literature is the employment of immigrants in low-skill, often peripheral, jobs. If only this kind of employment position is available and manageable for immigrants with a foreign education, culture, language, and economic philosophy, they may have difficulties in advancing into primary economic sectors and may be relegated to marginality in the absorbing society (Park 1928)—a state similar to what I have called maladjustment. Under these circumstances, work in itself may become a stressor.

Among the most frequently referred to types of immigration-related potential stressors are the problems aroused in family and primary relations in the wake of immigration. Westermeyer (1991:135-138) suggests an array of immigration-related family problems that can have a stress-arousing impact. Among those he enumerates are the following: role reversal as a consequence of the children's assumption of adult functions due to their more rapid acculturation than their parents; partial families and solo parents (a particularly stress-arousing situation could be when adolescent sons believe that they should dominate their single-parent mothers. Westermeyer feels that difficulties in single-father families are usually due to inadequate parenting skills or involvement rather than lack of parental authority); inter-generational conflicts, exacerbated by the more rapid acculturation of the children than their parent; changing gender roles, when, say, the wife assumes the role of major breadwinner (Cohon [1981] reports on extreme expressions of stress among immigrant-fathers who felt unable to fulfill their responsibilities and resented their loss of power); family structure and styles that were successful in the former culture may become stressors in the absorbing country if they are continued rigidly without respect for changed circumstances. Bavington and Majid (1986), in their study on Asian immigrants to the United Kingdom, highlight the lack of supportive family relations as one of the main factors leading to depression among immigrant women.

The Stress-Potential of Immigration-Related Demands

Not every demand confronting an immigrant is bound to become a stressor. Berry, though emphasizing the intrinsic stress-potential of the process of acculturation, insists that the problems causing acculturative stress "are not inevitable and seem to depend on a variety of group and individual characteristics that enter into the acculturation process. That is, acculturation sometimes enhances one's life chances and mental health, and sometimes virtually destroys one's ability to carry on; the eventual outcome for any particular individual is affected by other variables that govern the relationship between acculturation and stress" (Berry 1991:27). He further maintains that the acculturation experience is likely to vary, that different people are likely to perceive the same change differently, in terms of both its salience and stress-potential: "For some people, acculturative changes may all be in form of stressors, while for others they may be benign or even seem as opportunities. Various levels of stress may become manifest as a result of acculturation experience and stressors" (Berry 1991:28–29). The subjective appraisal of a demand's threat and insurmountability determine both the force of its stress-potential and its salience (see Kaplan 1983; Thoits 1983).

Immigration to Israel: Potential Stressors

What, then, is the stress-potential of the demands confronting new immigrants and veterans in Israeli society? According to the operational definition of a demand's stress-potential given earlier, the strength of the negative correlation (μ_2) between the respondents' emotional homeostasis, measured by the Scale of Psychological Distress (SPD), and the salience of demands was regarded as an indicator of a demand's stress-potential for the group under investigation: A strong negative correlation between a demand and the SPD suggests a high potential of that demand to become a stressor for that group. A lack of correlation means that the stress-potential of this demand is small. A positive relationship would mean that this demand has a stress-buffering capacity. But the extent to which a group's readjustment is threatened by a stressor is also dependent on the salience of the stressor for that group.

The data in Table 41 show the stress-potential of the demands investigated (that is, μ_2 between SPD and salience). The data suggest that almost all demands have some stress-potential, with the possible exception of underutilization of skills for both groups ($\mu_2 = -.05$), demands in the area of employment problems (.04), and unfamiliarity with bureaucracy (-.08) for immigrants, all three of which are virtually unrelated to emotional homeostasis. Intergroup comparison suggests that, for immigrants, "affective" and "cognitive" demands have the strongest stress-potential, while the stress-potential of "instrumental" demands is much smaller. For veterans, on the other hand, both "affective" and "instrumental" demands have fairly high stress-potential.

Table 41
Stress-Potential and Salience of Demands: Correlations (μ_2) Between SPD and
Salience of Demands, and Percentage in the Upper Three Levels of Salience by
Population Group[a]

| Mode of Demand | Veterans | | Immigrants | |
Demand	(μ_2)	(%)	(μ_2)	(%)
Instrumental				
Economic condition	-.40	17	-.19	60
Economic helplessness	-.39	23	-.17	25
Job/employment	-.35	15	.04	48
Dwelling	-.19	11	-.17	65
Contact with bureaucracy	-.27	11	-.38	12
Average μ_2	-.32		-.19	
Affective				
Family relations	-.38	6	-.35	9
Future of children	-.34	12	-.33	32
Education for children	-.47	2	-.47	9
Social relations	-.32	2	-.37	3
Emotional isolation	-.38	27	-.29	36
Leisure	-.39	4	-.33	22
Average μ_2	-.38		-.35	
Cognitive				
Know obligations & entitlements	-.22	20	-.29	64
Unfamiliar with bureaucracy	-.22	26	-.08	42
Underutilization of skills	-.05	15	-.05	51
Average μ_2	-.16		-.14	

a. Based on the data in Table 36.

Stress-Potential and the Salience of Demands

Up to now, I have analyzed separately the salience and stress-potential of
demands. Yet, as indicated earlier, to understand the threat to homeostasis, we
must consider these two simultaneously. Thus, in the following analysis, I
classify demands according to both criteria (Tables 42 and 43). For simplicity,
I divide each criterion into "high" and "low," yielding a four-fold cross-classification. So as to facilitate comparison between population groups, identical
cutting points for "high" and "low" were determined by the medians of each of
the two criteria according to their combined intergroup frequency.

Table 42
Cross-Classification of Demands by Stress-Potential and Salience: Immigrants

Salience (%)	Stress-potential (μ_2)					
	High ($\mu_2 \geq -.29$)			Low ($\mu_2 \leq -.28$)		
Demand	(μ_2)	(%)	Demand		(μ_2)	(%)
High ($\geq 22\%$)						
Future of children	-.33	32	Economic helplessness		-.17	25
Leisure	-.33	22	Job/Employment		.04	48
Emotional isolation	-.29	36	Dwelling		-.17	65
Know oblig's & entit's	-.29	64	Unfamiliar w. bureauc.		-.08	42
			Underutilization of skills		-.05	51
			Economic conditions		-.19	60
Low ($\leq 21\%$)						
Contact with bureaucracy	-.38	12				
Family relations	-.35	9				
Social relations	-.37	3				
Education for children	-.47	9				

Table 43
Cross-Classification of Demands by Stress-Potential and Salience: Veterans

Salience (%)	Stress-potential (μ_2)					
	High ($\mu_2 \geq -.29$)			Low ($\mu_2 \leq -.28$)		
Demand	(μ_2)	(%)	Demand		(μ_2)	(%)
High ($\geq 22\%$)						
Economic helplessness	-.39	23	Unfamiliar w. bureauc.		-.22	26
Emotional isolation	-.38	27				
Low ($\leq 21\%$)						
Economic condition	-.40	17	Dwelling		-.19	11
Job/employment	-.35	15	Contact with bureaucracy		-.27	11
Family relations	-.38	6	Know oblig's & entit's		-.22	20
Future children	-.34	12	Underutilization of skills		-.05	9
Social relations	-.32	2				
Education for children	-.47	2				
Leisure	-.39	4				

The data in Table 42 suggest that the demands that most threaten the immigrants' emotional homeostasis are mainly affective, namely, the future of their children, leisure, and emotional isolation. Ignorance of obligations and entitlements constitutes an additional homeostasis-threatening demand. The other affective demands, though having a high stress-potential, have relatively low salience so may constitute a lesser threat to homeostasis. Similarly, most of the instrumental demands, though highly salient, have a fairly low stress-potential. As for the veterans, isolation, both economic and emotional, is the major threat to their homeostasis. The other affective and instrumental demands, though having a relatively high stress-potential, are not a major threat to readjustment, perhaps due to their low salience.

Overall, the data indicate the usefulness of distinguishing between the stress-potential of a demand and its salience. As we saw, most of the investigated demands have some degree of stress-potential. Due to their low salience, few of them constitute a substantial threat to readjustment. Still, the risk of their materializing this stress cannot be disregarded, for two reasons: First, there are individuals, albeit only a few, for whom these demands are salient. Second, changing conditions (say in the field of employment) may increase the salience of demands such that they threaten readjustment.

At this point, an unexpected finding regarding the immigrants requires further consideration. How are we to understand the relatively low stress-potential of the instrumental demands, particularly in the areas of employment, dwelling and underutilization of skills—areas that are evidently highly salient and intuitively would be expected to have a strong stress-potential? In fact, however, the data corroborate evidence from other migratory movements, suggesting that problems in family and primary group relations aroused by immigration often overshadow other problems (Bavington and Majid 1986; Cohon 1981; Gold 1989; Sluzki 1979; Westermeyer 1991). This may be because of two factors. First, family and primary relations are often the major, if not the sole, source of support following immigration, such that immigrants need them for assistance and support, a need that would be difficult to meet in the best of circumstances. Second, however, the changes involved in immigration mean that immigrant families are prone to conflict and even disruption, just when they are needed most and become even less able to help the individual members. Under these circumstances, the economic and employment problems of the immigrants, despite their high salience, are less likely to constitute a threat to readjustment than is conflict in the immigrants' primary relations.

CONCLUSION: LIFE CHANGE, DEMANDS, AND STRESSORS

In this chapter, we examined the usefulness of the proposed paradigm (Figure 1) in helping to explain the function of demands in immigration-instigated life change. Specifically, we focused on the role of catalysts in the salience of demands, on the one hand, and the stress-potential of demands, on the other hand, in threatening the readjustment of immigrants and veterans.

Empirical investigation among new immigrants and veterans demonstrated the utility of the proposed framework for furthering the understanding of the factors promoting or impeding readjustment. First, with regard to the function of the catalysts, the data suggest the importance of the catalysts in affecting the salience of demands. Thus, as we saw (Tables 38 and 39), objective circumstances, such as time in the country, may moderate the salience of the demands confronting immigrants. The effect of age is less clear, seeming to have different effects in the two population groups. "Ideological" individual perspectives may have a salience-moderating function for immigrants, but not for veterans. On the other hand, belief in ideological societal perspectives may exacerbate the salience of the demands of immigrants but not veterans. These findings point to the need for identifying the relevant perspectives for specific population groups and specific situations. The data in Tables 42 and 43 emphasize the distinction between the stress-potential of a demand and the salience which, together predict the likelihood of the demand threatening readjustment. In the next chapter, we turn to coping as a means of reducing the salience of demands.

NOTE

1. There is a growing recognition that many phenomena in the social sciences can be better demonstrated by the recurrence of patterns than by arbitrarily-chosen "levels of significance" (Carver 1978; Guttman 1977). Thus, I did not use significance tests as indicators of meaningfulness in my analyses.

7

Coping and Resources

THE NOTION OF COPING

Coping Outcome: An Indicator of Coping

In Chapter 3, I defined coping as moderating the salience of a demand, hence reducing the likelihood that it will disrupt one's emotional homeostasis. This definition is similar to that of Lazarus and Folkman, who maintain that "in both the animal and psychoanalytic ego psychology models, coping is equated with adaptive success, which is also the popular meaning of the term. In the vernacular, to say a person coped with the demands of a particular situation suggests that the demands were successfully overcome; to say a person did not cope suggests ineffectiveness or inadequacy" (Lazarus and Folkman 1991:200). It is somewhat different from the definition of Kahn and colleagues, who contend that "the concept of coping is defined by the behaviors subsumed under it and not by the success of those behaviors," and, consequently, "definitions of coping must include efforts to manage stressful demands, regardless of outcome" (Kahn et al. 1964:201). Yet, even they conclude that "the best coping is that which changes the person-environment relationship for the better" (Kahn et al. 1964: 205). In any case, it seems plausible that the core of coping is its effectiveness in allowing the individual to perceive that the conditions in diverse areas of life have changed for the better. I would like to repeat that coping does not mean merely going through the motions of "instrumental" behavior. Rather, as indicated above, the essence of coping is the perception of having moderated the salience of a demand and thus having successfully overcome the threat inherent in that demand (Ben-Sira 1981, 1983a; Ben-Sira and Eliezer 1990; Lazarus and Folkman 1991). This involves calming the agitation aroused by that demand by either depreciating the significance of the demand or appreciating the effectiveness of the invested coping behavior.

As with catalysts, coping can involve three behavior modalities: "affective," "cognitive," and "instrumental." For instance, an individual encountering a demand in the form of a symptom having a strong stress-potential—say, a symptom of a chronic disease—may start with affective coping, that is, calming his/her agitation by moderating the assessment of its salience and evaluating it rationally. He/she may then apply cognitive coping, perhaps by assessing it as sporadic and/or attributing it to some behavior or physical effort. If the same symptom then recurred, he/she might apply the final step, namely, instrumental coping, by undergoing a physician's examination and a series of tests, and being assured that no pathogenic condition is involved. It is not, however, the examination and the tests in themselves but the belief in their effectiveness that moderates the salience of the demand and restores the individual's homeostasis.

Coping versus Defense

The affective dimension of coping should not be confused with defense. As stated elsewhere:

Coping, particularly its affective dimension, differs from defense in two distinctive features: confrontation versus avoidance, and endurance versus shortness of the effect. Coping . . . is characterized by a calculated assessment based on a deliberate and active confrontation with the demand. A defensive reaction implies maintenance or restoration of homeostasis by passively avoiding any thought about the demand through denial (that is, denying the existence of demand) or repression (that is, forgetting the demand). Defense occasionally may give immediate relief from a demand. In the long run, however, it is likely to be ineffective or even hazardous. (Ben-Sira 1991:54–55)

Referring again to the example above, affective coping would mean that the individual deliberately calmed his/her agitation in order to facilitate a rational appraisal of the meaning of that symptom and a consideration of the alternatives, leading, perhaps, to a decision to seek medical advice. Defense, on the other hand, would mean repressing any thought of the symptom. Such defensive reaction is likely to inhibit any action (rather than leading to instrumental steps), and, therefore, cannot moderate the salience of the symptom in the long term.

Immigration and Coping

Immigration studies point to the importance of immigrants' moderating the perceived salience of demands confronting them. Pollock (1989) terms the immigrants' coping with the consequences of the extreme life-change as a "mourning-liberation" process. One can interpret his psychoanalytically based report as referring to the centrality of perception in coping. In Pollock's words:

This [mourning-liberation] process . . . is involved in the migration-adaptation process. In fact, it is my belief that the total mourning-liberation process is involved in all situations of change and transition. . . . The stress and resulting strain of elective leaving [a familiar environment] resulted in responses very similar to . . . the mourning-liberation process—a normal, necessary, universal, transformational process that permits us to adapt to change (which is loss), loss of meaningful figures, loss of home, loss of resources, loss of physical and emotional-mental health, loss of memory—in other words, varied kinds of losses. (Pollock 1989:146)

Lobodzinska's study of immigrants from Poland in the United States further illuminates this point: "In addition to feeling estranged, some of the Polish immigrants . . . physically freed themselves from the Polish turmoil, but emotionally they are still there" (Lobodzinska 1986:429). This passage suggests both the dubious effectiveness of defensive reactions to the new environment and the significance of moderating the salience of the demands it imposes.

Gold's study of Russian Jewish and Vietnamese immigrants to the United States contains both instrumental and cognitive dimensions of coping in moderating the salience of the demands in the new country:

Many Soviet Jewish and Vietnamese refugees chose to enter small businesses because it allowed them to keep the family together, provided for the needs of family members, and made use of family based resources. . . . Small businesses were seen as especially desirable by Vietnamese families because such endeavours could be passed on to children. . . . [Conversely,] while certain Soviet Jewish proprietors encouraged their children's involvement in entrepreneurship, many others hoped that their offspring would have professional careers. These parents limited their children's connection with the family business. (Gold 1989:418–420)

In his analysis of immigrant acculturation, Berry implies that the experience of acculturation varies according to the person's perception. He thus alludes to the aspects of coping that we view as fundamental, namely, the role of perception and resources in moderating the salience of demands and consequently in readjustment. In Berry's words: "These relationships [between acculturation experience and stress] depend on a number of moderating factors. . . . Of particular importance among these psychological factors is the individual's ability to cope with the acculturative experience; individuals are known to vary widely in how they deal with major changes in their lives, resulting in large variations in the levels of stress experienced" (Berry 1991:28–29).

In contrast to the positive contribution of coping toward the immigrants' readjustment, Lobodzinska's study suggests the detrimental function of defense. She reports:

The newcomers changed their addresses, moving from one suburb to another, approximately from two to six times. This high mobility between countries, states, and suburbs can be considered an extension of the escape syndrome described by Slater. . . . The need to escape motivated their emigration from their homeland and is still exhibited in the frequent changes of place of residence. For some of them, it is also extended to frequent changes of the place of employment. (Lobodzinska 1986:425)

RESOURCES

The Essence of Resources

From the preceding analysis, we can see the centrality of resources for coping successfully with demands and restoring emotional homeostasis (Wheaton 1985). Resources can be defined so as to emphasize their significance for coping: "Innate or achieved traits or properties of an individual (such as physical stamina, self-esteem, education, skills, knowledge, experience, cultural characteristics, wealth, etc.) as well as environmental support (primary social support, professional assistance, etc.), that have the potential of facilitating effective coping with demands" (Ben-Sira 1985:397; see also Menaghan 1983:159).

There are two types of resources: personal resources, controlled by the individual, and environmental resources, derived from the environment. The latter are likely to be less effective than the former (Ben-Sira 1981, 1983a), for two reasons. First, environmental support is not always available. Second, it is ultimately the individual who must respond to the demand. In addition, overreliance on environmental support is apt to increase the probability that demands will be perceived as unresolvable.

Primary and Secondary Environmental Resources

Environmental resources are most likely to be used in situations in which personal resources are insufficient. Such situations are particularly characteristic of immigrants, who face unprecedented demands with resources developed for coping with other demands. Under such circumstances, they are forced to rely on resources controlled by others.

These others may be part of their primary group, including family and friends. Primary-group assistance is, to a great extent, based on reciprocity, since merely belonging to a group implies one's value for that group, and the help given to an individual is in part an exchange for the rewarding value of his/her membership. In terms of power relations: "The mutual dependence of actors on one another for valued resources provides the structural basis for their power over each other. . . . If A and B are equally dependent on each other, power in the relation is balanced" (Molm et al. 1994:99).

Such primary-group support may also be insufficient, however, especially for immigrants, whose primary-group members are often confronted with similar demands. In this case, moderating the salience of the demands may require the assistance of secondary sources, including bureaucratic agencies and professionals, such as social workers or psychologists. Use of such support highlights the person's inability to meet his/her needs alone and may be seen as an admission of inadequacy, that is, unequal dependence. In terms of power relations, "if dependencies are unequal, power is imbalanced. The less dependent and more powerful actor has a structural power advantage in the relation, . . . and the less powerful actor is power disadvantaged" (Molm et al. 1994:100). Admission of inadequacy thus implies, in terms of exchange theory, a cost for the recipient of that help, which may constitute a new demand requiring coping.

It follows that the benefit of bureaucratic or professional help is less than could be obtained from primary-group support, if the latter were effective. Though this support is necessary, reliance on it is likely to diminish the immigrants' belief in their "control," namely, their ability to change stressful situations (Thoits 1991). Consequently, reliance on such environmental support can lead to dependency and inferiority vis-à-vis "powerful" bureaucrats and professionals. Such dependence and inferiority undermines successful coping and increases the risk of maladjustment (Ben-Sira 1981, 1983a, 1985, 1986a, 1986b, 1989; Ben-Sira and Eliezer 1990). This risk can be minimized if assistance begins as soon as possible and focuses on resource enhancement, while providing resource compensation only as long as the immigrant does not yet have the necessary coping capacities (Ben-Sira 1983b). For instance, it is preferable to provide intensive vocational retraining and language teaching (resource enhancement), while steadily decreasing monetary assistance (resource compensation).

In addition, the immigrant may suspect that the assisting agent is pursuing his/her own self-interest (e.g., power, money) by deliberately perpetuating dependence or, conversely, withholding direct assistance (even when the actual goal is resource enhancement). Such suspicions are liable to be counter-productive to furthering the immigrants' coping capacities and consequent readjustment (Ben-Sira 1986a, 1986b, 1988b).

Primary Environmental Resources: Families and Ethnic Groups

In discussing the capacity of new immigrants to cope with the demands confronting them in the new country, the literature emphasizes the role of families and ethnic groups. These provide affective, cognitive, and instrumental resources. Gold focuses on the supportive role played by families in the readjustment of Russian Jewish and Vietnamese immigrants to the United States. With regard to the Vietnamese, the explanation Gold offers is the centrality of the family, reflecting a traditional type of culture:

[In] Vietnamese culture, family is everything. There are aspects which help us to readjust to this society. It is easy for us because of tradition of helping in the family. We solve problems because [the] family institution is a bank. Because if I need money—my brother and my two sisters are working—I tell them I need to buy a house. I need priority in this case. They say "okay," and they give it to me. And after only two years, I bought a house. . . . Now I help them. They live with me and have no rent. The family is [also] a hospital. If Mom is sick, I, my children and my brother and sisters care for her. (Gold 1989:416)

Gold also cites the example of a Russian Jewish entrepreneur who acquired funds from family members in order to open a restaurant: "I just said, 'I gotta have it' " (Gold 1989:419), and his numerous relatives felt obliged to help him.

"Family" includes not merely blood relations but also persons with whom a prolonged close contact had been maintained, such as persons who lived together in refugee camps in Southeast Asia, or persons living in ethnic enclaves in the United States. The latter method of creating "pseudo-families" evidently applied to Russian Jewish immigrants as well: "Refugees of both groups met co-ethnics in immigrant enclaves, coffee shops, at resettlement agencies, and while on job or in classes. . . . The inclusion of unrelated individuals in extended families facilitated the sharing of information, money, and emotional support among refugees" (Gold 1989:418).

In contrast, Lobodzinska indicates that immigrants who left Poland earlier were not eager to help the newcomers and reports similar observations with regard to Hungarian, Lithuanian and Czech immigrants. She concludes that, except between relatives, there is little communication among immigrants (Lobodzinska 1986:426). Nonetheless, she notes that in the Polish ethnic communities of Chicago, Detroit, New York City, and Buffalo, where most Polish immigrants live, there are Polish-language newspapers and Polish-American organizations which still function. She adds that immigrants of other nationalities also have particular urban centers where ethnic communities develop and which attract newcomers from the old countries, though many immigrants do not move to these ethnic communities (Lobodzinska 1986:411–412).

Palinkas, in his study of the adjustment of Chinese immigrants in San Diego, uses the concept "arena," which he defines as "the environmental, social and cultural context in which the actors experience sociocultural change" (Palinkas 1982:256), to describe a similar phenomenon. He contends that Chinatown "has served as the primary 'arena' for sociocultural change and adjustment to life in the United States for Chinese immigrants. . . . In [the] Chinatown arena, social organization is typically based on hierarchy of traditional, modernist, and 'activist' voluntary organizations" (Palinkas 1982:236).

Voluntary ethnic associations are another kind of environmental resource. According to Palinkas:

In the United States two institutions . . . have traditionally served to ease the process of adjustment as well as to mitigate the psychological stress experienced by the immigrant: the ethnic enclave or ghetto and the ethnic church. . . . While the Catholic church has played an important part in the maintenance of the ethnicity of European immigrants, . . . [Chinatown has] served a comparable function for Chinese immigrants. . . . However, as more and more Chinese move out of Chinatown, and Chinese immigrants move directly into other parts of the cities and suburbs, the Chinese church assumes these functions for Chinese immigrants in non-Chinese locales. (Palinkas 1982:235)

Palinkas concludes:

Many Mandarin speakers join these churches, particularly when they live in non-China-town settings, to seek an orderly and friendly world which will support them in this adjustment process. The Chinese church is useful in providing this support for three reasons. First, the church as a healing redemptive fellowship is inseparably concerned with mental health in both the preventive and therapeutic dimensions. Second, the Chinese church serves as a substitute for the Chinese kinship network, the traditional support system for adjustment to changes in the environment. Third, the Chinese church acts as an arena for sociocultural change whereas traditional Chinese ethnic identity is joined with modern Christian religious identity. (Palinkas 1982:255)

One might ask whether immigrants' confinement of their support relationships to their own ethnic group is not detrimental to their readjustment in the wake of the extreme life-change they have undergone. Kuo and Tsai (1986), in their study of Chinese, Filipino, Japanese, and Korean immigrants to the United States, observe that although there is a belief that assimilating structurally or socially with members of the host society will increase the immigrant's social or psychological well-being, the available empirical evidence on this point is far from conclusive. Portes (1981) has noted the importance of ethnic enclaves in permitting the immigrant to avoid economic exploitation. And several studies (Banchevska 1981; Koranyi 1981; H. B. M. Murphy 1973) have found that the ethnic subculture and community are vital for sheltering the immigrant from adaptation stresses, either by serving as a social support system or by functioning as an escape-hatch from psychiatric illness.

On the other hand, there are other studies suggesting, directly or indirectly, that certain types of social networks among immigrants may work against their social mobility and psychological well-being. Granovetter (1973), making a pioneering contribution by explicating the strength of "weak ties," implies that strong ties among ethnic groups led to political powerlessness, preventing them from stopping a public program that eventually destroyed their community. Further, Wilcox (1981) and Hirsch (1979) both report that among women undergoing major life transitions, lower-density networks (that is, with less interconnectedness among network members) were associated with positive adjustment.

Primary and Secondary Environmental Resources in the Readjustment of Immigrants in Israel

From the preceding analysis, the question arises as to the role of environmental support in the readjustment of immigrants to Israel. Some distinctive characteristics of Israeli society seem to lessen the relative importance of such support: the declared ideology viewing immigration as a national goal and, as such, in the interest of the society (even if the immigrants actually were driven by self-interest); and the declared values of collectivity orientation and equality (Ben-Sira 1988a, 1993; Eisenstadt 1967) as opposed to the prevailing values of achievement and self-orientation in the United States.

As we saw, new immigrants to Israel indeed tend to believe (more than do veteran Israelis) that immigration is a fundamental goal of Zionism (Table 1) and to hold immigration-favoring perspectives (Table 3). They also (like veterans) view Israeli society as characterized by a collectivity orientation (Table 5).

Included in these perspectives is the assumption that immigrants are entitled to assistance from the state. The onus of their adjustment is likely to be attributed predominantly to the state, thus relieving the family and primary relations of some of their responsibilities in this area.

The difficulty of secondary environmental resources in moderating the salience of demands confronting the immigrants can be seen in the following passage from Mirsky and Kaushinsky's study of the readjustment problems of Jewish immigrant students from the United States:

The [students'] ambivalence about longing for home and disappointment with it, about love of Israel and disappointment with it, leads to intense anger with both countries. Since Israel is the immediate source of frustration, the anger is directed mostly toward anything that represents Israel, including of course university and absorption authorities. The anger is particularly intense because the students know that they must depend on the absorption authorities. . . . [In addition,] adolescent immigrants need even more from their peer groups than do other adolescents because their internal rejection and external separation leaves them with impoverished internal resources. . . . And when they try to find a peer group within Israeli society, they are doomed to failure because of the vast differences between them and their Israeli peers: . . . Israelis serve three years in the army [and] are more mature, . . . [having passed the] individuation process in the army. . . . Furthermore, Israeli groups formed a long time before army [service] . . . hence view the immigrants as outsiders and often ridicule their behavior [and] language. (Mirsky and Kaushinsky 1989:737)

This passage illustrates the significance of both primary environmental resources—peers—and secondary environmental resources—Israeli society at large and formal organizations (absorbing authorities and university)—all providing affective and instrumental resources for the readjustment of the immigrants.

To what extent do these resources provide resource-compensation or even resource-enhancement for new immigrants from the former Soviet Union? It is to this question that I now turn.

Classification of Resources

As a first step in elucidating the resources that may help the immigrants to cope, it seems useful to consider what the different types of resources are. We can classify resources according to two facets, modality and source. In terms of modality, we can speak of affective (e.g., friendship, emotional support, feeling at home), cognitive (e.g., understanding, knowledge), and instrumental (work, income) resources. In terms of the source of the resources, we can speak of self-controlled resources and of those coming from the individual's primary and secondary environments. The resource referred to in the literature will be classified according to these categories.

Personal Resources

The personal resources in the instrumental modality include: employment of the immigrant or spouse, economic condition in itself, and home ownership (see Bach and Bach 1980; Ben-Barak 1989; Bouvier and Gardner 1986; Cochrane and Stopes-Roe 1977; Gold 1989; Lobodzinska 1986; Shin and Chang 1988; Shuval et al. 1975; Sluzki 1979; Westermeyer et al. 1983). In the cognitive modality, the resources generally considered most effective are: (i) education and (ii) knowledge of language (Ben-Sira 1982c; Ben-Sira 1988a; Burke 1969; Creed 1987; Gold 1989; Shuval et al. 1975; Simon 1985; Westermeyer 1991).

Environmental Resources

These include both primary and secondary environmental resources. In terms of instrumental resources, those in the primary environment include economic support by family and friends (Banchevska 1981; Gold 1989; Koranyi 1981; H. B. M. Murphy 1973); those in the secondary environment include formal agencies whose function is to assist immigration, as well as informal (mainly ethnic) mutual-help associations, which provide employment and economic assistance (Gold 1989; Kuo and Tsai 1986; Lobodzinska 1986; Palinkas 1982). In terms of affective resources, those in the primary environment include spouse, family, and friends, to the extent that they are available and functioning (Creed 1987; Westermeyer 1991); those in the secondary environment, in addition to the above-mentioned ethnic mutual help associations, include helping professionals (such as psychologists and social workers) and the supportive attitude of the society at large (Kuo and Tsai 1986; Lobodzinska 1986; Mirsky and Kaushinsky 1989; Palinkas 1982).

Resources Available to Immigrants and Veterans in Israel

Before turning to the role of resources in moderating the salience of demands among new immigrants from the former Soviet Union to Israel, let us first examine the extent to which these resources are available. The data in Table 44 suggest, as expected, that veterans have more of most personal resources. However, immigrants have more education; they are also similar to veterans in terms of many of the environmental resources. On the other hand, new immigrants have to struggle with language problems (only 8% of the immigrants compared to 81% of the veterans report having a very good knowledge of the Hebrew language), and three times more veterans than immigrants own apartments.

Assistance from the primary environment seems particularly problematic: The immigrants' families are much less likely to be seen as a source of either instrumental or affective resources. Also noteworthy is the social segregation of the immigrants from the veterans: The overwhelming majority of friends of each group are confined to their own group. Finally, the immigrants are less likely than the veterans to say that a desire to help needy individuals prevails in Israeli society (10% v. 33%, respectively).

Table 44
Availability of Resources by Population Group

Type of Resource Mode	Resource	Pole Indicator	Veterans (%)	Immigrants (%)	Total (%)
Personal					
Instrumental	Employment[a]	Employed	70	54	65
	Spouse employment[a]	Employed	51	47	50
	Apartment owner	Own apt.	65	21	51
	Income	≥3000 NIS	60	33	51
Cognitive	Education	≥ 13 yrs.	40	81	52
	Hebrew language[b]	Very good	81	8	65
Primary Environmental					
Instrumental	Family[c]	High	67	36	56
	Friends[c]	High	19	18	18
Affective	Spouse[d]	High	74	67	72
	Relatives[d]	High	45	33	41
	Friends[d]	High	50	36	45
	Meets friends[e]	High	79	52	69
	Has veteran friends[f]	Mainly	92	3	61
	Has immig. friends[f]	Mainly	4	84	31
Secondary Environmental					
Instrumental	Formal agency[c]	High	16	14	15
	Informal agency[c]	High	2	1	2
Affective	Psychologist[d]	High	2	—	1
	Society[g]	High	33	10	25

a. The percentage of unemployed includes housewives, students, drafted soldiers, and retirees.

b. Two top ranks on a scale of nine.

c. The question was: "When you needed help for a monetary or other economic problem, who mainly helped you?" The interviewer waited for a spontaneous answer; for those not mentioned, he/she probed: "Did you get help from . . . ?" And, if the answer was "Yes," the interviewer offered a range of extents, from "Much help" to "Very little help." The percentages indicate those who spontaneously mentioned the given party or who said they received much help.

d. The question was: "When you feel bad, are nervous and tense, and simply must talk to someone, to whom do you generally talk about your troubles?" Responses were coded as above, with the range of answers from "Frequently" to "Infrequently."

e. The question was: "How often do you meet friends or family?" The percentage indicates those who said they saw them once or more a week.

f. The question was: "Who are mainly your friends?" The percentages are those who said they are exclusively or mainly veteran Israelis and those who said they are exclusively or mainly new immigrants.

g. The question was: "In very general terms, to what extent is there a desire in Israeli society to help those who need help?" Response categories ranged from "To a very great extent" to "Not at all." Percentages refer to those responding "To a very great extent" or "To a great extent."

With regard to employment, the data in Table 45 suggest that the employment rate of immigrants in all occupational sectors is lower than that of veterans. Since the literature on immigration indicates numerous gender differences in employment (see Ben-Sira 1989; Gold 1989; Shin and Chang 1988; Westermeyer et al. 1983), I divided respondents by gender and compared the data for the two groups. The percentage of employed immigrant females is the smallest of all four groups. In this respect, the data corroborate those of Ben-Barak's (1989) Israeli study but differ from data on immigrants to the United States (Gold 1989; Westermeyer et al. 1983). As to the utilization of their skills and knowledge, the data in Table 46 suggest that the percentage of employed immigrants whose skills are utilized is less than the percentage among the veterans: 31 percent of the immigrant males, compared to 65 percent of the veteran Israeli males, say that their skills and knowledge are utilized in their job. Employed immigrant women are even less able than men to utilize their skills in their jobs.

Table 45
Level of Employment by Professional Status and by Gender by Population Group[a])

Population Group	Gender	Academic & Profess'nal (%)	Senior Executive (%)	White Collar (%)	Skilled Blue Collar (%)	Unskilled Blue Collar (%)	Total (%)
Immigrants	Male	63	[c]	73	58	[c]	64
	Female[b]	50	[c]	50	38	[c]	49
Veterans	Male	88	90	82	85	85	65
	Female[b]	82	97	85	87	74	62

a. The percentage of unemployed includes housewives, students, drafted soldiers, and retirees.

b. One percent of immigrant women and 18 percent of veteran women stated that their occupation was housewife.

c. N was too small (≤6) to derive meaningful conclusions.

Personal Resources and Coping

Turning finally to the major question of this chapter: What is the effectiveness of the investigated resources in helping immigrants cope successfully with the demands? Again, in this work, effectiveness of a resource refers to the its ability to moderate the salience of a demand. To operationalize this, correlation coefficients (μ_2) between the resources and demands were calculated; effectiveness of a resource was taken to mean that there is a negative correlation between the availability of that resource and the salience of a demand, or, the stronger the negative correlation, the more effective the resource. A positive relationship would imply that possessing the resource may increase the salience of a demand.

Table 46
Utilization of Skills by Occupational Status and by Gender by Population Group

Population Group	Gender	Academic & Profess'nal (%)	Senior Executive (%)	White Collar (%)	Skilled Blue Collar (%)	Unskilled Blue Collar (%)	Total (%)
Immigrants	Male	31	33	a	32	23	a
	Female	25	29	a	9	a	a
Veterans	Male	65	79	61	69	66	28
	Female	62	76	60	65	57	29

a. N was too small (≤ 3) to derive meaningful conclusions.

The overall picture based on the data in Tables 47 and 48 is that personal resources are less effective in moderating the salience of the demands for immigrants than for veterans. This is clear from a comparison of μ_2 in the two population groups. The differential effectiveness of the resources is particularly striking for education, employment, and knowledge of Hebrew language. The overall average μ_2 of education is $+.14$ for immigrants and $-.16$ for veterans; of employment, $-.19$ and $-.33$, respectively; and of Hebrew language, $.06$ and $-.22$, respectively. It seems, then, that for these immigrants, education is liable to exacerbate the salience of the demands confronting them, particularly in their work ($\mu_2 = .43$) and in the education of their children ($\mu_2 = .35$), but also in the areas of their economic condition ($\mu_2 = .23$), the future of their children ($\mu_2 = .28$), and their family relations ($\mu_2 = .27$).

Employment, apartment ownership, and income are the most effective resources, particularly for coping with the "instrumental" demands, but are apt to aggravate the salience of the demands confronting immigrants in their family relations. The salience-exacerbating effect of spouse's employment with regarding the demands confronting the immigrants in the areas of education and future of their children ($\mu_2 = .45$ and $.41$, respectively) is notable, with the latter effect evident among the veterans as well ($\mu_2 = .23$).

Environmental Resources and Coping

Can environmental resources compensate for the immigrants' limited personal resources (Table 44) and for the limited effectiveness of those resources (Table 47 and 48)? The data in Tables 49 and 50 suggest that the environmental resources studied—with the exception of perceiving the absorbing society as supportive—are even less effective than the personal resources, since the correlations in these tables are smaller (less negative) than those in Tables 47 and 48.

Table 47

Correlations (μ_2) between the Availability of Personal Resources and the Salience of Demands: Immigrants

Mode of Demand Demand	Employed (μ_2)	Spouse employed (μ_2)	Own apt. (μ_2)	Income ≥ 3000 (μ_2)	Educa- tion (μ_2)	Hebrew Language (μ_2)
Instrumental						
Economic helplessness	-.22	-.11	-.16	-.26	.20	.12
Economic condition	-.48	-.17	-.34	-.36	.23	-.12
Job/employment	-.76	.14	-.11	-.20	.43	.20
Dwelling	-.34	-.41	-.95	-.34	.13	-.27
Contact with bureaucracy	-.40	-.27	-.32	-.30	.08	-.15
Average μ_2[a]	-.40	-.16	-.38	-.29	.21	-.04
Cognitive						
Underutilization of skills	.23	-.24	.09	-.43	-.05	-.36
Know oblig's & entit's	-.22	-.14	-.18	-.34	-.16	-.43
Unfamiliar w. bureauc.	-.14	-.20	-.18	-.27	-.11	-.16
Average μ_2[a]	-.04	-.19	-.09	-.35	-.11	-.32
Affective						
Emotional isolation	-.25	-.11	-.13	-.29	.05	.05
Family relations	.10	.07	-.10	.09	.27	.11
Education for children	.18	.45	.18	.22	.35	.24
Future of children	.00	.41	.06	.23	.28	.16
Social relations	-.34	-.36	-.09	-.31	.13	-.17
Leisure	-.30	.01	-.03	-.22	.29	-.13
Average μ_2[a]	-.10	.08	-.02	-.07	.21	.04
Overall Average μ_2[a]	-.19	-.07	-.15	-.20	.14	-.06

a. The average coefficients were calculated only to facilitate an overall comparison and have no statistical meaning.

Beyond that overall characteristic, the data suggest that formal agencies are the most effective environmental resource for immigrants, and the supportive function of formal agencies for them appears not to be confined to alleviating the salience of the instrumental demands but to be effective for coping with the demands in all three life-areas. In other words, economic assistance by formal agencies is likely to assist immigrants in alleviating the salience not merely of instrumental demands (e.g., financial, employment, and dwelling problems) but also in the cognitive and affective fields (e.g., family life, social relations).

Table 48

Correlations (μ_2) between the Availability of Personal Resources and the Salience of Demands: Veterans

Mode of Demand Demand	Employed (μ_2)	Spouse employed (μ_2)	Own apt. (μ_2)	Income ≥ 3000 (μ_2)	Educa- tion (μ_2)	Hebrew Language (μ_2)
Instrumental						
Economic helplessness	-.42	-.18	-.15	-.32	-.34	-.22
Economic condition	-.61	-.14	-.31	-.47	-.23	-.27
Job/employment	-.85	-.25	.23	-.54	-.23	-.41
Dwelling	-.15	-.23	-.71	-.47	-.13	-.07
Contact with bureaucracy	-.36	-.09	-.23	-.29	.01	-.18
Average μ_2	-.47	-.18	-.33	-.42	-.18	-.23
Cognitive						
Underutiliz. of skills	-.01	-.01	-.23	-.35	-.36	-.08
Know oblig's & entit's	-.19	-.15	-.11	-.20	-.24	-.40
Unfamiliar w. bureauc.	-.24	-.03	-.19	-.21	-.08	-.31
Average μ_2	-.15	-.06	-.18	-.25	-.23	-.25
Affective						
Emotional isolation	-.38	-.04	-.21	-.20	-.26	-.11
Family relations	-.44	.05	-.15	-.20	-.15	-.20
Education for children	-.27	.23	.18	.08	-.13	-.20
Future of children	-.33	-.07	-.12	-.24	-.03	.07
Social relations	-.37	-.03	-.10	-.14	-.02	-.19
Leisure	-.06	.05	-.03	-.09	-.09	-.44
Average μ_2	-.31	-.06	-.13	-.16	-.11	-.18
Overall Average μ_2	-.33	-.10	-.21	-.27	-.16	-.22

For veterans, in contrast, the spouse's affective support appears to be the most effective environmental resource in alleviating the salience of the demands in the instrumental fields, as well as in the cognitive and affective fields. Friends, in both their instrumental (financial and other economic support) and affective (frequency of meeting friends) capacities, are likely to be relatively more effective for the immigrants' coping with their instrumental and cognitive demands than they are for veterans, while for the latter friends are more effective for coping with demands in the affective sphere. Reliance on instrumental support (from informal agencies—voluntary mutual-help associations), on affective support (by professionals—psychologists), and having friends mainly from the same population group, are likely to increase the salience of demands.

These conclusions are derived from the strength and direction of the correlations in Tables 49 and 50. Among immigrants, correlations between instrumental support of formal agencies and almost all types of demands are negative. This is not the case among veterans, for whom almost all negative correlations between affective support by the spouse and coping with instrumental demands are stronger than among the immigrants, where some of the demands are virtually unrelated with that type of support. Among immigrants, the negative correlations between instrumental support by friends, on the one hand, and coping with demands of dwelling (instrumental) ($\mu_2 = -.32$) and underutilization of skills (cognitive) ($\mu_2 = -.33$), on the other, are fairly strong. Meeting with friends and, to some extent, affective support by friends, evidently are more important for the immigrants' coping with instrumental demands than for veterans. Among veterans, instrumental assistance by friends is virtually unrelated with all modalities of demands. Most of the correlations of demands with having friends mainly from the same population group and with getting affective assistance from a psychologist are positive—alluding to their salience-exacerbating function. For both groups, perception of society as supportive has a relatively strong negative correlation with coping with instrumental and cognitive demands.

Summary: Resource Availability and Resource Effectiveness

To summarize, the data suggest not only that new immigrants have fewer resources than veterans (education being an exception), but also that the effectiveness of most of the resources available to immigrants in coping with the demands of life in the new society is rather limited.

Starting with the personal resources, the problem of formal education as a coping resource is particularly striking. On the one hand, the proportion of immigrants with more than high school education is more than twice that of veterans. On the other hand, and in contrast to the extensively documented effectiveness of education as a coping resource, its effectiveness for immigrants is rather limited. Indeed, the data suggest that education seems even to exacerbate the salience of the demands (Table 47). Presumably, the detrimental function of education is due to the immigrants' inability to utilize their knowledge. As suggested by the data in Table 46, immigrants are much less likely than veterans to feel that their skills are utilized in their current job. This situation corresponds with that of immigrants in various settings, including earlier waves of immigration to Israel as well as to the United States and other countries (see Bach and Bach 1980; Ben-Barak 1989; Bouvier and Gardner 1986; Gold 1989; Lobodzinska 1986; Shin and Chang 1988).

Table 49
Availability of Environmental Resources and Salience of Demands: Immigrants

	Instrumental Support						Affective Support				
	Primary		Secondary				Primary			Secondary	
Mode of Demand	Fam-		Forml	Infrml		Rela-	Meets	Vet.	Imm.	Psy-	Soci-
Demand	ily	Frnds	Agncy	Agncy	Spouse	tive	Frnds	Frnds	Frnds	chol.	ety
Instrumental											
Ec. helplessness	-.12	.00	-.24	-.08	-.19	-.20	.09	-.33	.05	.33	-.35
Ec. condition	-.16	-.11	-.17	.22	-.02	-.17	-.21	-.32	.30	.46	-.22
Job/employment	.05	-.04	-.18	.07	-.01	-.04	-.03	-.14	.25	.24	-.34
Dwelling	-.21	-.32	-.16	.16	-.02	-.02	-.17	-.11	.31	.27	-.18
Contact w. bur.	-.07	-.01	-.21	.08	-.20	-.11	-.10	-.19	.02	.22	-.28
Average μ_2	-.10	-.10	-19	.09	-.09	-.11	-.08	-.22	.19	.22	-.27
Cognitive											
Underutil. skills	-.04	-.33	-.07	.25	-.01	.04	-.05	-.16	.47	.07	-.37
Know obl's/ent's	.01	-.05	-.28	.01	-.14	-.02	-.25	-.17	.21	.31	-.22
Unfam. w. bur.	-.05	-.16	-.21	-.10	-.23	-.14	-.18	-.18	.22	.10	-.09
Average μ_2	-.03	-.18	-.19	.05	-.13	-.04	-.16	-.17	.30	.16	-.23
Affective											
Emot'l isolation	.08	.11	-.23	.05	-.52	-.17	.05	-.28	.07	.43	-.19
Family relations	.01	.17	-.14	.27	-.31	.09	.27	.00	-.03	.55	.13
Ed. for children	.05	.12	-.13	.04	.06	-.15	.05	.07	-.07	.33	.09
Fut. of children	.02	.14	-.11	.30	.21	-.27	-.10	-.09	.08	.33	-.14
Social relations	-.17	.01	-.23	-.24	-.37	-.10	.02	-.23	-.10	.35	-.05
Leisure	-.22	.14	-.22	-.08	-.06	-.06	-.14	-.34	.29	.38	-.09
Average μ_2	-.04	.08	-.18	.06	-.17	-.11	.03	-.15	.06	.34	-.04
Overall Average μ_2	-.06	-.04	-.18	.07	-.13	-.12	-.05	-.18	.15	.25	-.16

Lack of the skills needed in the absorbing society, cultural differences and difficulties in acculturation, and job unavailability have been offered as explanations for downward mobility (Bach and Bach 1980; Bouvier and Gardner 1986; Stevens et al. 1978; Westermeyer 1991). In any case, it seems that the frustration emanating from the inability to use one's education makes its impact on the "affective" life areas, in particular family life. These findings corroborate evidence by Gold (1989) and Westermeyer (1991), who emphasize the effect of such frustration on family life.

Table 50
Availability of Environmental Resources and Salience of Demands: Veterans

Mode of Demand / Demand	Instrumental Support				Affective Support						
	Primary		Secondary		Primary					Secondary	
	Family	Frnds	Forml Agncy	Infrml Agncy	Spouse	Rela-tive	Meets Frnds	Vet. Frnds	Imm. Frnds	Psy-chol.	Soci-ety
Instrumental											
Ec. helplessness	-.32	.08	.11	.32	-.22	-.10	-.05	-.24	.23	.31	-.33
Ec. condition	-.08	-.01	.09	.18	-.25	-.05	-.01	-.15	.36	.28	-.19
Job/employment	-.04	-.14	.00	-.02	-.23	-.07	.02	-.10	.43	.23	-23
Dwelling	-.10	-.03	-.16	.08	-.20	-.15	.03	-.03	.18	.23	-.28
Contact w. bur.	-.05	.09	-.05	.28	-.18	-.10	.06	-.12	.27	.20	-.16
Average μ_2	-.12	-.02	.00	.17	-.22	-.09	.00	-.13	.21	.25	-.24
Cognitive											
Underutil. skills	.03	.06	.08	-.04	-.24	.05	.00	-.04	-.14	-.13	-.07
Know obl's/ent's	-.02	-.04	-.13	.24	-.12	-.02	-.01	-.23	.25	.13	-.33
Unfam. w. bur.	-.01	.04	-.16	.16	-.12	-.01	.15	-.05	.16	-.06	-.29
Average μ_2	.00	.02	-.07	.12	-.16	.02	.05	-.11	.09	-.02	.23
Affective											
Emot'l isolation	-.11	.02	.08	.34	-.30	-.05	-.05	-.25	.17	.30	-.27
Family relations	-.16	.03	.10	.15	-.41	-.14	.19	.06	.20	.19	-.16
Ed. for children	.04	.24	.16	.37	.01	-.01	.00	-.26	.05	.24	-.10
Fut. of children	-.03	.07	.13	.06	-.06	-.03	.02	-.20	.31	.25	-.16
Social relations	-.02	.19	.14	.47	-.10	.01	-.16	-.38	.28	.21	-.27
Leisure	-.05	.14	.18	.26	-.23	.07	-.10	-.34	.33	.20	-.29
Average μ_2	-.06	.00	.13	.28	-.18	-.03	-.03	-.23	.22	.23	-.21
Overall Average μ_2	-.07	.00	.03	.20	-.19	-.04	.00	-.17	.12	.19	-.22

As to the environmental resources, the evidence generally points to the lesser effectiveness of secondary environmental resources. However, with regard to the immigrants, the relatively high effectiveness of support by formal agencies is noteworthy—a finding that contradicts the evidence from numerous studies among problem-laden populations (Ben-Sira 1981, 1983a, 1986a, 1986b, 1988b, 1989). Indeed, the data suggest the importance of "instrumental" (economic) support by formal agencies for the immigrants' coping with demands in all spheres of their life, and perhaps to their dependence on such support, since most primary support sources and informal agencies are evidently ineffective. For veterans, on the other hand, the spouse seems to be the most effective environmental support agent in coping not only with "affective" and "cognitive," but also with "instrumental," demands. The apparent salience-moderating effectiveness of the perception of society at large as a resource by both immigrants and veterans points to the centrality of society for coping with the demands of life. Nonetheless, few of the immigrants view society as supportive (Table 44)—thus suggesting their lack of an important environmental resource.

POTENCY AND LIFE CHANGE

The Notion of Potency

Immigrants have a high risk of maladjustment (Tables 11 and 13) due to their limitations in coping with the demands confronting them. Their vulnerability brings into focus the role of potency in reducing the stress-potential of unmet demands. Potency refers to a nonspecific mechanism characterized by an energy over and above other resources, based on both an accumulation of successful coping outcomes and encounters that foster trust in the social environment. It facilitates following an unmet demand, either by calling forth an experience-based confidence that a solution is bound to come up, or by reassessing the relative importance of the demand. As stated elsewhere: "Potency fulfills a delayed homeostasis-stabilizing function through its . . . capacity to prevent tension . . . from turning into a lasting stress. Potency is latently existent and activated by a failure in coping with a demand due to resource deficiency—a failure causing the demand to become a stressor" (Ben-Sira 1985:399). I suggest, then, that potency's stress-buffering capacity should be understood as a capacity to reduce the stress-potential of a demand. In operational terms, it is meant to weaken the relationship between demands and emotional homeostasis.

Evidence suggests that potency is effective in buffering the stress-potential of demands and hence promoting the readjustment among persons who have experienced a traumatic, debilitating change in their life situation such as disability or a heart attack (Ben-Sira 1989; Ben-Sira and Eliezer 1990). With regard to immigrants to the United States, Kuo and Tsai contend:

Personality characteristics indicative of psychological resources (mastery and self-esteem) are the most helpful in sustaining people facing strains arising out of conditions over which they may have little direct control. . . . [I]mmigrants' personality characteristics alone, perhaps are inadequate to explain fully how they cope with and master their new environments. However, self-esteem and mastery, which denote the belief that one's life changes are under one's own control instead of being fatalistically directed, would seem to be key immigrant characteristics if such exist. (Kuo and Tsai 1986:137)

Gitelman, writing of the political orientations of immigrants to Israel from the United States and the Soviet Union, contends that "the fundamental orientations relevant to politics do not change very much over the first years in Israel, and [I] suspect that they have not changed greatly from what they had been in the Soviet Union and the United States. These may be so firmly embedded as a result of socialization, or of 'imprinting' at critical stages of life, that they function like personality characteristics, not easily shaped by changing environments" (Gitelman 1989:259). Nonetheless, one might question the effectiveness of potency for immigrants confronting an entirely new social system.

Potency also has a societal component: confidence in and commitment to a social environment which is perceived as having a basically meaningful order and a just distribution of rewards. The logic underlying the concept of potency would lead us to expect a weakening of the immigrants' sense of potency. It is possible that the lower level of the immigrants' perception of the positiveness of Israeli society compared to that of the veterans (Tables 28 and 29), together with the contingence of potency on that conception of society (Table 33), as well as coping failures experienced in the new society, may undermine their ability to maintain a reasonable sense of potency.

Thoits's contention regarding the consequences of a continuous failure in coping may also allude to the vulnerability of the personal components of potency, namely, self-esteem and mastery. She maintains:

The maintenance and enhancement of self-regard is assumed either explicitly or implicitly to be a fundamental human need and to have important implications for one's psychological state. Negative events (and the persistent undesirable consequences of those events) may decrease self-regard in two ways. Failures to control the occurrence of events or their undesirable consequences may decrease the sense of mastery over life, . . . and the loss of valued social roles or inadequate performance in remaining roles may lower the value of individuals in their own and others' eyes. . . . Persistent role strains can confront people with dogged evidence of their own failures—or lack of success—and with the inescapable proof of their inability to alter the unwanted circumstances of their lives. Under these conditions people become vulnerable to the loss of self-esteem and to the erosion of [a sense of] mastery. (Thoits 1983:82–83)

Thoits's description comes rather close to conditions that may confront immigrants. In light of the inconclusive evidence, what conclusions can be derived from the data on the 1990s wave of immigration to Israel?

The Potency of Immigrants from the Former Soviet Union in Israel

Although we have no data on the potency of immigrants before arriving in Israel, their current level of potency in comparison to that of veteran Israelis may provide some indication of their capacity to avoid maladjustment. The data suggest that the sense of potency of new immigrants is weaker than that of veteran Israelis: 36 percent of the former, compared to 55 percent of the latter, are in the highest levels of potency (Table 51). Analysis by year of immigration (Table 52) indicates an increase in the immigrants' feeling of potency over time (from 32% high in the first year to 44% in the fourth), but the sense of potency of even fourth-year immigrants is still less than that of the veterans.

Table 51
Level of Potency[a] by Population Group

Level of Potency		Veterans (%)	Immigrants (%)	Total (%)
High	6	22	12	18
	5	17	10	15
	4	16	14	15
	3	17	24	19
	2	16	18	17
Low	1	13	22	16
(N)		(891)	(486)	(1377)

a. It should be recalled that these data refer to relative levels of potency and thus can be used only for comparison among groups and not as indicators of absolute levels of potency.

Table 52
Level of Potency by Veterans' Origin and Immigrants' Year of Immigration

Level of Potency		Veterans			Immigrants			
		East (%)	Israel (%)	West (%)	1993 (%)	1992 (%)	1991 (%)	1990 (%)
High	6	21	22	22	8	14	10	13
	5	15	15	20	9	9	10	12
	4	16	16	15	15	14	11	16
	3	17	16	18	36	25	24	20
	2	14	16	17	13	14	19	20
Low	1	16	14	7	19	23	27	19
(N)		(397)	(203)	(272)	(47)	(77)	(165)	(194)

Potency and the Stress-Potential of Demands

To what extent does a feeling of potency help buffer the stress-potential of demands (Table 53)? Operationally, I define the capacity of potency to buffer the stress-potential of demands to mean a reduction in the negative correlation between demands and stress, as sense of potency increases. I divided sense of potency into "high" and "low." The correlation coefficients (μ_2) between demands and stress (as measured by the SPD scale) were calculated for each.

Table 53

Correlations (μ_2) between Salience of Demands and SPD by Level of Potency and Population Group

Mode of Demand Demand	Veterans		Immigrants	
	High Salience (%)	Low Salience (%)	High Salience (%)	Low Salience (%)
Instrumental				
Economic helplessness	-.21	-.37	-.04	-.24
Economic condition	-.24	-.32	-.09	-.14
Job/employment	-.22	-.27	.12	.14
Dwelling	-.14	-.06	-.06	-.18
Contact w. bureaucracy	-.12	-.24	-.37	-.18
Average μ_2	-.19	-.25	.14	-.12
Cognitive				
Underutiliz. of skills	.03	-.01	-.03	-.12
Know oblig's & entit's	-.12	-.16	-.22	-.26
Unfamiliar w. bureauc.	-.18	-.11	-.02	-.11
Average μ_2	-.09	-.09	-.09	-.16
Affective				
Emotional isolation	-.21	-.39	-.16	-.32
Family relations	-.28	-.38	-.31	-.31
Education for children	-.38	-.42	-.47	-.37
Future of children	-.14	-.31	-.29	-.31
Social relations	-.30	-.18	-.36	-.20
Leisure	-.37	-.27	-.29	-.19
Average μ_2	-.28	-.33	-.31	-.28
Overall Average μ_2	-.21	-.25	.20	-.20

Overall, potency is more effective for veterans than for immigrants. However, careful examination suggests a more complex picture. In the instrumental sphere, among both the veterans and the immigrants, most of the correlations are weaker for the high-potency than for the low-potency respondents, implying the effectiveness of potency in buffering the stress-potential of the demands. The exception is among the immigrants for demands related to contact with bureaucracy. In this area, contrary to expectations, the high-potency respondents had a larger negative coefficient (-.37 v. -.18), suggesting that contact with bureaucracy is more stress-arousing for high-potency individuals. In the cognitive sphere, there is no consistent trend among the veterans, while among immigrants, the correlations are weaker for the high-potency than for the low-potency respondents. Finally, the affective sphere seems to be most problematic for the immigrants. While among the veterans, four out of six correlations are in the expected direction (demands in the areas of social relations and leisure being the exceptions), the direction of correlations among immigrants is reversed for three of the demands and virtually identical for two more.

The next question is: To what extent is potency effective in buffering the stress-potential of those demands that I defined as having a high stress-potential? For immigrants, a feeling of potency seems to buffer the stress-potential of one of the four demands that were identified (Table 42) as the most threatening, namely, emotional isolation (from -.32 to -.16). For leisure, another threatening stressor, the data suggest a slight stress-intensifying tendency. For the other demands that I identified as having a strong stress-potential but weak salience, the data imply that potency does not buffer, and may even exacerbate, their stress-potential. These latter demands include contact with bureaucracy (an increase from -.18 to -.37), education of children (from -.37 to -.47), and social relations (from -.20 to -.36). A feeling of potency, however, has a stress-buffering effect on most instrumental and cognitive demands that, according to the data in Table 42, I defined as having a low stress-potential (economic helplessness, economic condition, dwelling, underutilization of skills, and unfamiliar bureaucracy). For veterans, potency fulfills stress-buffering function for all high stress-potential demands (Tables 41 and 43), except one (leisure).

Summary: Immigration and the Level and Effectiveness of Potency

As we saw (Tables 51 through 53), immigrants have a lower level of potency than do veterans. Though the data suggest an increase in the potency of immigrants among fourth-year immigrants, even they have a much weaker sense of potency than do veterans. More important is the limited effectiveness of potency as a stress-buffering mechanism for demands with the highest stress-potential. How might we explain these two phenomena?

Lower Prior Level of Potency

It is possible that, even before their immigration, those coming from the former Soviet Union had a lower level of potency than did veteran Israelis. Horowitz (1979), in her study of immigration in the 1970s, found that, in two respects (friendly v. unfriendly world and politically responsive v. unresponsive world), immigrants from the Soviet Union do display a lower degree of internal locus of control than those from North America. Yet she, too, lacks data on whether the lower degree of internal locus of control of these immigrants is a prior trait or a consequence of the extreme change they had undergone, a change that may have been less extreme for immigrants from North America. In any case, this does not explain the more limited effectiveness of potency among immigrants from the former Soviet Union.

Trust in Society

Trust in society is an important component of potency. However, as we saw, the image of Israeli society held by the immigrants is much less positive than that held by the veterans (Table 24) and may even deteriorate with time (Table 25), particularly with respect to social relations (both between Ashkenazim and Sephardim and between veterans and immigrants; see Table 23).

CONCLUSION: THE EFFECT OF IMMIGRATION ON RESOURCES AND POTENCY

As stated several times, an acute threat to an individual's emotional homeostasis is a result of both the stress-potential and the salience of demands confronting that individual. Almost any demand, if inadequately met, has the potential of disturbing homeostasis (see Kessler 1983:268). This chapter, then, addresses the differential availability and effectiveness of resources for moderating the salience of demands. Specifically, it focuses on the ability of immigrants, relative to veterans, to cope effectively with the demands confronting them. The major findings from the data are that immigrants have fewer resources and that these resources are less effective, a problematic combination given the demands immigrants must face. The data suggest first, the inadequacy of individual and primary environmental resources to fulfill a compensatory function on the one hand, and a greater reliance on secondary environmental resources on the other; and second, the relative weakness of both the level and the effectiveness of the immigrants' feeling of "potency" as a stress-buffering mechanism. Because of all these, they are prone to the disruption of their emotional homeostasis (see Table 11, which points to their vulnerability to maladjustment, and Tables 13 to 15, which show their poorer level of health).

To what extent do these findings raise questions regarding the effectiveness of potency over and above that of resources in general? One would expect potency to contribute a certain degree of stability, despite the extreme life-change. For instance, Grove and Torbiorn maintain that "[A] person's level of mere adequacy and clarity is, in effect, a personality trait and therefore resistent to change. [However,] it is of course possible that the level's steady course could be disturbed by the shock of entering a new total environment" (Grove and Torbiorn 1985:211). Though the concepts of adequacy and clarity refer to a different content universe than that of potency, their work suggests that the effectiveness of personality traits which promote adjustment may be weakened in the wake of extreme life-changes.

The data may provide insights as to the factors underlying the complexity of family life in the wake of immigration (Bavington and Majid 1986; Cohon 1981: 263–265; Gold 1989:423–425; Sluzki 1979; Westermeyer 1991:135–138). Evidence presented here (Table 42) corroborates that documented in numerous studies suggesting the high stress-potential demands in the immigrants' family life. This stress-potential is understandable in view of the difficulties families face as a primary environmental resource (Table 44). As we saw, the data suggest the limited effectiveness of the family in helping the immigrants cope with the demands confronting them (Table 49) as well as the limited capacity of the immigrants' potency to buffer the stress-potential in the demands of family life (Table 53). We see, then, a vicious cycle that may evolve in the immigrants' family life. On the one hand, the family is likely to be the primary environmental resource most available to the immigrant. On the other hand, the family is often unable to provide the needed support and guidance.

A similar trend may be observed with regard to the capacity of the immigrants' social relations to buffer stress-potential (see Table 42). Extensive research has documented the effectiveness of primary relationships as a coping resource (Banchevska 1981; Gold 1989; Koranyi 1981; Kuo and Tsai 1986; H. B. M. Murphy 1973; Palinkas 1982; Portes 1981). In this case, however, primary relations with other immigrants may exacerbate the stress-potential of demands—including social relations—confronting the immigrants, thus corroborating those approaches that question the effectiveness of social relations with other immigrants and emphasize the importance of relations with members of the absorbing society (Granovetter 1973; Hirsch 1979; Mirsky and Kaushinsky 1989; Wilcox 1981). This may be because relations with members of the absorbing society are the least available resource for immigrants, and that veterans are not too likely to have extensive social relations with immigrants (Table 44). In addition, one component of potency, as I defined it, is the individuals' trust in, and belief in the meaningfulness of, their social environment. Problems in their social relations may thus upset one basis of their potency and, particularly for high-potency individuals, may thereby exacerbate the stress-potential of the demands arising from social relations (Table 53).

Finally, I noted the differential role of formal agencies as a secondary environmental resource for veterans and immigrants. Among veteran Israelis, the data (Table 50) suggest the limited effectiveness of formal agencies as an environmental resource—hence corroborating the evidence from numerous studies on this topic (see Ben-Sira 1981, 1983a, 1986a). However, among immigrants, the data (Table 49) suggest that formal agencies may be the most effective environmental resource—highlighting the problematic situation of the immigrant to Israel, whose readjustment is so dependent on these resources.

8

An Empirical Model of Readjustment

THE CONCEPTUAL FRAMEWORK

The Fundamentals of the Stress Process

This work has analyzed the issue of what factors inherent in immigration-instigated change have stress-buffering or stress-precipitating effects on immigrants and veterans, hence promoting or impeding their readjustment. The work is thus intended to identify the relative vulnerability to maladjustment of the two groups, and the factors aggravating or buffering their vulnerability. The literature emphasizes the stress-precipitating potential of the social change inherent in migration and its effect on both immigrants (see Rumbaut 1991) and members of the absorbing society (see Brym, 1992; Creed 1987). Yet, in view of the growing recognition that change per se does not cause stress (see Mirowsky and Ross 1989:125–130), I wanted to better understanding the factors that affect the stress-potential of extreme life-change.

The work is based on current approaches to the stress-coping relationship and focuses on two aspects of this relationship. First, considerable evidence indicates the stress-potential inherent in an extreme life-change, such as immigration. Second, research in the field of coping points to the difficulty of coping with unprecedented demands. Shuval and her colleagues maintain that, "migration is a form of social change which imposes new demands on the individual and renders much of his past expertise obsolete. . . . Response to the pressures generated by social change is a function of resources both external and internal available to the migrant" (Shuval et al. 1975:151–52).

A Summary of the Framework

The framework developed here derives from one developed earlier (Ben-Sira 1991). In terms of this framework, readjustment is viewed as successful culmination of the process of immigration and results from successful coping with demands. Underlying demands are catalysts, i.e., objective circumstances and relevant individual and perceived societal perspectives. If demands are inadequately coped with, they may disrupt the individual's emotional homeostasis and become stressors. All demands are potential stressors, although differing in their stress-potential and in their salience. The threat of a demand to an individual's emotional homeostasis, then, depends on both its stress-potential and its salience. Given the centrality of perception in determining the stress-potential and the salience of demands, coping does not mean merely going through the motions of "instrumental" behavior. Rather, the essence of coping is in the perception of having overcome the threat inherent in a demand by moderating its salience. Coping is accomplished by means of personal resources, reinforced by primary and secondary environmental resources. Prolonged failure to restore homeostasis—stress—is likely to result in breakdown, disease being one of its expressions. Yet not every tension results in stress. Potency can weaken the demand-stress relationship and restore homeostasis. In light of the societal component of potency, integration into the society is an important contributor to a feeling of potency and, thus, to readjustment.

The usefulness of this framework for furthering the understanding of the complexity of readjustment in the wake of immigration-instigated life-change has been examined by a study among new immigrants from the former Soviet Union to Israel and veteran Israelis.

AN EMPIRICALLY BASED PARADIGM OF READJUSTMENT

Smallest Space Analysis

The basic hypothesis underlying the proposed framework is that readjustment results from the interaction of a number of factors. In view of the complexity of the framework, its empirical verification requires a method of analysis that can properly demonstrate the causal interrelationship among the components of a multivariate content universe. The SSA (Smallest Space Analysis) method developed by Guttman (Brown 1985; Canter 1985a) is an ideal method for examining such a multivariate interrelationship, as it takes into consideration the multitude of mutually interacting factors determining various phenomena. This method also makes it easier to see the overall pattern ("structure") of the data, since the output is a map of the variables of a multivariate content universe, where the position of the variables is determined by the interrelations among them. (For further description of SSA, see Appendix C.)

The Structure of Readjustment: Veteran Israelis

The configuration of the SSA map in Figure 4 suggests the interrelationships among factors affecting the veterans' adjustment and lends support to the hypothesized framework of readjustment, implying the contributory role of emotional homeostasis in the maintenance of health and the stress-buffering function of potency. Integration is, as expected, an essential precondition for potency, yet its effect on readjustment is indirect.

Figure 4
The Structure of Readjustment: Veterans
SSA (Smallest Space Analysis) of the Correlations in Appendix D

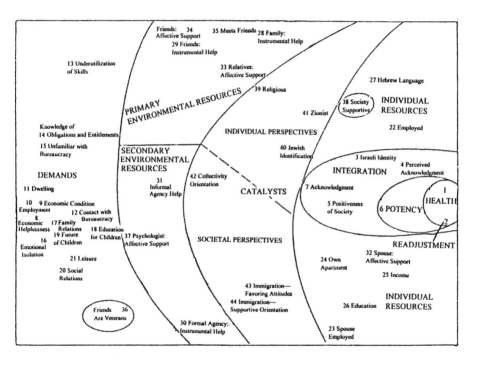

The map suggests that health is related to readjustment, which in turn is related to potency. Potency is predicted by integration, which is affected by the personal resources an individual has at his/her disposal. The effect of primary environmental resources on readjustment is, as hypothesized, weaker than that of personal resources. Furthermore, the effect of secondary environmental resources on readjustment is less than that of primary environmental resources, alluding to their potential negative impact on readjustment. However, perceiving society as supportive, which I view as a secondary environmental resource, seems to have a positive impact on integration and readjustment. Demands can impede readjustment, but resources—especially individual and primary environmental resources—can limit the negative impact of demands on readjustment. The catalysts studied—mainly ideological individual and societal perspectives— are irrelevant for the readjustment process of the veteran Israelis.

These conclusions are derived from the configuration of the variables on the SSA map (Figure 4). The clustering of the variables on the map reveals eight content-related regions. At the extreme right of the map is the variable denoting health (Variable #1), close (strongly related) to readjustment (Variable #2), which in turn is next to potency (Variable #6). These variables are closely surrounded by those comprising integration (Variables #3, 4, 5, and 7). Above and below the region of integration is the region comprising the variables representing personal resources, reflecting their relatively strong association with integration. The adjustment-promoting function of perceiving society as supportive (Variable #38) is indicated by its location close to the personal resources. The problematic nature of the catalysts is indicated by their location between the personal and primary environmental resources, suggesting a lack of significant relationship with demands. The primary environmental resources are grouped in the region to the immediate left to that of the catalysts. To the left of the primary environmental resources are the secondary environmental resources, their location suggesting a possibly negative effect on readjustment. Finally, at the extreme left of the map, furthest from readjustment, are the demands, indicating their negative relationship with readjustment. Their distance from personal resources implies a negative relationship between these sets of variables. The clustering of the demands fits in with their classification by the three modalities of human behavior. The cognitive demands are in the top subregion, with the instrumental demands. The affective demands are concentrated in the bottom subregion. The structure of readjustment of veteran Israelis, then, corroborates the conclusions of numerous studies on the readjustment of diverse population groups (Ben-Sira 1981, 1983a, 1985, 1986a, 1986b, 1989).

The Structure of Readjustment: New Immigrants

The structure of readjustment of immigrants as suggested by the SSA map in Figure 5, though in most general terms supporting the hypothesized framework, reveals a somewhat less systematic pattern, differing in some respects from that of the veterans. As with the veterans, the location of health (Variable #1) right next to readjustment (Variable #2) implies its dependence on emotional homeostasis, which in turn is affected by potency (Variable #6); integration fulfills an intervening role. Yet, contrary to the veterans, integration is related both to the control of personal resources (except education) and to individual perspectives. In contrast to both the hypothesis and the pattern characterizing the structure of the veterans' readjustment, support by formal agencies (Variable #30) is located in the region of the personal resources. Similar to the case of the veterans, but contradicting the hypothesis, perceiving society as supportive (Variable #38) is close to both personal resources and individual perspectives. The data also imply the limited effect of primary environmental resources, compared to personal resources, on readjustment. Demands can impede readjustment, but personal and primary environmental resources can limit this negative impact. Unlike their marginality for veterans, for immigrants catalysts are likely to affect the salience of demands. As we saw, individual perspectives clearly fulfill a salience-moderating function, leading to integration and potency, while societal perspectives are likely to exacerbate the salience of the demands. The role of support by formal agencies (Variable #30) in the immigrants' structure of readjustment is particularly noteworthy. The SSA structure suggests that in contrast to both the data on the veterans and the evidence from other societies, such support seems both to enhance the immigrants' personal resources and to moderate the salience of demands. Finally, education appears to exacerbate the salience of demands.

These conclusions are derived from the configuration of the variables on the SSA map (Figure 5). The clustering of the variables on the map again forms eight content-related regions but in a far less systematic pattern than that of the veterans. As with the veterans' structure, the variable denoting health (Variable #1) is located on the extreme right, close to readjustment (Variable #2). Similarly also, the variables representing demands are at the left of the map, furthest from readjustment, indicating their negative relationship with readjustment. Nearest to the readjustment variable is the variable representing potency (Variable #6), followed by the variables denoting integration (Variables #3, 4, 5, and 7). To the left of these variables are both variables comprising individual perspectives (at the lower edge) and those comprising personal resources (at the upper edge), suggesting the similar effect of these variables on integration and reflecting their strong negative relationship with demands. The role of integration is indicated by the location of this variable (#38) close to the individual perspectives. The inclusion of the variable denoting support by formal agencies (#30) suggests the readjustment-promoting function of such support for the immigrants. The primary environmental resources are located to the left of both the individual perspectives and individual resource variables. To the left of the variables representing primary environmental resources are the societal perspectives, followed by the region of the demand variables, suggesting the potential of the societal perspectives to exacerbate the salience of demands.

The scattering of the secondary environmental resource variables can be interpreted as follows. First, the fact that support by formal agencies (Variable #30) is within the region of personal resources suggests its resource-enhancing function for the immigrants. The closeness of psychologist support (Variable #37) to the variables denoting affective demands suggests the dependence of the immigrants on this kind of support. But at the same time, dependence on that support has a strong negative relationship with readjustment, suggesting a re-adjustment-countering effect. Finally, as indicated earlier, the location of education (Variable #26) in the region of demands suggests its function in exacerbating the salience of demands among the immigrants.

Figure 5
The Structure of Readjustment: Immigrants
SSA (Smallest Space Analysis) of the Correlations in Appendix E

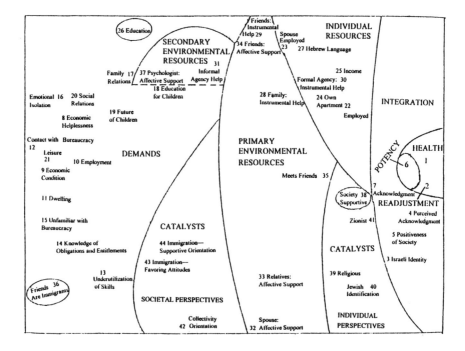

9

Conclusion

OVERALL TRENDS

The Structure of Readjustment

The results of my study indicate that readjustment is the outcome of interaction among a number of different factors, which can be said to create a "structure of readjustment." The figures below present a schematic display of the empirical structures in Figures 4 and 5. Comparison of the figures shows the intergroup differences both in the factors affecting readjustment and in the interactions among these factors.

The immigrants' readjustment, as for the veterans, is affected primarily by their potency, which in turn is dependent on their integration into the society. However, the immigrants' integration, unlike that of the veterans, is dependent on personal resources, support by formal agencies, and adherence to individual ideological perspectives. Education, rather than being a resource, is salient demand. Support by formal agencies (contrary to evidence in numerous studies) plays an important readjustment-promoting role for the immigrants. Immigrants are also more in need than veterans of professional support for meeting their affective demands. This dependence, however, seems counterproductive to their readjustment. Finally, and contrary to expectation, belief in the prevalence of immigration-supporting and collectivity-oriented perspectives in Israeli society is likely to exacerbate somewhat the salience of demands.

The immigrants' lower level of readjustment, and consequent poorer health, may be due to their worse position, compared to that of the veterans, on all components of the process that could moderate the deleterious salience of the demands. They have less potency than do the veterans; they are less integrated into Israeli society; both the availability and the efficacy of the resources they have at their disposal is inferior to those of the veterans; only a small minority either adhere to the ideological perspectives or perceive society as supportive. And yet, the salience of the demands confronting them exceeds that of the veterans. Moreover, the immigrants believe in immigration-supporting perspectives more than do the veterans and have a higher level of education than do the veterans. Both of these appear to be readjustment-countering factors. In most general terms, then, the immigrants' risk of stress and, consequently, of breakdown is "explained" by the interdependence among the factors constituting the process, the more limited resources available to the immigrants, and the higher salience of the demands confronting them.

As to the veterans, the data suggest that their emotional homeostasis may be negatively affected by their attitude toward immigration (see Table 40). Israelis of "Eastern" origin and second-generation Israelis are more likely than "Westerners" to have reservations about immigration (Table 4). The data further suggest a high degree of social separation between immigrants and veterans. The separation between the groups and interpretations attributed to intergroup relations may lead to an escalating cycle of discord.

Figure 6
Schematic Display of the Structure of Readjustment: Veterans
Based on the SSA in Figure 4

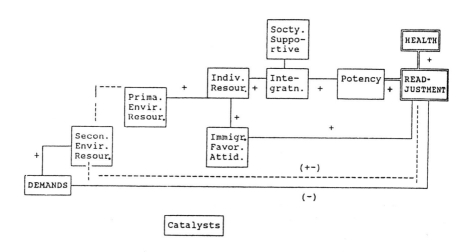

Figure 7
Schematic Display of the Structure of Readjustment: Immigrants
Based on the SSA in Figure 5

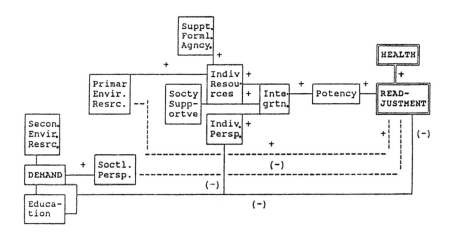

Immigrants' Vulnerability to Stress

I now turn to a more descriptive review of my findings. The immigrants' health is poorer than that of the veterans (Table 13). Time in Israel somewhat improves their health, but the health of even fourth-year immigrants is worse than that of the veterans (Table 14). Accumulating evidence regarding the stress-disease relationship, including the data in the current study (Table 15), indicate that emotional homeostasis is a contributory factor in health. Yet, the immigrants' level of emotional homeostasis is lower than that of the veterans (Table 11) and there is no indication of improvement over time (Table 12). Emotional homeostasis, in turn, is dependent on the individual's feeling of potency. The immigrants' potency is weaker than that of the veterans (Table 51). By the fourth year in Israel, the immigrants' feeling of potency improves, but it is still weaker than that of the veterans (Table 52). Moreover, the efficacy of the immigrants' feeling of potency in buffering the stress-potential of the demands is weaker than that of the veterans (Table 53). Integration into a society is a crucial element underlying potency. However, the immigrants' integration is weaker than that of the veterans (see Tables 18, 20, 24, 28). The improvement over four years is negligible (Tables 19, 21, 25), and one of the facets of integration, the perceived "positiveness of the society," of integration, even decreases (Table 29).

The personal and primary environmental resources that immigrants have at their disposal are generally more limited than those of the veterans (Table 44) and are also less effective than those of the veterans in moderating the salience of the demands (Tables 47 and 48). Moreover, contrary to expectations, in this study, the immigrants' higher level of education constitutes not a resource but a demand—possibly because of the underutilization of their skills (Tables 44 and 46). Support by formal agencies is an effective resource for the immigrants, for moderating the salience of the instrumental demands, and also of the affective and cognitive demands, confronting them (Table 49). This finding differs from both the evidence in the current study regarding the veterans (Table 48) and numerous studies on various other populations.

The salience of most demands confronting the immigrants exceeds that of the veterans (Table 34). The salience of these demands decreases by the fourth year in Israel but still exceeds that of the veterans. The affective demands have a higher stress-potential for the immigrants than do the instrumental and the cognitive demands, though all are fairly salient (Table 42). Several individual perspectives moderate the salience of the demands for the immigrants but not for the veterans (Tables 38 and 39). Yet only a small minority of the immigrants adhere to these perspectives (Tables 32 and 33). On the other hand, the immigrants' belief in immigration-supporting perspectives, which exceeds that of the veterans (Tables 1 and 3), may exacerbate the salience of their demands, perhaps because it arouses unrealistic expectations. The positive correlation between belief in these perspectives and the salience of demands confronting the immigrants (Tables 38 and 39) provides some support for this contention. The stronger feeling of deprivation among the immigrants than among the veterans (Table 7) may be a further expression of frustrated expectations. In fact, the more the immigrants believe in immigration-supporting perspectives, the more deprived by society they feel (Table 10). Feelings of deprivation do not appear to change over the period in Israel covered by the study.

However, it is not just the immigrants' worse position with regard to almost all components making up the process of immigration that hinders their readjustment. Gordon (1964) suggests that mutually hostile attitudes, and misinterpretations of overt and covert behavior can also hinder immigrants in achieving a reasonable level of adjustment. In fact, the data suggest that veteran Israelis have some reservations with regard to the influx of immigrants and that these may harm adjustment by means of an escalating cycle of discord.

The Immigrants' Perception of Society and the Implications for Integration

I noted earlier that the absorbing society's image in the immigrants' eyes is an important factor in their readjustment (Table 33). Yet, a number of factors may hamper the crystallization of a positive image of society in the immigrants' eyes. First is the discrepancy between the immigrants' and the veterans' belief in immigration-supporting perspectives (Tables 1 and 3). This discrepancy may lead to unrealistic expectations, resulting in the higher salience of demands (Tables 38 and 39) and may thus explain the negative correlation between the immigrants' readjustment and their belief in immigration-supporting perspectives (Table 40). Viewing society as supportive of people in need can also be a resource: the stronger the belief in the society's inclination to assist people in need, the weaker the salience of the demands confronting an individual (Tables 51 and 52). Yet few of the immigrants believe that Israeli society does, in fact, help the needy (Table 46).

Integration into the society and, in particular, perceived positiveness of society, are powerful predictors of potency and readjustment. Yet, the immigrants are much less likely than the veterans to have a positive image of Israeli society, with fourth-year immigrants being the least likely to hold such an image (Table 29). Perceived positiveness of the society affects the other facets of integration—with this effect being stronger among the immigrants than that among the veterans (Tables 31 and 32). The evidence suggests that the immigrants' likelihood of assuming an Israeli identity decreases over the period of four years—perhaps because of the decline in the perceived positiveness of society (Table 30). Moreover, given the importance of the perceived positiveness of society for the immigrants' potency and readjustment (Table 33), the decline in the perceived positiveness of the absorbing society is especially problematic.

Contradictions within the Absorbing Society's Position toward Immigrants

The immigrants are evidently exposed to contradicting messages from the absorbing society. On the one hand, Israeli society is more likely to acknowledge immigrants as members than the immigrants are to feel that they are indeed acknowledged (Table 20). On the other hand, evidence suggests a relative separation between the groups as far as primary relations are concerned: Very few of the immigrants report that their friends are mainly Israelis, and very few of the veterans say that their friends are mainly immigrants (Table 44). Thus, both the social separation and unstated reservations about immigration prevailing in Israeli society (Table 3) may explain the immigrants' doubts about their actual acknowledgement as members of that society.

Perceived Intergroup Relations

A further explanation of the immigrants' image of society and consequent integration and readjustment may lie in their perception of the prevailing relations between immigrants and veterans. Few define this relationship as positive (Table 28), and the proportion who do so declines over time.

How do these perceptions of the immigrants conform with the prevailing attitudes among the veterans? First, fewer than half of the veteran Israelis define veteran-immigrant relations as positive. Second, not only do fewer veterans than immigrants hold immigration-supporting perspectives, but second-generation Israelis and "Easterners" are even less likely to hold such attitudes than are "Westerners" (Table 4). The data suggest further that the veterans' attitudes toward immigration may affect their own emotional homeostasis (Table 40). Since second-generation Israelis and "Easterners" are less likely than Westerners to hold immigration-favoring perspectives (Table 4), they are more likely to be distressed by the wave of immigration. It stands to reason, then, that the discrepancy between the expected and actual attitudes as well as the reservations about immigration prevailing among some groups may influence intergroup interaction, which may, in turn, have an impact on the immigrants' sense that they are acknowledged as members of Israeli society.

Moreover, the overwhelming majority of the immigrants from the former Soviet Union are "Westerners." The reservations among the "Easterners" regarding this immigration (Tables 2 and 4) conform, to some extent, to the problems documented in studies of interethnic relations in Israeli society. In the past, these problems became particularly salient at times of a substantial influx of "Western" immigrants (Ben-Sira 1988a; Bernstein 1979; Cohen 1980). The immigrants seem to be quite sensitive to the problematic intergroup relations— especially Ashkenazi-Sephardi relations—within Israeli society (Table 26). Their perception of the positiveness of this relationship deteriorates with the length of stay in Israel. From the immigrants' perspective, then, being "Ashkenazi" may explain both their doubts of their being acknowledged members of the society and the low level of their appraisal of the positiveness of that society.

The Emergence of an Escalating Cycle of Discord

The analysis above implies that the combination of the veterans' attitudes toward immigration and the immigrants' feelings of, and response to, such attitudes may set into motion an escalating cycle of discord. Immigration-instigated change may affect the lives of both immigrants and members of the absorbing society and may arouse reciprocal reservations and/or misinterpretations of behavior and intentions. These are likely to create stress-arousing demands for both groups, over and above those caused by the change itself. Even when members of the absorbing society do not display hostile attitudes but merely ignore the immigrants, the latter may perceive this behavior as indifference. Members of the absorbing society, in turn, may interpret certain unfamiliar verbal and non-verbal expressions of the immigrants as aloofness. Such a perception of the immigrants' behavior could be an outcome of the immigrants' efforts to maintain "a sense of their own basic reasonableness and normalcy." Moreover, while members of the absorbing society may expect to see the immigrants grateful, impressed, excited, and happy, in reality many of them are confused (Lobodzinska 1986). This may be interpreted as ingratitude and lack of appreciation for the "sacrifices" made in absorbing them, in particular when such perception is accompanied by a feeling that immigration came at the absorbing society's expense.

Breaking this cycle requires implicit and explicit mutual acceptance (Gordon 1964), that is, a reasonable level of concomitant readjustment. Overtly welcoming activities by the veterans, such as establishing primary intergroup networks, can contribute to the immigrants' feeling of being welcomed into the absorbing society, enhancing their integration and readjustment. The emphasis of researchers on "joining with the dominant society" (Berry 1991:24) and on establishing social networks in the new society (Kuo and Tsai 1986) both point to the significance of the immigrants' seeing themselves as acknowledged members of that society. In the short term, support by formal agencies can also help to moderate the salience of demands (Table 49) and promote readjustment of immigrants (Appendix E). In the long term, however, failure to establish fruitful and rewarding social relations could result in isolation from the absorbing society, together with dependency on institutional support, both of which are counterproductive to successful readjustment.

GENERALIZABILITY OF THE EMPIRICALLY SUPPORTED PARADIGM

To what extent do these conclusions contribute to an understanding of the factors promoting and impeding readjustment of immigrants into other social systems? It seems that there are similarities, in terms of the paradigm developed, between immigrants to Israel of the 1990s and immigrants in other migratory movements.

Some scholars have denied the legitimacy of drawing generalizations from specific immigration studies (see H. B. M. Murphy 1977), because of major differences among migratory movements with respect to both the reasons for emigration and the relevant characteristics of the migrants and the absorbing societies. However, as documented throughout this work, the decisive factors in readjustment are the demands confronting the immigrants, the availability and effectiveness of resources, the individual perspectives of the immigrants, the societal perspectives prevailing in the absorbing society, and the perception of these perspectives by the immigrants. Many of the studies cited in this work bring evidence of stress and maladjustment, feelings of frustration, difficulties in meeting unprecedented demands, and inappropriateness of resources at the immigrants' disposal.

One might argue that even if many components constituting the conceptual framework I describe are relevant to the readjustment process in other migratory movements, immigrants to Israel may believe that immigration is central to the state's legitimation and may therefore have higher expectations of society. Indeed, such expectations can lead to frustration when reality proves to be different. Yet immigrants to the United States, also an immigration-based society, are similarly prone to frustration due to often-unrealistic expectations. In addition, while ideological individual perspectives unique to the Israeli context may moderate the salience of the demands confronting immigrants to Israel, we saw that only a small minority of immigrants believe in these ideologies; overall, the Russian immigration to Israel was not motivated by ideological considerations (see Table 17). Thus, despite these presumably unique perspectives, immigration to Israel may not differ significantly from immigration to other countries.

In conclusion, then, the paradigm developed here may contribute to an understanding of the complex readjustment process in the wake of an extreme life-change, such as immigration. Viewing readjustment as an indicator of successful culmination of immigration may further our understanding of the factors underlying the much-documented stress among immigrants and the weight of the various components of that process in exacerbating and moderating this stress. Applying this paradigm to other societal and cultural contexts will require adding relevant cultural and structural factors. However, the paradigm may serve as a useful conceptual framework for introducing these factors and may provide insights regarding the role of veterans in the readjustment of immigrants, the role of immigrants in the emotional homeostasis of the absorbing society, and the possible reciprocal maladjustment that could set into motion an escalating cycle of discord.

Some Caveats Regarding the Empirical Evidence

At this stage, some weaknesses of the empirical evidence ought to be noted. In terms of the study itself, first, the conclusions derived from the empirical investigation do not go beyond the four-year period studied. Thus, no inferences may be drawn as to the immigrants' readjustment over longer periods of time. Second, my conclusions are based on a particular interpretation of the data. Thus, though with regard to many specific components this interpretation corroborates findings documented in many other studies, other interpretations are possible. Third, the conclusions regarding changes over time are based not on a follow-up longitudinal study but on an investigation of immigrants arriving in Israel in different years. The consistency of the findings and the logic underlying the differences provides some confidence in the validity of the conclusions. In addition, the cohorts are fairly similar with regard to their relevant background traits (Appendix A). Still, it is possible that intervening factors characterizing the year of their arrival may have affected some of the results.

In terms of the data analysis, one could question the use of SSA (Smallest Space Analysis). As indicated earlier, this approach assumes that one can draw conclusions about social behavior and attitudes from the empirical structure produced by the interplay among the multitude of variables constituting the content universe (Brown 1985; Canter 1985a). Such an approach is particularly appropriate to the current study, the goal of which was to understand the interplay among the variables and bring to light the mutual effect of each factor on all the others. Because of the critical importance of this understanding process, methods which merely explain the variance in dependent variables would therefore be inadequate.

The statistical significance of the correlations presented in this work may also seem problematic. However, there is a growing recognition that the significance of phenomena in the social sciences can be established by the recurrence of patterns rather than by arbitrarily defined "significance levels" (Bartram 1980; Canter 1985b; Carver 1978; Guttman 1977). The patterns in the present work correspond largely with those in other studies among problem-laden populations to which I refer throughout this work. This consistency, especially if sustained by accumulating evidence from future studies, may lend support to the validity of the paradigm.

Finally, survey research of the type commonly used in the social sciences has its weaknesses. It may be argued that responses reflect the norms in the investigated population rather than the actual situation. If indeed this is the case, that in itself would emphasize the pressures confronting the immigrants in comparison to those of the veterans. Kessler's discussion of the difficulty of arriving at valid conclusions is noteworthy. According to Kessler:

The most difficult phase of stress research is that associated with . . . probing the reasons for variation in adjustment to particularly serious life crises. Here we must not only contend with the problems of imputing causality to the event, but we must also do so while simultaneously considering intervening variables that can modify the effect of the event on . . . outcome measures. There are not only issues of causal ambiguity here, but also serious problems of estimation and interpretation. . . . Many of the methodological problems . . . would be resolved if it were possible to conduct experiments in which exposure to a stressful event is randomly assigned. . . . The stressors found in laboratory studies are very tame compared to those encountered in the real world. . . . It is not at all clear that results obtained with mild stressors of this sort generalize to the more serious life crises that are of interest to applied researchers. As a result of this and other problems of external validity, the present use of laboratory experiments is minimal in stress research. . . . [On the other hand,] on occasion, natural variation in exposure to some disaster makes it possible to analyse the impact of a serious life event as if exposure were assigned randomly. [For instance, naturally occurring circumstances] provide the best evidence available to date that life events can in fact cause illnesses. . . . In cross-sectional surveys, causal inferences are made on the assumption that the people who do not experience the strain under investigation stand as proxies for how people who are strained would have been if they had not experienced the strain. In this way the difference in the rates of ill health in the strained and unstrained groups is interpreted as the effect of strain on health. (Kessler 1983:269–271)

In summary, then, the systematic approach of the current work may be regarded as taking an additional step in the understanding of the factors underlying the life-change-stress relationship in general, and of the factors underlying readjustment in the wake of immigration in particular. Studies of immigration in other social systems are clearly imperative. Yet the paradigm suggested here may serve as a conceptual framework for a systematic approach to such studies.

APPENDICES

Appendix A

Study Design

THE SAMPLE

The data presented in this work are based on an interview study carried out among two cross-sectional representative samples of Israeli Jewish adults, aged twenty years or older. One sample (N = 892) consisted of veteran Israelis; for some analyses, it was subdivided into "East," if the respondent or his/her father was born in Asia or North Africa; "West," if the respondent or his/her father was born in Europe or America; and "Israel," if the respondent was at least second-generation Israeli-born. The other sample (N = 486) consisted of immigrants from the former Soviet Union who arrived in Israel between 1990 and 1993; for some analyses, it was subdivided by year of immigration. In the tables based on a single question, sample sizes for that question are listed.

The sampling was based on data obtained from Israel's Central Bureau of Statistics (including the Statistical Yearbook) and comprises forty-four townships (including the four major cities: Jerusalem, Tel Aviv, Haifa, and Beer Sheva) which represent the geographic distribution and socioeconomic characteristics of the entire Jewish population (except for kibbutz residents). Each township was divided into precincts according to social and economic variables. The number of respondents in each precinct was determined by the population in that precinct (see "Sample Characteristics," below).

DATA COLLECTION

The interviews were carried out by trained interviewers at the respondents' homes using interview schedules with close-ended questions. The same questions were used for both population groups. The immigrant questionnaires were translated into Russian, and their identity with the Hebrew version was ascertained. The interviews were carried out simultaneously in all locations between September 23 and November 4, 1993.

SAMPLE CHARACTERISTICS

Veteran Israelis

The sample is representative of the Jewish Israeli adult population: 46.5 percent were male and 53.5 percent female; 67 percent were Israeli-born (22% at least second-generation Israeli, 30% North African or Asian origin, 15% European or American origin), 33 percent were born abroad (16% in North Africa or Asia, 15% in Europe or America, and 2% elsewhere); 89 percent of the latter had immigrated to Israel after the establishment of the state in 1948 (34% in the years of the mass immigration between 1948 and 1956, 26% after 1974, that is, after the Yom Kippur war); the average age was approximately thirty-six years old (28% were 20–24, and 4% were 65 or older); 5 percent had partial or complete elementary education, 11 percent had partial high school education, 44 percent had completed high school, and 40 percent had 13 or more years of formal education; 71 percent were gainfully employed, 3 percent retired, 12 percent were enlisted soldiers or students, 9 percent were housewives, and 5 percent were unemployed.

Immigrants

The sample is representative of immigrants from Russia during the period studied: 45.7 percent were male, and 54.3 percent were female; 40 percent immigrated in 1990, 34 percent in 1991, 16 percent in 1992, and 10 percent in the first half of 1993; 41 percent came from Russia, 21 percent from Ukraine; 23 percent from Belaruss, Moldavia, and the Baltic republics, and 15 percent from the Asian republics; the average age was approximately forty-three years old (11% were 20–24, 12% were sixty-five or older); 2 percent had partial or complete elementary education, 9 percent had partial high school education, 8 percent had completed high school, and 81 percent had 13 or more years of formal education; 55 percent were gainfully employed, 18 percent retired, 5 percent were enlisted soldiers or students, 1 percent were housewives, and 21 percent were unemployed. Comparison of immigrant samples according to year of immigration reveals a high degree of similarity with regard to the central demographic variables, except for gainful employment.

Table A1

Description of the Immigrant Sample by Year of Immigration

Variable	Category	1993	1992	1991	1990
Age	Average[a]	42	42	44	44
Age	20–24 years	11	11	10	11
	65+ years	11	11	13	12
Education	Elementary and less	–	1	2	2
	Partial high school	13	12	5	11
	Complete high school	7	8	10	7
	Post high school	80	79	83	80
Employment	Employed	31	48	57	62
	Retired	16	18	18	18
	Soldier/Student	2	4	4	8
	Housewife (only)	8	1	1	–
	Unemployed	44	28	20	12

a. The numbers in this row are not percentages but average age for the given year of immigration.

Appendix B

Composite Variables

IMMIGRATION-FAVORING ATTITUDES

Eight statements asking respondents for their opinion of the responsibility of
Israeli society toward immigrants and other citizens.

Statements of Immigration-Favoring Attitudes

Statement	Factor Loading
1. The State should ensure that all immigrants have housing (agree).	.41
2. The government should ensure housing first for young couples and soldiers and only then for immigrants (disagree).	.78
3. Immigrants should have priority in finding appropriate employment (agree).	.39
4. Immigrants are a burden on the State (disagree).	.64
5. Ex-soldiers should have preference over immigrants in finding jobs (disagree).	.78
6. Immigration contributes to the economic development of the State (agree).	.65
7. Every immigrant should take care of him/herself. The State has no obligation to do so (disagree).	.48
8. Immigrant absorption justifies raising taxes (agree).	.51

Cutting points between categories of the composite variable were determined
according to sectiles of the averages of the accumulated responses to all items.

COLLECTIVITY ORIENTATION

Five statements asking for the respondents' degree of agreement with each.

Statements of Collectivity Orientation

Statement	*Factor Loading*
1. As matters stand today, citizens should first contribute to the State and only then worry about the needs of their families (agree).	.44
2. The State is responsible for everyone having what he needs to live (agree).	.56
3. Citizens should worry first about the needs of their families and only then contribute to the State (disagree).	.40
4. Every citizen is responsible for himself; the State need not help anyone (disagree).	.48
5. The State should use taxes to transfer money from the wealthy to the needy (agree).	.57

Cutting points between categories of the composite variable were determined according to sectiles of the averages of the accumulated responses to all items.

THE SCALE OF PSYCHOLOGICAL DISTRESS (SPD)

In the literature, a wide variety of scales for measuring distress is available. Rumbaut measured psychological adaptation (or psychological distress) by a widely used screening scale, the General Well-Being Index (GWB), developed and validated by the National Center for Health Statistics in the 1970s (Rumbaut 1985, 1989, 1991:61–63; Link and Dohrenwend 1980). This scale contains indicators of the frequency of affective symptoms experienced by the respondent over the past month. Eight items, accounting for 40 percent of the variance, reflect dysphoric symptoms and a sad, anxious, and depressed mood; these constitute the measure of psychological distress used in his study on the readjustment of refugees. Wethington and Kessler (1991:18) measured psychological adjustment, following the literature on coping, by self-reported symptoms of anxiety and depression. They used items from the anxiety and depression subscales of the revised Hopkins Symptom Checklist.

A widely used measure of distress is Langner's (1962) Mental Health Index (MHI). It is a typical index of distress indexes and was the standard in community research for many years. Recently, there has been a shift from this scale to those asking more about mood, such as feeling afraid, lonely, or sad. "Researchers have discovered that people are more willing to report their emotional feelings, . . . so that questions about headaches, sweaty palms, and heart palpitations, which were used to mask the intent of measuring a respondent's emotional state are unnecessary. . . . [Furthermore,] the use of physiological symptoms of distress could bias results in favor of an association between distress and disease" (Mirowsky and Ross 1989:21–23).

On the other hand, it is precisely the danger of "breakdown" resulting from a prolonged failure to restore emotional homeostasis (Antonovsky 1972) that justifies the application of a scale that represents both psychological and bodily responses. Stress leads to major outpourings of powerful hormones, creating dramatic alterations in bodily processes, many of which we sense; examples are pounding heart, sweating, trembling, and fatigue (Monat and Lazarus 1991). It is desirable to use a composite scale that reflects the stress-response.

In the current study, we used the six-item Scale of Psychological Distress (SPD) (Ben-Sira 1979, 1982a). The scale contains five items from the original MHI (heart palpitations, fainting, insomnia, headache, hand trembling), and one from the Cornell index (nervous breakdown). These six items, which have been used in a considerable number of studies, formed a Guttman scale of an almost identical order, indicating their relation to the same content universe. The SPD was validated by using the MHI as a criterion (Ben-Sira 1982a). It has been used in numerous studies investigating reaction to life change events (Ben-Sira 1982b), readjustment of traumatically disabled persons (Ben-Sira 1981, 1983b, 1986a, 1989), well-being of persons receiving welfare assistance (Ben-Sira 1986b), intergroup relations (Ben-Sira 1986b, 1988a), stress-resolving component of primary medical care (Ben-Sira 1987, 1988b), readjustment of convalescents after heart attack (Ben-Sira and Eliezer 1990), and readjustment of aged (Ben-Sira 1991). The SPD was also found to differentiate between population groups according to their emotional state (see Aviram et al. 1984). Consequently, it was considered a valid measure of psychological distress.

DISEASE SCORE

As in other studies on the behavioral consequences of disease (see Ben-Sira 1982b, 1985, 1987, 1988b), respondents' self-reports of physician-diagnosed prolonged or chronic health problems were used as a measure of state of health. This approach seems more appropriate than that of reports on "complaints" or self-reports of the effect of illness (see Kessler and Cleary 1980; Melick 1978). Respondents were presented a list of diseases, and the interviewer asked: "Here is a list of diseases and other conditions. Has a physician told you of or have you been diagnosed to have that such a condition?"

Statements of Medical Conditions

Medical condition
1.   High blood pressure
2.   Heart disease
3.   Other diseases of the blood circulation
4.   Diabetes

5. Diseases of the nervous system
6. Rheumatism
7. Stomach ulcer
8. Chronic eye disease
9. Cancer
10. Liver disease
11. Kidney disease
12. Other chronic disease of the digestive system
13. Bone disease
14. Other chronic disease
15. Permanent disability as a consequence of injury

Each respondent was assigned a score based on the number of reported diagnosed conditions.

ISRAELI IDENTITY SCALE (IIS)

As in an earlier study (Ben-Sira 1988a), Israeli identity was measured by the five questions listed below. Response options were on a scale of five, ranging from very positive through very negative. A composite measure was constructed from the items.

Questions for Israeli Identity Scale (IIS)

Modality	Item	Factor loading
Affective	1. To what extent do you feel at home in Israel?	.80
Cognitive	2. To what extent do you feel yourself part of the State of Israel and its problems?	.68
Instrumental	3. If you could, would you prefer to live outside of Israel?	.62
	4. Are you sure you will stay in Israel?	.50
	5. Do you want your children to live permanently in Israel?	.63

Cutting points between categories of the composite variable were determined according to sectiles of the averages of the accumulated responses to all items.

SOCIETAL ACKNOWLEDGMENT SCALE (SAS)

Perceived acknowledgement, like identity, has affective, cognitive, and instrumental components. It was measured by three questions listed below. Response options were on a scale of six, ranging from very positive through very negative. A composite measure was constructed from the items.

Questions for Societal Acknowledgment Scale (SAS)

Modality	Item	Factor loading
Affective	1. How often do you feel that Israeli society rejects you?	.67
Cognitive	2. How often do you feel that you do not understand this society at all?	.71
Instrumental	3. How often do you feel that Israeli society deprives you?	.63

Cutting points between categories of the composite variable were determined according to sectiles of the averages of the accumulated responses to all items.

REFERENCE POSITIVITY SCALE (RPS)

Positiveness of reference society was measured by the four questions listed below. Response options were on a scale of four, ranging from very good to very bad. A composite measure was constructed from the items.

Questions for Reference Positivity Scale (RPS)

Item	Factor loading
1. What is the situation in Israel in general?	.67
2. What is the social situation in Israel?	.71
3. How are relations between the Ashkenazi and Sephardi ethnic groups in Israel?	.63
4. How are relations between new immigrants and veterans?	.61

Cutting points between categories of the composite variable were determined according to sectiles of the averages of the accumulated responses to all items.

POTENCY SCALE

The potency scale includes elements of the mastery and self-confidence scales (Pearlin et al. 1981; Rosenberg 1979), which measure confidence in one's capacities, and also of the alienation and anomie scales (Seeman 1972; Srole 1956), which measure trust in the meaningfulness of society (see also Ben-Sira 1985: 399). The scale contains nineteen items. Mastery and self-confidence items refer to the frequency with which respondents have the feelings expressed in given statements (very frequently to never). Alienation and anomie items were presented as statements asking about the respondents' agreement with each (definitely agree to definitely disagree).

Questions for Potency Scale

Mastery
1. I have little control over things that happen to me (never).
2. I feel that I am being pushed around in my life (never).
3. I can do about anything I set my mind to (very frequently).
4. I often feel helpless in dealing with the problems of life (never).
5. What happens to me in the future mostly depends on me (very frequently).
6. There is really no way I can solve some of the problems I have (never).

Self-confidence[a]
1. I certainly feel useless at times (never).
2. All in all I am inclined to feel that I am a failure (never).
2. I am able to do things as well as most other people (very frequently).

Alienation[b]
1. Nowadays a person has to live pretty much for today and let tomorrow take care of itself (definitely disagree).
2. In spite of what some people say, the lot of the average man is getting worse and not better (definitely disagree).
3. It is hardly fair to bring children into the world with the way things look for the future (definitely disagree).
4. Party membership is more important than talent for achieving something in this society (definitely disagree).
5. Having the right connections is more important than talent for achieving something (definitely disagree).

Anomie
1. Community leaders are indifferent to one's needs (definitely disagree).
2. Little can be accomplished in this society which is basically unpredictable and lacking order (definitely disagree).
3. Life goals are receding rather than being realized (definitely disagree).
4. Life is futile (definitely disagree).
5. Nowadays one cannot count even on closest personal associates for support (definitely disagree).

---

[a] Items from the self-confidence scale were chosen only if they referred to coping efficacy.

[b] This scale was modified for conditions in Israel, where political patronage and individual favoritism are often considered the most widespread form of discrimination against those who are not affiliated with the "right" party or who do not have the "right" connections.

Cutting points between categories of the composite variable were determined according to sectiles of the averages of the accumulated responses to all items.

Appendix C

Methodology

WEAK MONOTONICITY COEFFICIENT (μ_2)

In the present study, I used the weak monotonicity coefficient (μ_2), which expresses the extent to which variance in one variable corresponds with the variance in another variable in a particular direction, without specifying the exact nature of the regressive function. A weak monotonicity coefficient is particularly appropriate in the social sciences, where linearity cannot be assumed, as there is no supposition of equal distances among the categories in each of the variables and the number of effective categories differs from item to item (Rave 1986).

The formula for μ_2 is as follows: Given n pairs of observations on numerical variables (x, y,), (x_i, y_i) (i = 1, . . . , n), then,

$$\mu_2 = \frac{\displaystyle\sum_{h=1}^{n} \sum_{i=1}^{n} (x_h - x_i)(y_h - y_i)}{\displaystyle\sum_{h=1}^{n} \sum_{i=1}^{n} |x_h - x_i| \, |y_h - y_i|}$$

SMALLEST SPACE ANALYSIS (SSA)

The SSA (Smallest Space Analysis) method developed by Guttman (Brown 1985; Canter 1985a) facilitates the examination of a multivariate interrelationship and the drawing of theoretically justified and empirically supported conclusions promoting the understanding of factors determining human behavior. The method takes into consideration the multitude of often mutually interacting factors determining behavior. It facilitates drawing conclusions from the overall "structure," which is seen as the outcome of those interacting forces and reflected in the mapping of the variables of a multivariate content universe, where the position of the variables is determined by the interrelations among them. The presentation thus reflects the positive or negative predictive power of each variable vis à vis all the others. The efficacy of the method lies in the graphic presentation of the interrelationships among the variables, facilitating a simultaneous perception of the entire multivariate universe and the interplay among its components.

The computer "translates" the strength of the interrelations between the variables into relative distances among them and prints all variables as numbered points on a map. The distance between the points is based on the relation of each variable to all the others. In general, the stronger the positive relation between two variables, the shorter the distance between the points representing them; the weaker the positive relation (or the stronger the negative relationship), the longer the distance between the points. However, the location of a point (that is, a variable) on the map is determined not merely by a pairwise correlations but by the relation of each variable to all other variables, thereby reflecting the complex interplay of the variables.

Appendix D

Correlations (μ_2) among Components of the Readjustment Process: Veterans

VARIABLE	#	1	2	3	4	5	6	7	8	9	10	11	12	13	14	15	16	17	18	19	20
Health	1	-																			
Readjustment	2	.52	-																		
Integration																					
Israeli identity	3	.03	.10	-																	
Perceived acknowledg.	4	.19	.28	.39	-																
Positivity of society	5	-.01	.11	.23	.28	-															
Potency	6	.30	.57	.33	.50	.36	-														
Acknowledgement	7	.20	.09	.12	.32	.24	.15	-													
Demands																					
Economic helplessness	8	-.17	-.39	-.21	-.38	-.14	-.49	.01	-												
Economic condition	9	-.10	-.40	-.14	-.29	-.20	-.58	-.04	.64	-											
Job/employment	10	-.07	-.35	-.23	-.31	-.18	-.55	-.16	.48	.80	-										
Dwelling	11	.04	-.19	-.22	-.39	-.12	-.40	-.21	.46	.73	.66	-									
Contact w. bureauc.	12	-.16	-.27	-.15	-.48	-.10	-.41	-.17	.42	.53	.54	.65	-								
Underutiliz. of skills	13	.11	-.05	-.29	-.07	-.09	-.24	-.06	.25	.23	.32	.07	.03	-							
Know oblig's/entit's	14	-.04	-.22	-.20	-.31	-.31	-.39	-.17	.20	.36	.40	.28	.46	.23	-						
Unfamil. w. bureauc.	15	-.07	-.22	-.15	-.23	-.28	-.36	-.11	.20	.32	.29	.35	.37	.19	.61	-					
Emotional isolation	16	-.30	-.38	-.24	-.53	-.13	-.45	-.16	.59	.36	.38	.31	.36	.14	.24	.23	-				
Family relations	17	-.15	-.38	-.17	-.27	.02	-.33	.19	.48	.56	.38	.47	.48	.08	.17	.33	.45	-			
Education for children	18	-.29	-.47	-.09	-.34	-.10	-.42	-.21	.39	.43	.28	.22	.53	-.02	.17	.24	.40	.68	-		
Future of children	19	-.22	-.34	-.09	-.31	-.17	-.49	-.19	.43	.65	.53	.46	.49	-.03	.28	.29	.28	.48	.83	-	
Social relations	20	-.18	-.32	-.29	-.46	-.09	-.47	-.20	.39	.49	.41	.35	.49	.03	.21	.34	.50	.63	.67	.52	-
Leisure	21	-.39	-.39	-.18	-.27	-.05	-.48	-.13	.44	.48	.35	.39	.45	.05	.19	.34	.38	.53	.57	.53	.88
Resources																					
Employment	22	.07	.21	.21	.22	.16	.36	.01	-.42	-.61	-.85	-.15	-.36	-.02	-.19	-.24	-.38	-.44	-.27	-.33	-.37
Spouse employment	23	-.12	.04	-.04	.09	.13	.06	-.04	-.16	-.14	-.25	-.23	-.09	-.01	-.15	-.03	-.04	.05	.23	-.07	-.03
Apartment owner	24	.21	.00	.34	.18	.05	.03	.27	-.15	-.31	-.23	-.71	-.23	-.23	-.11	-.19	-.09	-.15	.18	.01	-.10
Income	25	-.01	.15	.21	.27	.01	.28	.07	-.32	-.47	-.54	-.47	-.29	-.35	-.20	-.21	-.20	-.15	-.13	-.07	-.14
Education	26	.21	.22	-.01	.14	.03	.40	-.06	-.34	-.23	-.23	-.13	.01	-.36	-.24	-.08	-.20	-.15	-.13	-.12	-.02
Hebrew language	27	.28	.12	.23	.18	-.03	.16	.06	-.22	-.27	-.41	-.07	-.18	-.08	-.40	-.31	-.26	-.20	-.20	-.24	-.37
Family help	28	.26	-.01	-.05	-.05	.09	.11	-.08	-.32	-.08	-.04	-.10	-.05	-.03	-.02	-.01	-.11	-.16	.04	-.03	-.02
Friends help	29	-.01	-.07	-.11	-.25	-.06	-.11	-.04	.08	-.01	-.14	-.03	.09	.06	-.04	.04	.02	.03	.24	.07	-.19
Formal agency	30	-.21	-.04	.03	.03	.00	.05	.11	.11	.09	.00	-.16	-.05	.08	-.13	-.16	.08	.10	.16	.13	.14
Informal agency	31	-.06	-.19	.01	-.37	-.27	-.28	.41	.32	.18	-.02	.08	.28	-.04	.24	.16	.34	.15	.37	.06	.47
Spouse support	32	.12	.07	.00	.12	.06	.29	.13	-.22	-.25	-.23	-.20	-.18	-.24	-.12	-.12	-.30	-.41	.01	-.06	-.10
Relatives support	33	.04	-.06	.04	-.05	.11	-.03	.03	-.10	-.05	-.07	-.15	-.10	.05	-.02	-.01	-.05	-.14	-.01	-.03	.01
Friends support	34	.14	-.03	-.05	-.14	.01	.02	-.12	-.05	-.01	.02	.03	.06	.00	-.01	.15	-.05	.19	.00	.02	-.16
Meet friends	35	.38	.11	-.11	.07	-.03	.18	-.15	-.24	-.15	-.10	-.03	-.12	-.04	-.23	-.05	-.25	.06	-.26	-.20	-.38
Veteran friends	36	.20	-.02	-.14	-.06	.02	.05	-.06	.23	.36	.43	.18	.27	-.14	.25	.16	.17	.20	.05	.31	.28
Psychologist support	37	-.38	-.56	-.24	-.28	.12	-.24	.14	.31	.28	.23	.23	.20	-.13	.13	-.06	.30	.19	.24	.25	.21
Societal support	38	.07	.08	.20	.41	.29	.41	.16	-.33	-.19	-.23	-.28	-.16	-.07	-.33	-.29	-.27	-.16	-.10	-.16	-.27
Catalysts																					
Religious	39	-.01	-.01	.33	.07	-.15	-.10	.30	.06	.00	-.07	-.05	.04	.02	.08	-.08	-.06	-.25	-.01	-.02	-.17
Jewish identity	40	.06	-.03	.58	.16	.20	.09	.23	-.02	.04	.01	-.05	.05	-.29	-.10	-.18	-.13	-.13	.12	.04	-.23
Zionist identity	41	.00	-.02	.74	.27	.24	.19	.19	-.07	-.03	-.12	-.10	-.03	-.22	-.22	-.14	-.17	-.12	.01	.00	-.21
Collective orientation	42	-.05	-.02	.22	-.09	.03	-.01	.03	.06	.07	.04	.00	.19	-.05	-.04	.05	.12	.19	.02	.02	.12
Favor immigration	43	-.02	.28	.26	.18	.22	.43	.08	-.09	-.08	-.07	-.16	.06	-.18	-.02	-.04	.03	.08	-.06	-.07	.17
Support immigration	44	-.15	.05	.08	-.04	.15	.15	-.02	-.03	-.06	-.02	-.12	.03	-.17	.02	-.03	.04	-.07	-.06	.06	.15

```
-.06   -
 .05  .50   -
-.03  .36  .05   -
-.09  .68  .55  .54   -
-.09  .26  .26 -.03  .22   -
-.44  .50  .40 -.06  .18  .10   -
-.05  .16  .11 -.11 -.07  .20  .18   -
-.14  .13 -.10 -.08 -.15 -.04  .11  .19   -
 .18 -.02  .26  .10  .15 -.04 -.15 -.40 -.14   -
 .26  .07 -.42  .25 -.18  .02  .24  .15  .64  .26   -
-.23  .10  .12  .30  .28  .18  .19  .31  .07  .07  .09   -
 .07 -.02  .13  .00 -.14  .13 -.05  .45  .22  .00  .16  .17   -
-.10  .03 -.10 -.31 -.19  .23  .02  .19  .41 -.13 -.03 -.19  .27   -
-.34  .03  .02 -.38 -.08  .06  .23  .17  .28 -.15 -.23 -.03  .07  .50   -
 .33 -.33 -.21 -.04 -.21  .38 -.75 -.21 -.03  .26  .04 -.10 -.04  .03 -.15   -
 .20 -.27  .17 -.08 -.22 -.21  .07 -.03  .20  .35  .64  .05  .30  .11 -.18 -.18   -
-.29  .10 -.15  .01  .04  .12  .16  .28  .08  .07  .00  .11  .06  .16  .22  .04 -.02   -

-.08  .01 -.32  .16  .00 -.11  .12 -.08  .06 -.13  .66 -.01 -.05 -.20 -.20 -.12 -.40  .09   -
-.11  .17 -.20  .13 -.02 -.09  .07 -.08 -.01 -.09  .17 -.02  .00 -.06 -.13  .04 -.02  .12  .51   -
-.16 -.10 -.20  .13  .06 -.06  .25 -.04 -.06 -.06 -.05  .02  .09  .07  .00 -.17  .07  .11  .38  .71   -
 .13 -.12 -.21  .03 -.16 -.04  .03 -.04  .00 -.05  .20 -.27  .02  .04 -.04  .15  .06  .06  .17  .16  .23   -
 .11 -.10 -.16  .13  .07  .30 -.43 -.10 -.05  .04  .08 -.08 -.06 -.01 -.21  .61  .03  .19 -.10  .16  .11  .34   -
 .08 -.17 -.06  .01 -.04  .18 -.21  .05  .01 -.07 -.13 -.08 -.02  .14 -.04  .39  .15  .04 -.13  .16  .03  .16  .45   -
```

Appendix E

Correlations (μ_2) among Components of the Readjustment Process: Immigrants

VARIABLE	#	1	2	3	4	5	6	7	8	9	10	11	12	13	14	15	16	17	18	19	20
Health	1	-																			
Readjustment	2	.68	-																		
Integration																					
Israeli identity	3	-.11	.12	-																	
Perceived acknowledg.	4	.06	.20	.67	-																
Positivity of society	5	-.06	.30	.59	.60	-															
Potency	6	.26	.50	.48	.57	.52	-														
Acknowledgement	7	-.05	.00	.32	.49	.57	.46	-													
Demands																					
Economic helplessnes	8	-.03	-.17	-.31	-.47	-.22	-.49	-.12	-												
Economic condition	9	.13	-.19	-.33	-.45	-.36	-.47	-.41	.46	-											
Job/employment	10	.23	.04	-.44	-.52	-.33	-.09	-.29	.36	.66	-										
Dwelling	11	-.24	-.17	-.26	-.32	-.21	-.33	-.18	.24	.59	.34	-									
Contact w. bureauc.	12	-.11	-.38	-.25	-.40	-.27	-.46	.01	.20	.43	.20	.40	-								
Underutiliz. of skills	13	-.29	-.05	-.32	-.28	-.15	-.36	-.24	.21	.21	.74	.14	.03	-							
Know oblig's/entit's	14	-.32	-.29	-.16	-.20	-.30	-.41	-.23	.03	.27	.23	.20	.24	.38	-						
Unfamil. w. bureauc.	15	-.08	-.08	-.13	-.18	-.19	-.31	-.19	.16	.34	.15	.15	.33	.11	.63	-					
Emotional isolation	16	-.03	-.29	-.39	-.38	-.28	-.46	-.12	.61	.32	.28	.15	.21	-.02	.17	.27	-				
Family relations	17	-.05	-.35	-.12	-.13	-.19	-.32	-.02	.26	.32	.16	.11	.30	-.12	.12	.14	.46	-			
Educat'n for children	18	.03	-.47	-.11	-.18	-.15	-.24	.16	.23	.21	.35	.01	.26	.04	.06	.08	.18	.69	-		
Future of children	19	.09	-.33	-.24	-.42	-.24	-.30	.02	.30	.46	.52	.23	.28	.15	.23	.12	.27	.40	.82	-	
Social relations	20	-.04	-.37	-.32	-.35	-.09	-.36	.03	.56	.37	.31	.19	.40	-.03	.09	.24	.66	.65	.41	.39	-
Leisure	21	-.03	-.33	-.41	-.38	-.43	-.44	-.29	.26	.51	.45	.19	.36	.39	.31	.28	.32	.35	.33	.46	.61
Resources																					
Employment	22	.31	.25	.00	.30	.23	.33	.13	-.22	-.48	-.76	-.34	-.40	.34	-.22	-.14	-.25	.10	.18	.00	-.34
Spouse employment	23	-.55	.21	-.24	.05	.08	.17	.04	-.11	-.17	.41	-.41	-.27	-.24	-.14	-.20	-.11	.07	.45	.41	-.36
Apartment owner	24	.28	.00	.11	.21	-.15	.21	.03	-.16	-.34	-.11	-.95	-.32	.09	-.18	-.13	-.10	.18	.06	-.09	-.03
Income	25	.34	-.06	.14	.10	.32	.15	-.26	-.36	-.20	-.34	-.20	-.43	-.34	-.27	-.29	.09	.22	.23	-.31	
Education	26	.30	.04	-.31	-.27	-.37	-.22	-.24	.20	.23	.43	.13	.08	-.05	-.16	-.11	-.05	.27	.35	.28	.13
Hebrew language	27	.55	.34	.06	.04	.02	.37	.06	.12	-.12	.20	-.27	-.15	-.36	-.43	-.16	.05	.11	.24	.16	.22
Family help	28	.08	.00	-.10	.02	.03	.12	.02	-.12	-.16	.05	-.21	-.07	-.04	.01	-.05	.08	.01	.05	.02	-.17
Friends help	29	.08	.00	-.07	-.01	-.03	.09	.06	.00	-.11	-.04	-.32	-.01	-.33	-.05	-.16	.11	.17	.12	.14	.01
Formal agency	30	.01	.03	.21	.18	.23	.19	.14	-.24	-.17	-.18	-.16	-.21	-.07	-.28	-.21	-.23	-.14	-.13	-.11	-.23
Informal agency	31	-.07	-.22	-.11	-.17	-.24	-.09	.14	-.08	.22	.07	.16	.08	.25	.01	-.10	.05	.27	.04	.30	-.24
Spouse support	32	.02	.03	.00	-.07	-.05	.03	-.14	-.19	-.02	-.01	-.02	-.20	-.01	-.14	-.23	-.52	-.31	.06	.21	-.37
Relatives support	33	-.10	-.07	.17	.09	.02	.13	.08	-.20	-.17	-.04	-.02	-.11	-.04	-.02	-.14	-.17	.09	-.15	-.27	-.10
Friends support	34	.02	.00	-.05	.14	.12	.18	.19	.09	-.21	-.03	-.17	-.10	-.05	-.25	-.18	.05	.27	.05	-.10	.02
Meet friends	35	.07	.11	.26	.20	.09	.35	.25	-.33	-.32	-.14	-.11	-.19	-.16	-.17	-.18	-.28	.00	.07	-.09	-.23
Veteran friends	36	-.11	-.03	-.49	-.41	-.28	-.27	-.32	.05	.30	.25	.31	.02	.47	.21	.22	.07	-.03	-.07	.08	-.10
Psychological support	37	-.37	-.71	-.05	-.19	-.36	-.24	-.30	.33	.46	.24	.27	-.22	.07	.31	.10	.43	.55	.33	.33	.35
Societal support	38	.15	.13	.53	.65	.63	.42	.35	-.35	-.22	-.34	-.18	-.28	-.37	-.22	-.09	-.19	.13	.09	-.14	-.05
Catalysts																					
Religious	39	.08	-.23	.58	.25	.32	.28	.31	-.10	-.25	-.20	-.12	-.18	.09	-.13	-.22	-.21	-.33	-.21	-.28	-.24
Jewish identity	40	-.19	.06	.75	.43	.50	.16	.23	-.13	-.23	-.46	-.22	-.07	-.38	-.13	-.13	-.23	-.11	-.05	-.26	-.18
Zionist identity	41	-.08	.09	.74	.42	.48	.27	.41	-.11	-.30	-.29	-.22	-.05	-.14	-.25	-.24	-.04	.14	-.11	-.05	
Collective orientation	42	-.24	-.03	.08	-.01	.04	-.09	.01	.01	.08	.07	.12	-.03	.17	.23	.04	.01	-.15	-.13	.08	-.26
Favor immigration	43	-.34	-.17	-.29	-.27	-.15	-.22	-.12	.15	.23	.09	.29	.15	.01	.18	.21	.15	.04	.01	.11	.18
Support immigration	44	-.05	-.07	-.03	.00	-.01	-.07	-.14	-.10	.09	.01	.40	.13	.09	.19	.17	-.11	.19	.16	.04	.14

21	22	23	24	25	26	27	28	29	30	31	32	33	34	35	36	37	38	39	40	41	42	43	44
-.30	-																						
.01	.54	-																					
-.03	.37	.36	-																				
-.22	.77	.83	.45	-																			
.29	-.30	.06	-.16	.14	-																		
-.13	.41	.60	.34	.54	.22	-																	
-.22	.16	.19	.28	.09	-.08	.19	-																
-.14	.05	.32	.20	.24	-.27	.05	.34	-															
-.22	.29	.03	.33	.31	-.11	-.05	-.26	-.02	-														
-.08	.62	.32	.45	.48	.54	.40	.39	.32	.18	-													
-.06	.21	-.08	.23	.32	.25	-.15	-.04	-.05	.11	.01	-												
-.06	-.17	.04	-.06	-.09	.04	-.06	.37	-.04	.03	.20	.02	-											
-.14	.10	.27	-.04	.07	-.03	.12	.10	.33	.26	.14	-.32	.13	-										
-.34	.05	.02	.04	.06	.04	.14	.16	.18	.15	.09	-.01	.22	.33	-									
.29	-.09	.00	-.33	-.16	.21	-.46	-.10	-.31	-.08	-.05	.03	.11	.00	-.11	-								
.38	.09	.30	.02	-.15	.48	-.18	.04	.47	-.01	.15	-.10	.08	.37	.00	-.18	-							
-.09	.16	.06	.07	.15	-.16	.09	.01	.03	.24	-.03	.08	.10	.03	.22	-.30	.40	-						
-.32	.15	-.03	.14	.05	-.35	-.03	.05	-.09	.20	-.09	.06	.05	-.12	-.05	-.35	.08	.24	-					
-.24	.04	-.27	.14	-.11	-.19	-.14	-.07	-.13	.03	-.31	-.05	.05	-.12	-.06	-.35	-.21	.29	.57	-				
-.41	.33	-.13	.18	.04	-.29	.16	.02	.03	.34	-.24	-.11	.05	.18	.15	-.47	-.11	.32	.63	.63	-			
.09	-.15	-.26	-.06	-.11	-.25	-.25	.00	-.11	-.04	-.08	.05	-.04	-.13	-.04	.03	.16	-.08	.18	.10	.11	-		
.06	-.25	-.15	-.33	-.22	-.11	-.25	.12	.02	-.33	-.16	-.08	.10	-.07	-.17	.22	-.16	-.25	-.01	-.04	-.19	.26	-	
.11	.19	-.05	-.45	.02	-.07	-.05	-.11	.08	.05	-.11	.01	-.05	.00	-.08	.06	.06	.10	-.05	-.03	.00	.06	.10	-

Bibliography

Aaronson, A. M. 1984. "Southeast Asian refugees in Rhode Island." *Rhode Island Medical Journal* 67:309.

Achanfuo-Yeboah, D. 1993. "Grounding a theory on African migration in recent data on Ghana." *International Sociology* 8:215-26.

Adler, S. 1977. "Maslow's need hierarchy and the adjustment of immigrants." *International Migration Review* 11(4):441-51.

Agarwal, V. B., and D. R. Winkler. 1984. "Migration of professional manpower to the United States." *Southern Economic Journal* 50(3):814-30.

Alma, W. 1986. "Psycho-social problems of migrants." In *Migration and Health*, edited by M. Colledge, H. A. van Geuns, and P. G. Svensson, pp. 187-95. Copenhagen: World Health Organization, Regional Office for Europe.

Antonovsky, A. 1972. "Breakdown: A needed fourth step in the conceptual framework armamentarium of modern medicine." *Social Science and Medicine* 6(5):537-44.

———. 1979. *Health, Stress, and Coping*. San Francisco: Jossey-Bass Publishers.

Antonovsky, A., and A. D. Katz. 1979. *From the Golden to the Promised Land*. Jerusalem: Academic Press.

Anumonye, A. 1970. *African Students in an Alien Culture*. New York: Black Academy Press.

Aviram, U., Z. Ben-Sira, I. Shoham, and I. Stern. 1984. "Bodily complaints with no identified organic cause among women: Psychosocial resources as buffers." In *Social Psychiatry*, edited by V. Hudolin, pp. 821-41. New York: Plenum Press.

Bach, R. L., and J. B. Bach. 1980. "Employment patterns of Southeast Asian refugees." *Monthly Labor Review* October 103(10):31-38.

Bach, R. L., J. B. Bach, and T. Triplett. 1982. "The flotilla 'entrants': Latest and most controversial." *Cuban Studies* 11:29-48.

Back, K. W. 1980. "Uprooting and self-image: Catastrophe and continuity." In *Uprooting and Development*, edited by G. V. Coelho and P. I. Ahmed, pp. 117-30. New York: Plenum Press.

Bagley, C. 1971. "Mental illness in immigrant minorities in London." *Journal of Bio-social Science* 3(4):449–59.

Banchevska, R. 1981. "Uprooting and settling: The transplanted family." In *Strangers in the World*, edited by L. Eitinger and D. Schwarz, pp. 107–31. Bern: Hans Huber.

Bar-Yosef, R., and Y. Varsher. 1977. *A Follow-up Study on the Professional Absorption of Engineers.* Jerusalem: Hebrew University, Institute for Work and Welfare (Hebrew).

Barret, K. C., and J. J. Campos. 1991. "A diacritical function approach to emotions and coping." In *Life-Span Developmental Psychology: Perspectives on Stress and Coping*, edited by E. M. Cummings, A. L. Greene, and K. H. Karraker, pp. 21–41. Hillsdale, NJ: Lawrence Erlbaum Associates.

Barth, F. 1969. "Introduction." In *Ethnic Groups and Boundaries*, edited by F. Barth, pp. 9–38. Boston: Little, Brown and Company.

Bartram, D. 1980. "Do you really need your null hypothesis?" *British Psychological Society Bulletin* 33:318–21.

Bavington, J., and A. Majid. 1986. "Psychiatric services for ethnic minority groups." In *Transcultural Psychiatry*, edited by J. L. Cox, pp. 270–90. London: Croom Helm.

Beiser, M. 1985. "A study of depression among traditional Africans, urban North Americans and Southeast Asian refugees." In *Culture and Depression*, edited by A. Kleinman and B. Good. Berkeley and Los Angeles: University of California Press.

Ben-Barak, S. 1989. "Attitudes toward work and home of Soviet immigrant women." In *The Soviet Man in an Open Society*, edited by T. R. Horowitz, pp. 115–22. Lanham, MD: University Press of America.

Ben-Gurion, D. 1969. *The Renewed State of Israel.* Tel-Aviv: Am Oved (Hebrew).

Ben-Sira, Z. 1979. "A scale of psychological distress." *Research Communications in Psychology, Psychiatry and Behavior* 4:337–56.

———. 1981. "The structure of readjustment of the disabled: An additional perspective on rehabilitation." *Social Science and Medicine* 15A:565–80.

———. 1982a. "The scale of psychological distress (SPD): Cross-population invariance and validity." *Research Communications in Psychology, Psychiatry and Behavior* 7: 329–41.

———. 1982b. "Life change and health: An additional perspective on the structure of coping." *Stress* 3:18–28.

———. 1982c. "The structure of stratification: A revised bimodal approach." *Quality and Quantity* 16:171–96.

———. 1983a. "Loss, stress and readjustment: The structure of coping with bereavement and disability." *Social Science and Medicine* 17(21):1619–1632.

———. 1983b. "Social integration of the disabled: Power struggle or enhancement of individual coping capacities." *Social Science and Medicine,* 17:1011–60.

———. 1984. "Chronic illness, stress and coping. *Social Science and Medicine* 8(9): 725-736.

———. 1985. "Potency: A stress-buffering link in the coping-stress-disease relationship." *Social Science and Medicine* 21(4):397–406.

———. 1986a. "Disability, stress, and readjustment: The function of the professional's latent goals and affective behavior in rehabilitation." *Social Science and Medicine* 23(1):43–55.

———. 1986b. "The latent functions of welfare and need-satisfaction of the disadvantaged." *Journal of Sociology and Social Welfare*, 13(2):418–44.

———. 1987. "The stress bounding capacity of the physician's affective behavior: An additional dimension of health promotion." In *Human Stress: Current Selected Research*, edited by J.H. Humphrey, pp. 15–36. New York: AMS Press.

———. 1988a. *Alienated Identification in Israeli Society*. Jerusalem: Magnes Press, The Hebrew University (Hebrew).

———. 1988b. *Politics and Primary Medical Care: Dehumanization and Overutilization*. Aldershot, England: Gower.

———. 1989. "Potency: A readjustment-promoting link in the rehabilitation of disabled persons." *Sociology of Health and Illness* 11(1):41–61.

———. 1991. *Regression, Stress, and Readjustment in Aging*. New York: Praeger.

———. 1993. *Zionism at the Close of the Twentieth Century: A Dilemma*. Lewiston, NY: The Edwin Mellen Press.

Ben-Sira, Z., and R. Eliezer. 1990. "The structure of readjustment after heart attack." *Social Science and Medicine* 30(5):523–36.

Bernstein, D. 1979. "Conflict and protest in Israeli society." *Megamot* 25:65–79 (Hebrew).

Berry, J. W. 1991. "Refugee adaptation in settlement countries: An overview with an emphasis on primary prevention." In *Refugee Children: Theory, Research, and Services*, edited by F. L. Ahearn and J. L. Athey, pp. 20–38. Baltimore and London: The Johns Hopkins University Press.

Bieliauskas, L. A. 1982. *Stress and its Relationship to Health and Illness*. Boulder, CO: Westview Press.

Blau, P. M. 1977. *Inequality and Heterogeneity: A Primitive Theory of Social Structure*. New York: The Free Press.

Bouvier, L. F., and R. N. Gardner. 1986. "Immigration to the United States: The unfinished story." *Population Bulletin* 41(4):3–50.

Bridges, K., and D. P. Goldberg. 1985. "Somatic presentation of DSM-I psychiatric disorders in primary care." *Journal of Psychosomatic Research* 29:627–39.

Brody, E. B. 1970. "Migration and adaptation: The nature of the problem." In *Behavior in New Environments: Adaptation of Migrant Populations*, edited by E. B. Brody, pp. 13–22. Beverly Hills, CA: Sage Publications.

Brown, J. 1985. "An introduction to the uses of facet theory." In *Facet Theory: Approaches to Social Research*, edited by D. V. Canter, pp. 26–57. New York: Springer-Verlag.

Brown, M. C., and B. D. Warner. 1992. "Immigrants, urban politics and policing in 1900." *American Sociological Review* 57(3):293–305.

Brownstein, R. 1993. "Polarization marks debate on immigration policy." *Los Angeles Times* November 30:A1, A20.

Brownstein, R., and R. Simon. 1993. "Hospitality turns into hostility." *Los Angeles Times* November 14:A1, A6–A7.

Brym, R. J. 1992. "The emigration potential of Czechoslovakia, Hungary, Lithuania, Poland and Russia: Recent survey results." *International Sociology* 7(4):387–95.

Budzynski, T. H., and K. E. Peffer. 1980. "Biofeedback training." In *Handbook on Stress and Anxiety: Contemporary Knowledge, Theory, and Treatment*, edited by I. L. Kutash, L. B. Schlesinger, and Associates, pp. 413–27. San Francisco: Jossey-Bass.

Burawoy, M. 1976. "The functions and reproduction of migrant labor: Comparative material from southern Africa and the United States." *American Journal of Sociology* 81(5):1050–87.

Burke, K. 1969. *A Rhetoric of Motives*. Berkeley and Los Angeles: University of California Press.

Caldwell, J. C. 1969. *African Rural-Urban Migration: The Movement to Ghana's Towns*. New York: Columbia University Press.

Campbell, A., P. E. Converse, and W. L. Rodgers. 1976. *The Quality of American Life*. New York: Russell Sage.

Cannon, W. B. 1929. *Bodily Changes in Pain, Hunger, Fear and Rage*. New York: Appleton and Company.

Canter, D. 1985a. "How to be a facet researcher." In *Facet Theory: Approaches to Social Research*, edited by D. V. Canter, pp. 265–75. New York: Springer-Verlag.

―――. 1985b. "Introduction." In *Facet Theory: Approaches to Social Research*, edited by D. V. Canter, pp. 4–13. New York: Springer-Verlag.

Carpenter, L., and I. F. Brockington. 1980. "A study of mental illness in Asians, West Indians and Africans living in Manchester." *British Journal of Psychiatry* 137: 206–11.

Carver, R. O. 1978. "The case against statistical significance testing." *Harvard Educational Review* 48(3):378–99.

Cassel, J. 1975. "Studies in hypertension in migrants." In *Epidemiology and the Control of Hypertension*, edited by O. Paul, pp. 41–61. New York: Straton.

Castles, S., and G. Kosack. 1973. *Immigrant Workers and Class Structure in Western Europe*. London: Oxford University Press.

Chalmers, B. E. 1981. "A selective review of stress: Some cognitive approaches taken a step further." *Current Psychological Reviews* 1:325–44.

Cheung, F., and M. Dobkin de Rios. 1982. "Recent trends in the study of the mental health of Chinese immigrants to the United States." *Research in Race and Ethnic Relations* 3:145–63.

Chiswick, B. R. 1978. "The effect of Americanization on the earnings of foreign-born men." *Journal of Political Economy* 86(5):897–921.

Cochrane, R. 1985. "Schizophrenic and paranoid disorder in migrants to England." Paper presented at the Second Annual Symposium on Paranoid Disorders, Birmingham, AL.

Cochrane, R., and M. Stopes-Roe. 1977. "Psychological and social adjustment of Asian immigrants to Britain: A community survey." *Social Psychiatry* 12(4): 195–206.

Cohen, E. 1980. "The Black Panthers and Israeli society." In *Studies of Israeli Society*, Vol. 1, *Migration, Ethnicity and Community*, edited by E. Krausz, pp. 147–64. New Brunswick, NJ: Transaction Books.

Cohen, F. 1991. "Measurement of coping." In *Stress and Coping: An Anthology*, 3rd edition, edited by A. Monat and R. S. Lazarus, pp. 228–44. New York: Columbia University Press.

Cohen, J., and C. Cordoba (eds.). 1982. *Psychological Factors in Cancer*. New York: Raven.

Cohon, J. D., Jr. 1981. "Psychological adaptation and dysfunction among refugees." *International Migration Review* 15(1-2):255–75.

Cooper, C. L. 1983. *Stress Research: Issues for the Eighties*. New York: J. Wiley.

———. (ed.) 1984. *Psychosocial Stress and Cancer*. New York: J. Wiley.

Coser, L. 1964. *The Functions of Social Conflict*. New York: The Free Press.

Cox, J. 1976. "Psychiatric assessment of the immigrant patient." *British Journal of Hospital Medicine*, July:38–40.

Cox, T. 1978. *Stress*. Baltimore: University Park Press.

Coyne, J. C., and K. Holroyd. 1982. "Stress, coping and illness: A transactional perspective." In *Handbook of Clinical Health Psychology*, edited by T. Millon, C. Green, and R. Meagher. New York: Plenum Press.

Creed, F. H. 1987. "Immigrant stress." *Stress Medicine* 3:185–92.

Creed, F. H., and M. Carstairs. 1982. "Problems arising with patients from other cultures." In *Medicine and Psychiatry: A Practical Approach*, edited by F. H. Creed and J. M. Pfeffer, pp. 171–85. London: Pittman.

DaCosta-Bagot, P. 1985. *Culture Change, Ethnicity and Socio-Cultural Context: Acculturative Stress among Jamaican Immigrants*. Unpublished Ph.D. dissertation. Los Angeles: University of California.

David, H. P. 1970. "Involuntary international migration: Adaptation of refugees." In *Behavior in New Environments: Adaptation of Migrant Populations*, edited by E. B. Brody, pp. 73–95. Beverly Hills, CA: Sage Publications.

Dean, G., D. Walsh, H. Downing, and E. Shelley. 1981. "First admissions of native-born and immigrants to psychiatric hospitals in South East England 1976." *British Journal of Psychiatry* 139:506–12.

DeJong, G. F., and J. T. Fawcett. 1981. "Multidisciplinary framework and models of migration decision making." In *Migration Decision Making*, edited by G. F. DeJong and R. W. Gardener, pp. 13–58. New York: Pergamon Press.

DeJong, G. F., and R. W. Gardner (eds.). 1981. *Migration Decision Making*. New York: Pergamon Press.

DeVos, G. 1980. "Growing up within a culture." In *People in Culture: A Survey of Cultural Anthropology*, edited by I. Rossi, pp. 170–208. New York: Praeger.

Dohrenwend, B. S., and B. P. Dohrenwend. 1970. "Class and race as status related sources of stress." In *Social Stress*, edited by S. Levine and N. A. Scotch, pp. 111–40. New York: Aldine de Gruyter.

———. 1974. "A brief historical introduction to research on stressful life events." In *Stressful Life Events: Their Nature and Effects*, edited by B.S. Dohrenwend and B. P. Dohrenwend, pp. 1–5. New York: J. Wiley.

Editorial (unsigned). 1993. "A few points here, a few there—The immigration debate continues." *Daily Bruin* (UCLA), November 15:16.

Eisenbruch, M. 1988. "The mental health of refugee children and their cultural development." *International Migration Review* 22(2):282–300.

Eisenstadt, S. N. 1954. *The Absorption of Immigrants*. London: Routledge and Kegan Paul.

———. 1956. *From Generation to Generation: Age Groups and Social Structure*. Glencoe, IL: The Free Press.

———. 1967. "Israeli identity: Problems in the development of the collective identity of an ideological society." *Annals of the American Academy of Political and Social Science* 370 (March):116–23.

———. 1967. *Israeli Society: Background, Development and Problems*. Jerusalem: Magnes Press, The Hebrew University (Hebrew).

————. 1980. "Introduction: Some reflections on the study of ethnicity." In *Studies of Israeli Society*, Vol 1., *Migration, Ethnicity and Community*, edited by E. Krausz, pp. 1-4. New Brunswick, NJ: Transaction Books.

————. 1985. *The Transformation of Israeli Society*. Boulder, CO: Westview Press.

Eitinger, L. 1960. "The symptomatology of mental illness among refugees in Norway." *Journal of Mental Sciences* 106:947-66.

Eitinger, L., and D. Schwarz (eds.). 1981. *Strangers in the World*. Bern: Hans Huber.

Emerson, R.M. 1972a. "Exchange theory, part I: A psychological basis for social exchange." In *Sociological Theories in Progress*, Vol. 2, edited by J. Berger, M. Zelditch, Jr., and B. Anderson, pp. 38-57. Boston: Houghton-Mifflin.

————. 1972b. "Exchange theory, part II: Exchange relations and network structures." In *Sociological Theories in Progress*, Vol. 2, edited by J. Berger, M. Zelditch, Jr., and B. Anderson, pp. 58-87. Boston: Houghton-Mifflin.

Erikson, E. H. 1968. *Identity: Youth and Crisis*. New York: W. W. Norton.

Espino, C.M. 1991. "Trauma and adaptation: The case of Central American children." In *Refugee Children: Theory, Research, and Services*, edited by R. L. Ahearn and J. L. Athey, pp. 106-24. Baltimore and London: Johns Hopkins University Press.

Farago, U. 1978. "The ethnic identity of Russian immigrant students in Israel." *The Jewish Journal of Sociology* 20(2):115-27.

————. 1979. "Changes in the ethnic identity of Russian immigrant students in Israel." *The Jewish Journal of Sociology* 21:37-52.

Folkman, S., and R. S. Lazarus. 1991. "Coping and emotion." In *Stress and Coping*, 3rd edition, edited by A. Monat and R. S. Lazarus, pp. 207-27. New York: Columbia University Press.

Furnham, A., and S. Bochner. 1986. *Culture Shock: Psychological Reactions to Unfamiliar Environments*. New York: Methuen.

Gitelman, Z. 1989. "Changing political orientations and attitudes." In *The Soviet Man in an Open Society*, edited by T. R. Horowitz, pp. 259-70. Lanham, MD: University Press of America.

Gitelman, Z., and D. Naveh. 1976. "Elite accommodation and organizational effectiveness: The case of immigrant absorption in Israel." *The Journal of Politics* 38(4): 963-86.

Goffman, E. 1959. *The Presentation of Self in Everyday Life*. New York: Doubleday.

Gold, S. J. 1989. "Differential adjustment among new immigrant family members." *Journal of Contemporary Ethnography* 17:408-34.

Gordon, M. M. 1964. *Assimilation in American Life: The Role of Race, Religion, and National Origins*. New York: Oxford University Press.

Gottesmann, M. 1988. "Introduction." In *Cultural Transition: The Case of Immigrant Youth*, edited by M. Gottesmann, pp. 7-10. Jerusalem: Magnes Press, The Hebrew University.

Granovetter, M. S. 1973. "The Strength of Weak Ties." *American Journal of Sociology* 78(6):1360-80.

Grant, I., G. C. Kyle, A. Teichman, and J. Mendels. 1974. "Recent life events and diabetes in adults." *Psychosomatic Medicine* 36(2):121-28.

"Great Divide: Immigration in the 1990s." 1993. *Los Angeles Times*, 14-30 November.

Grove, C. L., and I. Torbiorn. 1985. "A new conceptualization of intercultural adjustment and the goals of training." *International Journal of Intercultural Relations* 9: 205-33.

Guttman, L. 1977. "What is not what in statistics." *The Statistician* 26:81–107.

Haberkon, G. 1981. "The migration decision-making process: Some social-psychological considerations." In *Migration Decision Making*, edited by G. F. DeJong and R. W. Gardener, pp. 13–58. New York: Pergamon Press.

Hallowell, A. I. 1955. *Culture and Experience*. New York: Schocken.

Handlin, O. 1951. *The Uprooted: The Epic Story of the Great Migrations that Made the American People*. Boston: Little, Brown.

Hanegbi, R., and S. Menuchin-Itzigson. 1988. "Problems of cultural and developmental passage for Ethiopian-Jewish adolescents in an Israeli environment." In *Cultural Transition*, edited by M. Gottesmann, pp. 140–49. Jerusalem: Magnes Press, The Hebrew University.

Harvey, M. E. 1975. "Interregional migration studies in tropical Africa." In *People on the Move*, edited by L. Kosinski and R. M. Prothero, pp. 151–63. London: Methuen and Company Studies on Internal Migration.

Hinkle, L. H. 1970. "The effect of exposure to culture change, social change, and changes in interpersonal relationships on health." In *Social Stress*, edited by S. Levine and N. A. Scotch, pp. 9–44. New York: Aldine de Gruyter.

Hiok-Boon, E. L., L. J. Ihle, and L. Tazume. 1985. "Depression among Vietnamese refugees in a primary care clinic." *American Journal of Medicine* 78:41–44.

Hirsch, B. J. 1979. "Psychological dimensions of social networks: A multimethod analysis." *American Journal of Community Psychology* 7(3):263–77.

Holmes, T. H., and R. H. Rahe. 1967. "The Social Readjustment Rating Scale." *Journal of Psychosomatic Research* 11:213–18.

Homans, G. C. 1974. *Social Behavior: Its Elementary Forms*, revised edition. New York: Harcourt Brace Jovanovich.

Horowitz, R. T. 1979. "Jewish immigrants to Israel: Self-reported powerlessness and alienation among immigrants from the Soviet Union and North America." *Journal of Cross-Cultural Psychology* 10(3):366–74.

Impellizeri, L. 1993. "A city's open arms close as tensions rise." *Los Angeles Times* December 1:A5.

Jensen, M. M. 1981. "Emotional stress and susceptibility to infectious diseases." In *Stress and Cancer*, edited by K. Bammer and B. H. Newberry, pp. 59–70. Toronto: C. J. Hogrefe.

Jones, E.E., and S. J. Korchin. 1982. *Minority Mental Health*. New York: Praeger.

Kahn, R. L., D. M. Wolfe, R. P. Quinn, J. D. Snoek, and R. A. Rosenthal. 1964. *Studies in Role Conflict and Ambiguity*. New York: J. Wiley.

Kaplan, H. B. 1983. "Psychological distress in sociological context: Toward a general theory of psychosocial stress." In *Psychosocial Stress: Trends in Theory and Research*, edited by H. B. Kaplan, pp. 195–264. New York: Academic Press.

Keesing, R. M. 1981. *Cultural Anthropology: A Contemporary Perspective*, 2nd edition. Fort Worth, TX: Holt, Rinehart and Winston.

Kessler, R. C. 1983. "Methodological issues in the study of psychosocial stress." In *Psychosocial Stress: Trends in Theory and Research*, edited by H. B. Kaplan, pp. 267–341. New York: Academic Press.

Kessler, R. C., and P. D. Cleary. 1980. "Social class and psychological distress." *American Sociological Review* 45(3):463–78.

Kiev, A. 1965. "Psychiatric morbidity of West-Indian immigrants in an urban group practice." *British Journal of Psychiatry* 111:51–56.

Kinzie, D. J., and W. D. Sack. 1991. "Severely traumatized Cambodian children: Research findings and clinical implications." In *Refugee Children: Theory, Research, and Services*, edited by F. L. Ahearn and J. L. Athey, pp. 92–105. Baltimore and London: Johns Hopkins University Press.

Klaff, V. Z. 1980. "Residence and integration in Israel: A mosaic of segregated groups." In *Studies in Israeli Society*, Vol. 1, *Migration, Ethnicity and Community*, edited by E. Krausz, pp. 53–71. New Brunswick, NJ: Transaction Books.

Kleinman, A., and J. Kleinman. 1985. "Somatization." In *Culture and Depression*, edited by A. Kleinman and B. Good, pp. 429–90. Berkeley and Los Angeles: University of California Press.

Kobasa, S. C., S. R. Maddi, and S. Courington. 1981. "Personality and constitution as mediators in the stress-illness relationship." *Journal of Health and Social Behavior* 22(4):368–78.

Koranyi, E. K. 1981. "Decline and stress: Immigrant's adaptation in aged population." In *Strangers in the World*, edited by L. Eitinger and D. Schwarz, pp. 220–32. Bern: Hans Huber.

Kraut, A. M. 1994. *Silent Travelers: Germs, Genes and the "Immigrant Menace."* New York: Basic Books.

Kunz, E. F. 1973. "The refugee in flight: Kinetic models and forms of displacement." *International Migration Review* 7(2):125–46.

Kuo, W. 1976. "Theories of migration and mental health: An empirical testing on Chinese Americans." *Social Science and Medicine* 10(6):297–306.

Kuo, W. H., and Y-M. Tsai. 1986. "Social networking, hardiness and immigrants' mental health." *Journal of Health and Social Behavior* 27(2):133–49.

Lambo, T. A. 1967. "Adolescents transplanted from their traditional environment: Problems and lessons out of Africa." *Clinical Pediatrics* 6:438–45.

Langner, T. S. 1962. "A twenty-two item screening score of psychiatric symptoms indicating impairment." *Journal of Health and Human Behavior* 3:269–76.

Lawson, L. H. 1993. "Scorned outsiders of another era." *Los Angeles Times* December 28:B7.

Lazarus, R. S. 1981. "The stress and coping paradigm." In *Models for Clinical Psychopathology*, edited by C. Eisdorfer, D. Cohen, A. Kleinman, and P. Maxim, pp. 177–214. New York: Spectrum Publications.

Lazarus, R. S., and J. B. Cohen. 1977. "Environmental Stress." In *Human Behavior and Environment: Advances in Theory and Research*, Vol. 1, edited by I. Altman and J. F. Wohlwill, pp. 90–127. New York: Plenum Press.

Lazarus, R. S., and S. Folkman. 1984. *Stress, Appraisal and Coping.* New York: Springer Publishing Company.

———. 1991. "The concept of coping." In *Stress and Coping*, 3rd edition, edited by A. Monat and R. S. Lazarus, pp. 189–206. New York: Columbia University Press.

Lee, E. 1966. "A theory of demography." *Demography* 3:45–59.

Leff, J. P., M. Fischer, and A. Bertelsen. 1976. "A cross-national epidemiological study of mania." *British Journal of Psychiatry* 129:428–37.

Lehman-Wilzig, S. 1985. "Hollow at the core: Manifestations of the Israeli ideological decay." *Forum* 54/55:25–32.

Leiper de Monchy, M. 1991. "Recovery and rebuilding: The challenge for refugee children and service providers." In *Refugee Children: Theory, Research, and Services*, edited by F. L. Ahearn and J. L. Athey, pp. 163–80. Baltimore and London: Johns Hopkins University Press.

Levy, S., and L. Guttman. 1974. *The Desire to Remain in Israel*. Jerusalem: The Israel Institute of Applied Social Research (Hebrew).

———. 1976. "Worry, fear and concern differentiated." *Israel Annals of Psychiatry and Related Disciplines* 14(3):211–28.

Lin, K. M. 1986. "Psychopathology and social disruption in refugees." In *Refugee Mental Health in Resettlement Countries*, edited by C.L. Williams, and J. Westermeyer, pp. 61–73. New York: Hemisphere Publishing Company.

Lin, N., R. S. Simeone, W. M. Ensel, and W. Kuo. 1979. "Social support, stressful life events and illness." *Journal of Health and Social Behavior* 20(2):108–19.

Link, B., and B. P. Dohrenwend. 1980. "Formulation of hypotheses about the true prevalence of demoralization." In *Mental Illness in the United States: Epidemiological Estimates*, edited by B. P. Dohrenwend, pp. 114–32. New York: Praeger.

Linton, R. 1936. *The Study of Man: An Introduction*. New York: Appleton-Century Company.

Littlewood, R., and M. Lipsedge. 1981. "Some social and phenomenological characteristics of psychotic immigrants." *Psychological Medicine* 11:289–302.

Lobodzinska, B. 1986. "Post-war immigration in the United States and the State of Minnesota." *International Migration* 24(2):411–39.

Lowry, I.S. 1966. *Migration and Metropolitan Growth: Two Analytical Models*. San Francisco: Chandler Publishing Company.

Lundberg, U., T. Thorell, and E. Lind. 1975. "Life changes and myocardial infarction: Individual differences in life change scaling." *Journal of Psychsomatic Research* 19:27–32.

Magnusson, G., and G. Aurelius. 1980. "Illness behavior and nationality: A Study of Hospital Care Utilization by Immigrants and Natives in a Stockholm District." *Social Science and Medicine* 14A(4):357–62.

Marris, P. 1980. "The uprooting of meaning." In *Uprooting and Development*, edited by G. V. Coelho and P. I. Ahmed, pp. 101–16. New York: Plenum Press.

McFarlane, A. H., G. R. Norman, D. L. Streiner, and R. G. Roy. 1983. "The process of social stress: Stable, reciprocal and mediating relationships." *Journal of Health and Social Behavior* 24(2):160–73.

Mechanic, D. 1976. "Stress, illness, and illness behavior." *Journal of Human Stress* 2(2):2–6.

Meisner, D. M. 1993. "Solving the problem." *Los Angeles Times* November 30:A20.

Melick, M. E. 1978. "Life change and illness: Illness behavior of males in the recovery period of a natural disaster." *Journal of Health and Social Behavior* 19(3):335–42.

Menaghan, E. G. 1983. "Individual coping efforts: Moderators of the relationship between life stress and mental health outcomes." In *Psychosocial Stress: Trends in Theory and Research*, edited by H. B. Kaplan, pp. 157–91. New York: Academic Press.

Merton, R. K. 1968. *Social Theory and Social Structure*, 1968 enlarged edition. New York: The Free Press.

Mirowsky, J., and C. E. Ross. 1989. *Social Causes of Psychological Distress.* New York: Aldine de Gruyter.

Mirsky, J., and F. Kaushinsky. 1989. "Migration and growth: Separation-individuation process in immigrant students in Israel." *Adolescence* 24(95):727–40.

Molm, L. D., T. M. Quist, and P. A. Wisely. 1994. "Imbalanced structures, unfair strategies: Power and justice in social exchange." *American Sociological Review* 59(1):98–121.

Monat, A., and R. S. Lazarus. 1991. "Introduction: Stress and coping—Some current issues and controversies." In *Stress and Coping: An Anthology,* 3rd edition, edited by A. Monat and R.S. Lazarus, pp. 1–15. New York: Columbia University Press.

Murphy, F., and J. W. Brown. 1980. "Life events, psychiatric disturbance and physical illness." *British Journal of Psychiatry* 136:326–38.

Murphy, H. B. M. 1973. "The low rate of hospitalization shown by immigrants to Canada." In *Uprooting and After . . .*, edited by C. A. Zwingman and M. Pfister-Ammende, pp. 221–31. New York: Springer-Verlag.

———. 1977. "Migration, culture and mental health." *Psychological Medicine* 7(4):677–84.

Murphy, J. M. 1977. "War stress and civilian Vietnamese: A study of psychological effects." *Acta Psychiatrica Scandinavica* 56(2):92–108.

Myint, H. 1968. "The underdeveloped countries: A less alarmist view." In *The Brain Drain,* edited by W. Adams, pp. 233–46. New York: Macmillan.

Nann, R. C. 1982. *Uprooting and Surviving.* Dordrecht, Holland: D. Reidel.

Norbeck, J. S. and V. P. Tilden. 1983. "Life stress, social support, and emotional disequilibrium in complications of pregnancy: A prospective multivariate study." *Journal of Health and Social Behavior* 24(1):30–46.

Oh, Myung Jun. 1994. "The key is 'to meet challenges head on'." *Los Angeles Times* January 3:B4.

Oodegaard, O. 1932. "Emigration and insanity." *Acta Psychologica and Neurologica Scandinavia,* Supplement 4.

Palinkas, L. A. 1982. "Ethnicity, identity and mental health: The use of rhetoric in an immigrant Chinese church." *The Journal of Psychoanalytic Anthropology* 5:235–58.

Papajohn, J., and J. P. Spiegel. 1971. "The relationship of culture value orientation change and Rorschach indices of psychological development." *Journal of Cross-Cultural Psychology* 2(3):257–72.

Park, R. E. 1928. "Migration and the Marginal Man." *American Journal of Sociology* 33(3):241–247.

Parkes, C. M. 1971. "Psycho-social transitions: A field for study." *Social Science and Medicine* 5:101–15.

Parsons, T. 1951. *The Social System.* New York: The Free Press.

———. 1975. "Social structure and the symbolic media of interchange." In *Approaches to the Study of Social Structure,* edited by P. M. Blau, pp. 94–120. New York: The Free Press.

Pearlin, L. I. 1983. "Role strains and personal stress." In *Psychosocial Stress: Trends in Theory and Research,* edited by H. B. Kaplan, pp. 3–32. New York: Academic Press.

———. 1991a. "Life strain and psychological stress among adults." In *Stress and Coping: An Anthology,* 3rd edition, edited by A. Monat and R. S. Lazarus, pp. 319-36. New York: Columbia University Press.

————. 1991b. "The study of coping: An overview of problems and directions." In *The Social Context of Coping*, edited by J. Eckenrode, pp. 261-76. New York: Plenum Press.

————. 1993. "The social context of stress." In *Handbook of Stress: Theoretical and Clinical Aspects*, 2nd edition, edited by L. Goldberger and S. Breznitz, pp. 303-35. New York: The Free Press.

Pearlin, L. I., M. A. Lieberman, E. G. Menaghan, and J. T. Mullan. 1981. "The stress process." *Journal of Health and Social Behavior* 22:337-56.

Pearlin, L. I., and C. Schooler. 1978. "The structure of coping." *Journal of Health and Social Behavior* 19:2-21.

Pollock, G. H. 1989. "On migration—Voluntary and coerced." *Annual of Psychoanalysis* 17:145-58.

Portes, A. 1981. "Modes of structural incorporation and present theories of labor immigration." In *Global Trends in Migration: Theory and Research on International Population Movements*, edited by M. M. Kritz, C. B. Keely, and S. M. Tomasi, pp. 279-97. Staten Island, NY: Center for Migration Studies.

Portes, A., D. Kyle, and W. W. Eaton. 1992. "Mental illness and help-seeking behavior among Mariel Cuban and Haitian refugees in South Florida." *Journal of Health and Social Behavior* 33:283-98.

Pryor, R. 1981. "Integrating international and internal migration theories." In *Global Trends in Migration*, edited by M. M. Kritz, C. B. Keely, and S. M. Tomasi, pp. 110-29. Staten Island, NY: Center for Migration Studies.

Rave, A. 1986. "On measures of monotone association." *The American Statistician* 40: 117-23.

Ravenstein, E. G. 1885. "The laws of migration, part I." *Journal of the Royal Statistical Society* 48:167-235.

————. 1886. "The laws of migration, part II." *Journal of the Royal Statistical Society* 52:241-305.

Redfield, R., R. Linton, and M. J. Herskovits. 1936. "Memorandum on the study of acculturation." *American Anthropologist* 38:149-52.

Rosenberg, M. 1979. *Conceiving the Self.* New York: Basic Books.

Rossi, I. (ed.) 1980. *People in Culture.* New York: Praeger.

Rotenstreich, N. 1972. *Tradition and Reality: The Impact of History on Modern Jewish Thought.* New York: Random House.

Rumbaut, R. G. 1985. "Mental heath and the refugee experience: A comparative study of Southeast Asian refugees." In *Southeast Asian Mental Health*, edited by T.C. Owan, pp. 433-86. Rockville, MD: National Institute of Mental Health.

————. 1989. "Portraits, patterns and predictors of the refugee adaptation process." In *Refugees as Immigrants: Cambodians, Laotians and Vietnamese in America*, edited by D. W. Haines, pp. 138-82. Totowa, NJ: Rowman and Littlefield.

————. 1991. "The agony of exile: A study of the migration and adaptation of Indochinese refugee adults and children." In *Refugee Children: Theory, Research and Services*, edited by F. L. Ahearn and J. L. Athey, pp. 53-91. Baltimore and London: Johns Hopkins University Press.

Sarafino, E. P. 1990. *Health Psychology: Biopsychosocial Interactions.* New York: J. Wiley.

Schleifer, S. J., A. H. Schwartz, J. C. Thornton, and S. L. Rosenberg. 1979. "A study of American immigrants to Israel using the SRRQ." *Journal of Psychosomatic Research* 23(4):247–52.

Seeman, M. 1972. "Alienation and engagement." In *The Human Meaning of Social Change*, edited by A. Campbell and P. E. Converse, pp. 467–527. New York: Russell Sage.

Seligman, M. E. P. 1975. *Helplessness: On Depression, Development, and Death.* San Francisco: Freeman.

Selye, H. 1976. *The Stress of Life*, revised edition. New York: McGraw-Hill.

Shin, E. H., and K-S. Chang. 1988. "Peripherization of immigrant professionals: Korean physicians in the United States." *International Migration Review* 22(4):609–26.

Shumsky, A. 1955. *The Clash of Cultures in Israel: A Problem for Education.* New York: Bureau of Publications, Teachers College, Columbia University.

Shuval, J. T. 1962. "Emerging patterns of ethnic strain in Israel." *Social Forces* 40(4):323-30.

———. 1963. *Immigrants on the Threshold.* New York: Atherton Press.

———. 1970. *Social Functions of Medical Practice: Doctor-Patient Relationships in Israel.* San Francisco: Jossey-Bass.

———. 1983. *Newcomers and Colleagues: Soviet Immigrant Physicians in Israel.* Houston: Cap and Gown.

———. 1992. *Social Dimensions of Health: The Israeli Experience.* Westport, CT: Praeger.

Shuval, J. T., E. J. Markus, and J. Dotan. 1975. "Age patterns in the integration of Soviet immigrants in Israel." *The Jewish Journal of Sociology* 71(2):151–63.

Simon, R. J. (ed.) 1985. *New Lives: The Adjustment of Soviet Jewish Immigrants in the United States and Israel.* Lexington, MA: Lexington Books.

Sklar, L. S., and H. Anisman. 1981. "Contributions of stress and coping to cancer development and growth." In *Stress and Cancer*, edited by K. Bammer and B. Newberry, pp. 98-136. Toronto: C. J. Hogrefe.

Slater, Philip. 1970. *The Pursuit of Loneliness: American Culture at the Breaking Point.* Boston: Beacon Press.

Sluzki, C. E. 1979. "Migration and family conflict." *Family Process* 18:381-94.

Smooha, S. 1978. *Israel: Pluralism and Conflict.* London: Routledge and Kegan Paul.

"Soviet Jews: Get Thee to Israel." 1990. *The Economist.* June 9:51-52.

Srole, L. 1956. "Social integration and cohesion corollaries: An exploratory study." *American Sociological Review* 21(6):709-16.

Srole, L., T. S. Langner, and S. T. Michael, P. Kirkpatrick, M. K. Opler, and T. A. C. Rennie. 1962. *Mental Health in the Metropolis: The Midtown Manhattan Study*, Vol. 1, revised edition. New York: New York University Press.

Stein, B. N. 1986. "The experience of being a refugee: Insights from the research literature." In *Refugee Mental Health in Resettlement Countries*, edited by C. L. Williams and J. Westermeyer, pp. 5–23. New York: Hemisphere Publishing Company.

Stevens, R., L. W. Goodman, and S. S. Mick. 1978. *The Alien Doctors: Foreign Medical Graduates in American Hospitals.* New York: J. Wiley.

Stonequist, E. V. 1937. *The Marginal Man: A Study in Personality and Culture Conflict.* New York: Russell and Russell, Inc.

Stotland, E. 1987. "Stress." *Concise Encyclopedia of Psychology*, edited by R. Corsini, pp. 1085-86. New York: J. Wiley.

Sue, S., and J. K. Morishima. 1982. *The Mental Health of Asian Americans*. San Francisco: Jossey-Bass.

Thoits, P. A. 1982. "Conceptual, methodological and theoretical problems in studying social support as a buffer against life stresses." *Journal of Health and Social Behavior* 23(2):145-59.

———. 1983. "Dimensions of life events that influence psychological distress: An evaluation and synthesis of the literature." In *Psychosocial Stress: Trends in Theory and Research*, edited by H. B. Kaplan, pp. 33-103. New York: Academic Press.

———. 1991. "Patterns in coping with controllable and uncontrollable events." In *Life Span Developmental Psychology: Perspectives in Stress and Coping*, edited by M. Cummings, A. L. Greene, and K. H. Karraker, pp. 235-58. Hillsdale, NJ: Lawrence Erlbaum Associates.

Thomas, W. I., and D. S. Thomas. 1928. *The Child in America*. New York: Alfred A. Knopf.

Thomas, W. I., and F. Znaniecki. 1927. *The Polish Peasant in Europe and America*. New York: Alfred A. Knopf.

Tienda, M., and K. Booth. 1991. "Gender, migration and social change." *International Sociology* 6(1):51-72.

Tiryakian, Edward A. 1980. "Sociological dimensions of uprootedness." In *Uprooting and Development*, edited by G. V. Coelho and P. I. Ahmed, pp. 132-52. New York: Plenum Press.

Todaro, M. P. 1969. "A model for labor migration and urban unemployment in less developed countries." *American Economic Review* 59(1):138-48.

Turner, K. 1993. "Viewpoint." *Daily Bruin* (UCLA) November 15:16.

Tylor, E. B. 1874. *Primitive Culture: Research into the Development of Mythology, Philosophy, Religion, Language, Art and Customs*. New York: Henry Hold & Co.

United Nations. 1973. *The Determinants and Consequences of Population Trends*. New York: United Nations.

Valdes, T. M., and J. C. Baxter. 1976. "The Social Readjustment Rating Questionnaire: A study of Cuban exiles." *Journal of Psychosomatic Research* 20(3):231-36.

Watson, J. L. 1977. *Between Two Cultures: Migrants and Minorities in Britain*. Oxford: Blackwell.

Weber, M. 1968. *Economy and Society: An Outline of Interpretive Sociology*, edited by G. Roth and T. Wittich. New York: Bedminster Press.

Weil, S. 1988. "The influence of caste ideology in Israel." In *Cultural Transition: The Case of Immigrant Youth*, edited by M. Gottesmann, pp. 150-61. Jerusalem: Magnes Press, The Hebrew University.

Weingrod, A. (ed.) 1985. *Studies in Israeli Ethnicity: After the Ingathering*. New York and London: Gordon and Breach Science Publishers.

Westermeyer, J. 1991. "Psychiatric services for refugee children: An overwiew." In *Refugee Children: Theory, Research and Services*, edited by F. L. Ahearn and J. L. Athey, pp. 127-62. Baltimore and London: Johns Hopkins University Press.

Westermeyer, J., T. F. Vang, and J. Neider. 1983. "Refugees who do not seek psychiatric care." *Journal of Nervous and Mental Diseases* 171:86-91.

Wethington, E., and R. C. Kessler. 1991. "Situations and processes of coping." In *The Social Context of Coping*, edited by J. Eckenrode, pp. 13–29. New York: Plenum Press.

Wheaton, B. 1985. "Models for the stress-buffering functions of coping resources." *Journal of Health and Social Behavior* 26(2):352–64.

Wilcox, B. L. 1981. "Social support, life stress and psychological adjustment: A test of buffering hypothesis." *American Journal of Community Psychology* 9:371–86.

Williams, C. L. 1991. "Toward the development of preventive interventions for youth traumatized by war and refugee flight." In *Refugee Children: Theory, Research and Services*, edited by F. L. Ahearn and J. L. Athey, pp. 201–17. Baltimore and London: Johns Hopkins University Press.

Wills, T. A., and T. S. Langner. 1980. "Socioeconomic status and stress." In *Handbook on Stress and Anxiety: Contemporary Knowledge, Theory and Treatment*, edited by I. L. Kutash, L. B. Schlesinger, and Associates, pp. 159–73. San Francisco: Jossey-Bass.

Wolff, H. G., S. G. Wolff, and C. C. Hare. (eds.) 1950. *Life Stress and Bodily Disease*. Baltimore: Williams and Wilkens.

Wolpert, J. 1965. "Behavioral aspects of the decision to migrate." *Papers of the Regional Science Association* 5:159–69.

Zborowski, M. 1969. *People in Pain*. San Francisco: Jossey-Bass.

Zelinsky, W. 1971. "The hypothesis of the mobility transition theory." *Geographical Review* 61:219–43.

Zwingmann, C., and A. Gunn. 1983. *Uprooting and Health: Psychosocial Problems of Students from Abroad*. Geneva: World Health Organization, Division of Mental Health.

Index

About the Author

ZEEV BEN-SIRA (1925–1995) was Chair of the Department of Behavioral Sciences at Ben-Gurion University of the Negev, Director of the School of Social Work at the Hebrew University of Jerusalem and for many years a Senior Research Associate at the Louis Gutman Israel Institute of Applied Social Research. He also served as a central committee member of the Israeli Sociological Association. In addition, he was Visiting Professor at Rutgers University, at Washington University in Seattle, and at UCLA's School of Public Health. He was the author of many papers and books, including *Regression Stress and Readjustment in Aging* (Praeger, 1991).